N 0072915 9

FAIRNESS IN CHILDREN

FAIRNESS IN CHILDREN

A Social-Cognitive Approach to the Study of Moral Development

Michael Siegal

Department of Psychology
University of Queensland
St Lucia, Australia

1982

ACADEMIC PRESS
A Subsidiary of Harcourt Brace Jovanovich, Publishers

LONDON NEW YORK
PARIS SAN DIEGO SAN FRANCISCO SÃO PAULO
SYDNEY TOKYO TORONTO

Academic Press Inc. (London) Ltd
24–28 Oval Road
London NW1

US edition published by
Academic Press Inc.
111 Fifth Avenue,
New York, New York 10003

British Library Cataloguing in Publication Data
Siegal, M.
Fairness in children.
1. Fairness 2. Child psychology
I. Title
155.4'18 BJ1533-F2

ISBN 01-12-641380-0

LCCCN 81-68968

Typeset by Page Bros (Norwich) Ltd, Norwich, Norfolk

Preface

IT HAS NOW BEEN FIFTY YEARS since Piaget's book *The Moral Judgment of the Child* was first published. Since then a great amount of work has been devoted toward appraising Piaget's ideas. This book follows in scrutinizing theory and research germane to moral judgment development, but departs in widening its focus to include the development of moral behaviour. The contents are particularly directed at examining the development of that type of behaviour by which children demonstrate a sense of fairness toward others in considering the intentions and interests of the socially or economically disadvantaged. As such, the book is primarily written for those who have taken introductory courses in children's development and in the psychological study of social issues.

In exploring the predictability of children's fairness towards others, attention is given to variations in cognitive development, to children's perceptions of their parents, to adult influences on peer-group interaction, and to processes through which parent–child relations become linked with changing socioeconomic conditions. These features of development will be discussed in terms of an orientation which is neither predominantly Piagetian nor cognitive, nor predominantly one of social learning but which combines selected elements of the two (together with the work of others such as that of J. M. Baldwin) from the standpoint of a "social cognitive approach". The aim is to point out research possibilities, practicalities, and applications.

I have been helped by a great many people. I owe a debt to Professor Peter Bryant whose research is a model of clarity and precision. I have learned much from my co-workers and friends, Michael Boyes, Jim Chapman, Robin Francis, Lynn O'Donoghue, Jackie Rablin, and Carol Thorley. The moral support I have received from my colleagues at the University of Queensland, Boris Crassini, Ray Pike, and Wes Snyder, has been very much appreciated. Special thanks are due to Graeme Halford, James Russell, and Peter Sheehan for reading sections of the manuscript. Their extensive comments were extremely helpful in guiding me to correct the faults and inaccuracies which were contained in earlier drafts. The flaws which remain, of course, belong to me alone. Irene Hall and Jan Stewart expertly and patiently retyped the manuscript at least half a dozen times and the computing skills of Ross Gayler were an invaluable help in assembling the text on magnetic tape.

The research reported in the book was supported in part by the Australian Research Grants Committee, the Canada Council, the Social Sciences and Humanities Research Council of Canada, and the research committees of the Universities of British Columbia, Queensland, and Toronto. Parts of Chapters 5 and 7 are drawn from articles previously published in the *British Journal of Educational Psychology* (1980, *50*, 105–113) and the *Merrill-Palmer Quarterly* (1980, *26*, 285–297).

My wife, Sharon Winocur, went through each paragraph line by line correcting both the form and content of what I was trying to say. As usual, she was terrific. This book arises from her love and devotion.

Michael Siegal

Brisbane
January, 1982

CONTENTS

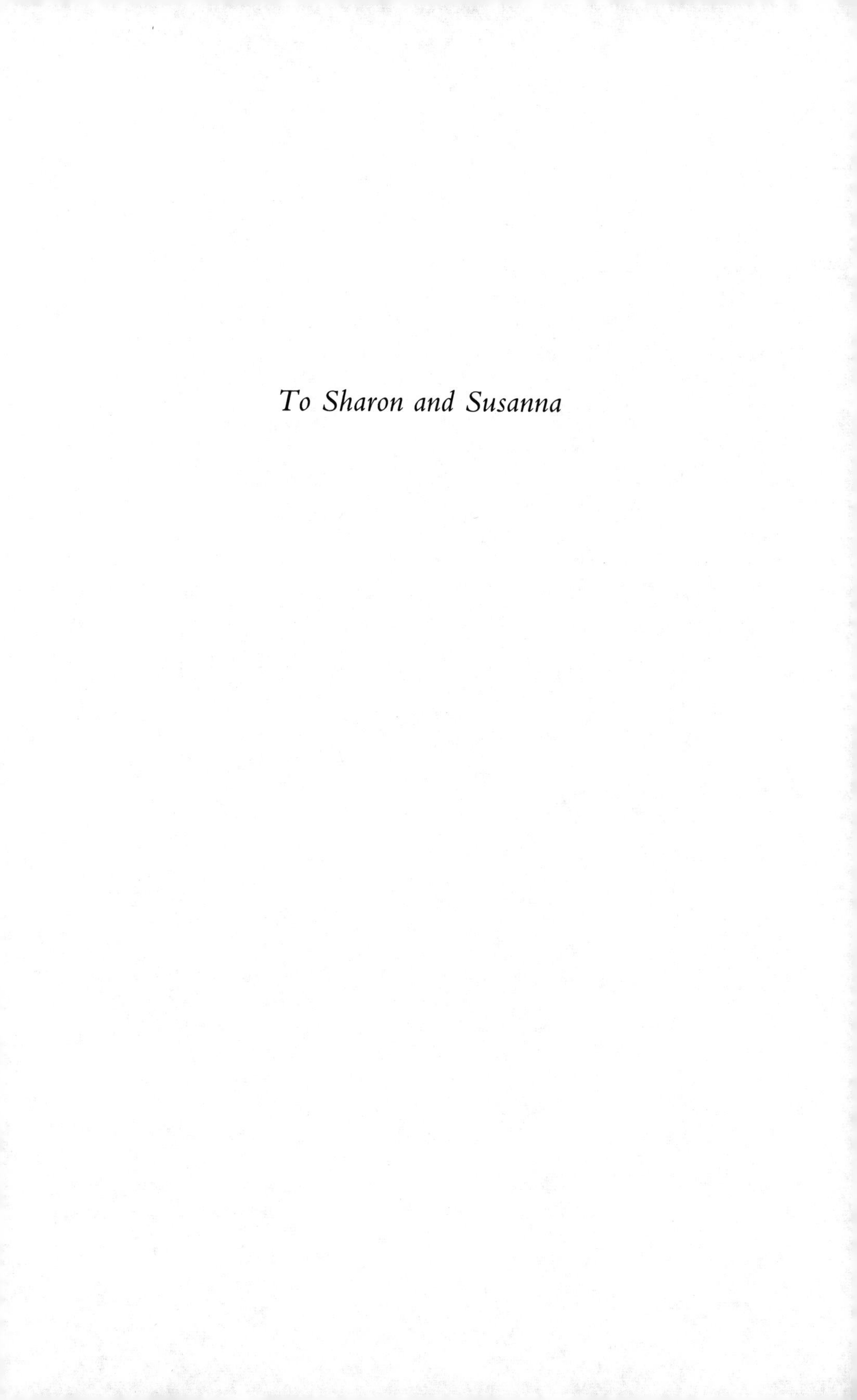

To Sharon and Susanna

Chapter One

INTRODUCTION

1.1 *How can Children's Fairness be Studied?*

A SENSE of fairness in children comes at the culmination of their general moral development. How children develop this sense has been the subject of many experimental studies. Many writers have agreed that it involves an ability to consider consistently and without contradiction the interests and intentions of others: to act bearing these in mind and without the guidance of a superior authority and to generalize fully this behaviour in all relevant situations. Fair acts are aimed to better the conditions of disadvantaged persons in a very wide variety of circumstances; freely volunteering to provide the poor with food, shelter and medical care is one reasonably clear example. To treat others in ways similar to treating oneself is both consistent and at the heart of the concept of fairness; it is especially indicative of a moral development towards systematically distinguishing between right and wrong.

There are many acts which are both fair and altruistic, and both fair and empathic. But an act of altruism is not necessarily one which is fair. As Krebs (1970) notes, psychologists researching "altruism" have generally employed everyday definitions. One which has been commonly used is that given by Leeds (1963): an altruistic act (a) is an end in itself and is not directed at gain, (b) is emitted voluntarily, and (c) does good. By this account, a child who helps a friend rob a candy store and is uninterested in partaking of the spoils is performing an altruistic act, but at the same time he may be unfair to a disadvantaged store proprietor. Similarly, a professional person who agrees to hear in confidence a criminal's confession is also performing an altruistic act but one which may be unfair to the public at large. Thus, to demarcate fair acts from those which can be termed in a way altruistic, it is necessary to amend Leeds' point (c): a fair act "does good" insofar as it is consistently founded on a consideration of the interests and intentions of the disadvantaged. In this connection it should be emphasized that a fair act must be deliberately planned and not accidental or fortuitous.

Likewise, it would be a serious mistake to use some sort of conceptual gerrymandering device for equating fairness with a sense of empathy. While empathy can be defined as a shared, vicarious response to others' feelings (Ford, 1979; Hoffman, 1977), an empathically motivated act is not necessarily a fair one. For example, newborns may demonstrate some degree of empathic distress when hearing the cries of other infants (Sagi and Hoffman, 1976). But it would be absurd to say that babies can act fairly. As another case in point, a judge in a court of law may be tempted to empathize with a delinquent's plight, pronouncing a lenient sentence which is unfair to the public at large and even to other offenders convicted of the very same crime. At the same time, a parent may selectively empathize with a delinquent offspring and unfairly neglect the interests of his victims.

Though a sense of empathy can be an invaluable aid in arriving at a fair course of action, there is nothing to prevent some empathically motivated acts from being characterized as misguided, narrowly channelled, and irrational. By contrast, it should be recognized that there is an essential element of rationality in fairness. Moreover, there is the sound argument that it is precisely this rationality which provides a foundation for principles of justice and impartiality; and that justice—as one paramount virtue of moral development—can be best conceptualized in terms of fairness (Rawls, 1958). This is not to deny that there remain important and serious differences of opinion on this question, but only to maintain that moral judgment and cognition are necessary for moral actions (i.e., actions deliberately taken without the force of an external authority).

Despite the rational and deliberate character of fairness, another equally prominent school of thought exists (Blasi, 1980). This school does not view morality in terms of fairness and does not see moral failure as resulting from a defect in moral judgment and cognition. In some circles within this school, it has become fashionable in recent years to explain human social behaviour in terms of biological and neurological processes (see for example the critique by Rose and Rose, 1973). Certain writers have even suggested that man's inhumanity to man is largely due to a fault in the neurological constitution of the brain. Arthur Koestler (1967, p.382), for one, has concluded that because we have been "let down by nature" we should "use our brain to cure its own shortcomings". An alternative but still extreme approach has been to reduce virtually all human social behaviour to that exhibited by other primates. From a wide variety of sources have come reports of what may be termed self-sacrificing behaviour in animals. For example, it appears that monkeys will share their food with others of their species and will protect their mates and peers against harm even with danger to themselves. Monkeys can be responsive to signs of distress; in one laboratory study (Masserman, Wechkin and Terris, 1964), monkeys were able to obtain food by pulling a chain which at the same time delivered an electric shock to their cagemates. The monkeys did not pull.

Though some of those who have carried out such studies were extremely reluctant to credit animals with altruistic behaviour (Nissen and Crawford, 1936, p.415), there are contemporary psychologists who claim that reports of self-sacrifice in primates lend "reasonably good evidence" for this notion (Hoffman, 1976, p.124). Certainly, the social behaviour of an animal may help others at considerable cost to himself. But in stark contrast to the vast array of rule-guided and principled behaviour of man, animal social behaviour may be construed merely as a response to particular patterns of stimuli—and there is no simple way to rule out this possibility (Hinde, 1974, p.336).

While some cogent explanations in certain areas in psychology may be located in the relationship between psychology and micro-level findings in sciences, such as biology and neurology, macro-level psychological processes contributing to children's fairness cannot be determined in this way. In fact, a great many such processes cannot be reduced and distilled into the laws of micro-level sciences for these laws are relatively unchanging and do not vary greatly from society to society. Though human biology can be assumed to have remained largely unchanged in the course of recorded history, fair acts have varied enormously across cultures and generations. Fair acts are certainly compatible with the laws of biology and neurology but they cannot be deduced from a knowledge of the function and organization of the brain, the digestive tract, and the respiratory system. To maintain the contrary would be to posit a mechanistic, predetermined outcome for human social behaviour providing an impoverished source for specific behavioural predictions. This of course is unwarranted.

What is at issue here has been eloquently voiced by Hilary Putnam (1973). In opposition to the doctrine of reductionism, Putnam offers the following example. Suppose we have two objects: a square peg which is a fraction less than one inch across, and a board with a square hole one inch across, and a round hole one inch in diameter. That the peg fits through the square hole and not the round one can be attributed to the size and rigidity of the two objects. Whatever the rigid microstructure of the board may be, whether it consists of wood, stone, or marble, is irrelevant to why the peg fits through the square; the explanation cannot be reduced to the physical composition of the board material.

In a parallel fashion, much psychology cannot be reduced to micro-level scientific processes. That is not to deny that *some* psychology is reducible. Very close to neurology, for example, are topics such as amnesia and aphasia. The convenient solution would be to draw a line between what is reducible and what is not. Putnam implies that these "two sides to psychology" can be clearly specified: that the study of pain is biologically rooted, in contrast to the study of aggression which is irreducible and irrelevant to biology and can be explained in terms of its relationship to societal beliefs. Yet often this demarcation line is more artificial than real. Aggression can cause pain; the two areas interact and can be profitably studied using both psychological and biological methodologies (Peele, 1981).

But more clearly on the non-reductionist side of the line is the study of fairness, a behaviour which cannot be determined by the mechanistic laws of micro-level sciences. In this case, a biological approach may be relevant but not necessarily so and to force the study of such social phenomena into predominantly "biological moulds is simply to deform them" (Baldwin, 1899/1973, p.522). Conversely, because fair acts are rational and deliberate and vary across both cultures and generations, they can be studied in terms of their relationship to cognition and to social influences emanating from parents and peers which are embedded in the political and economic framework of society (cf. the discussion on the nature and evolution of sociocultural systems in Cohen, 1978).

That fairness can be defined as possessing properties of rationality and logic has important ramifications for the study of moral development. Above all, it implies that measures of variables which contribute to fairness can be related to external criteria of behaviour, and that these can be clearly specified. In theory, it should be possible to establish the predictive validity of variables (such as intelligence, empathy, and parental identification) which would likely be associated with fair behaviour. In turn, the external criteria of fair behaviour are specifiable as voluntary acts which are consistently founded on a consideration of others' interests and intentions, such as the following of school rules designed to protect others' interests and the participation in civil rights marches designed to change rules which endanger others' interests.

It is instructive to contrast the concept of fairness with other concepts studied in psychology. Take the concept of anxiety as an example. Compared to fairness, anxiety is not clearly definable in terms of rational and logical properties. Consequently, external criteria for validating measures of anxiety behaviour are rather unclear. In fact, we may be unable to say what anxiety is until we gain a knowledge of the laws governing anxiety. Until that time, our definition of anxiety will remain "disturbingly loose" (Cronbach and Meehl, 1955, p.294). The way to solve this problem (i.e., to validate the construct of anxiety) is through an interplay between theory and test results. This may be an expensive and time-consuming task, and may even be an unrewarding one, for if theory and evidence do not match, either the theory or the test must be revised or scrubbed. It is very fortunate that fairness is unlike anxiety in that its rational properties foster an evaluation of qualities contributing to performance on relatively clear behavioural criteria (though this is not to suggest that fairness is in all respects less difficult to investigate than anxiety).

These then are the grounds upon which to search for a social-cognitive approach to the study of moral development in general, and fairness in particular. The term "fairness" refers to a rationalist approach to the study of moral development; this is in contrast to a non-cognitive, biological approach, or an approach which does not involve affect or motivation. Fairness is a rational attribute not reducible to mechanistic processes. Actions taken without cognition cannot be considered moral. A decision taken at the highest level of moral development is most rational and consistent; it corresponds to what is just and fair. And while it is true that the vagueness and lack of agreement on what constitutes "moral behaviour" has served to impair research since before the turn of the century, there is a distinguished line of psychologists who have worked in the rationalist tradition and have specialized in the study of issues to which fairness is relevant.

1.2 *The Theoretical Framework*

Beyond the possible prospect of reaching agreement on a definition of fairness, there is no widespread consensus over just when and how children do become fair. Some are inclined to believe that the critical period of development, if there is one, is during the preschool years; but for others, it is the first years of elementary school which are critical. Some have maintained that development can be attributed primarily to peer-group influence; but for others, it can be attributed primarily to the examples portrayed by adult models who are much revered in the eyes of young children.

The position advocated in this book proposes that a sense of fairness is generally developed through a combination of at least four ingredients: (1) cognitive development; (2) the structure of the problems which the child confronts; (3) adult instruction and identification; and (4) peer-group influence. It is almost a truism to assert that cognitive development must play a key role here. To imagine others' interests and intentions implies a considerable degree of intellectual awareness. This is the approach represented by the cognitive-developmental tradition as exemplified through the years by the work of Baldwin (1899/1973), Piaget (1932/1977), Peck and Harighurst (1960), and Kohlberg (1976). It asserts that the more advanced the cognitive development, the more abstract and difficult are the problems which the child is able to solve fairly. If cognition were all there was to developing a sense of fairness, it would be possible in theory to predict a child's behaviour from a knowledge of his level of cognitive development and the difficulty of the problem.

At the present, the study of cognitive processes has achieved a prominent position in psychology. But there is little doubt that cognition is far from synonymous with fairness. Ever since the time of Aristotle, the intellectual and moral virtues have been held to be at least partially separate. Some of the greatest villains in history have had brilliant intellects and it is certainly no contradiction to say that a certain criminal has a brilliant mind.

Therefore it is imperative to extend and refine the cognitive-developmental approach in exploring other normative or social factors which might contribute to the development of fairness. In this regard, a repetition of the past errors may be avoided through an examination of the history of psychology and its changing ideologies. Moreover, as Mary Henle (1976) points out, history contains many forgotten treasures. In an era where we have become increasingly absorbed in our own specialities, there is a trend toward becoming fragmented in our interests, operating in isolation from those working in cognate fields. We are often deeply immersed in our own ideas and short-term aims to the exclusion of much else. For this reason, we need the study of history to give us a wider theoretical insight and distance from our immediate pressing concerns.

Such distance is provided, for example, by a distinction made continuously for over two hundred years: a trilogy of mind consisting of cognition, affection, and conation. This division surfaced time and time again in eighteenth- and nineteenth-century writings on both sides of the Atlantic. Earlier in the present century, McDougall (1931, p.23) was able to discuss instincts by confidently proclaiming that "every instance of instinctive behaviour involves a knowing of some thing or object, a feeling in regard to it, and a striving toward or away from that object".

Yet with the emergence of cognitive psychology, the affective and conative designations have fallen on hard times. Indeed it appears possible that, owing to an enchantment with cognition, the once familiar division may be in danger of being dropped altogether. In some quarters a "cool" cognitive psychology has won pre-eminence in which cognition is studied in terms of information-processing and computer-simulation techniques. But at the same time, room should still be allowed for the thoughts and decisions that have high affective or conative importance to the person, what Hilgard (1980, p.115) terms "hot" cognition.

In the study of fairness, this hot cognition is located at the intersection of affective and motivational factors underlying the rate and nature of moral development. It involves important aspects of self-definition and, as such, can be characterized by the relationship of the child to the adult and peer group. According to the theory, these influences play complementary roles throughout childhood. Adult influences act primarily through verbal instructions and modelling which first implore children to behave fairly through considering the interests and intentions of others. Such abstract, esoteric instructions may be removed from actual real-life situations until children have been immersed in personal experiences which often involve peer-group influence. It is these experiences which can impart a conscious true-to-life meaning or content to the words and examples of the adult. The embryo of the theoretical model as formulated thus far is shown schematically in Fig. 1.

Time 1 (preschool/early childhood) The "shell" of morality is acquired through formal adult instruction	*Time 2* (middle childhood onwards) The "filling" of morality is acquired through practical experience often acquired in the peer group. The effectiveness of adult instruction does not decline

Fig. 1. *The preliminary model*

To be sure, there are of course many experiences which do not encourage fairness. For example, to deprive children of a wide and varied participation in play and games may possibly result in delinquency later. Yet there are peer-group experiences which are positive ones in that they give rise to a concern for the disadvantaged. These can involve situations which encourage practice and self-direction in taking the role of others. The intention is to mark these off and discuss each in some detail.

Peer-group influence is obviously important. But as children grow older, it still does not necessarily replace the influence of the adult which can remain strong throughout childhood. Adult instruction can have a particularly effective impact on peer-group relationships, especially as an identification with certain adults may deepen with age. In deciding how to resolve moral conflicts which carry weighty consequences, children may identify with an adult's rules and standards for behaviour and adopt these as their own.

At the core of this approach, then, is the development of a wide range of practical experience. Preschool children are in frequent day-to-day contact with their parents. Their range of experience is limited in no small way by a lack of mobility. The problems they face are simple ones, and do not lead to sophisticated notions of right and wrong. For example, restricted in their meeting of other children and in their knowledge of unfamiliar neighbourhoods, preschoolers are not fully conscious of what actions are deemed to be socially correct. They still have to learn collective rules which govern the relationships among large numbers of children. For the preschool child, problems are often about sharing toys with one other child rather than about playing fair in a team situation—which is far more complicated and allows for a wider range of problematic situations. While appearances can be used to classify persons into age groups, there is no such thing as deprivation in the child's peer-group relationships because the child does not yet have a concept of status. For example, it has been shown that if one asks the preschool child "Who is the toughest?" the child will almost invariably say "me" regardless of whether he is a weakling or superbly musclebound (Edelman and Omark, 1973; Omark and Edelman, 1975). The child does not usually understand what it means to be left out of the group or to be among the weaker of the group members because his experience of other children is so limited. If asked to say what is good and bad behaviour, he or she often faithfully repeats the teachings of his parents: sharing is good and lying is wrong. The child's moral psychology is innocent, simple and at times unyieldingly rigid.

Once children enter school, a dramatic change occurs: they spend much less time with adults and far more time with peers (Fig. 2). Children become initiated into the collective rules and conventions of the school and find that these are aimed to promote harmony among their classmates. Social situations become more complex and problematic. Children are rewarded and punished for their behaviour by an ever-increasing number of acquaintances, teachers, and other children. They are exposed to multiple models of behaviour, more adult models and more peer models. These models will probably display conflicting behaviours. Perhaps most importantly, children acquire the ability to infer accurately the absolute ages of others and to use age as a factor in rank-ordering persons' social positions (Edwards and Lewis, 1979). They develop an understanding of status and deprivation. When asked "Who is the toughest?", they are capable of naming the toughest child in their class and now know what it means to be on the top or at the bottom. Through the self-perceptions acquired in the peer group, the child comes to judge how well he or she is capable of meeting prospective stressful situations.

At the same time, though their cognitive development progresses, the number and the types of problems faced by children greatly increases. Their original definitions of right and wrong were acquired from their parents and were adequate for their preschool years, but these no longer provide an unequivocal yardstick. Children who have become initiated into the group meet with complex problems (i.e., whether to root for their school's

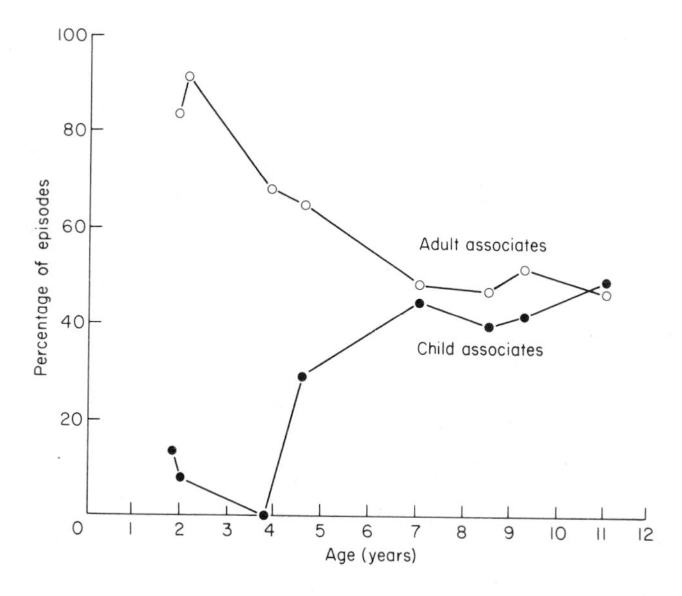

Fig. 2. *Percentage of episodes involving adult and child associates. (From Wright 1967.)*

team or the team for which a brother or sister plays, whether to tell on a best friend who has stolen some change or to remain quiet). Conflicts are encountered which consist of clashes between principles and rules as well as between rules and their own individual desires. Thus children are forced to redefine their sense of right and wrong, to decide what action to take, which model to follow. To do this fairly, they must be able to experience and take the role of the disadvantaged person in real-life conflict situations. Principles must be generated which involve a hierarchy of moral values and an evaluation of the goodness of rules. In the course of this often daunting enterprise, the products of their own intellectual development meet with wobbly and varied success and children often turn back to the adult for wise counsel. It is the adult's responsibility to meet this challenge with all the wisdom he or she can find: to promote and direct in a non-indoctrinative, authoritative manner the child's identification with rules and standards.

How precisely do these complementary roles of adults and peer-group influence relate to intellectual development and problem difficulty? A starting point is to characterize both the cognitive capacities of children and the complexity of moral conflicts by borrowing from the terminology of Jean Piaget (1970). The well-known designations of preoperational, concrete operational, and formal operational intelligence can be used to denote hierarchically organized stages of cognitive development. As children pass through each level of intelligence, they become cognitively more sophisticated and so are able to solve progressively more abstract problems. During the preoperational stage, young children's performance is constrained by the inexperienced use of their ability to take the role of others and consider their interests and intentions. In contrast, concrete operational children are better able to use their perspective-taking abilities in demonstrating an appreciation of the spirit of rules governing behaviour but their understanding is restricted to immediate, real-life situations. During the formal operational stage, a number of hypothetical alternative solutions to abstract problems can be considered systematically. The transition from preoperational to concrete operational intelligence occurs at 6–7 years and that from concrete to formal operational intelligence occurs at 11–12 years, but these are approximate ages only which are subject to substantial individual variation.

The range of increasingly complex moral conflicts can also be sub-divided into three categories: individual rituals, collective rules, and principles. These distinctions are less well-known and merit definition. The term "ritual" does not refer to ritualistic patterns of animal behaviour nor to religious or cultural rituals such as those which prohibit the eating of certain meats. It is used by Piaget and here to describe a kind of idiosyncratic prerule, experienced by cognitively unsophisticated, preoperational children as endowing certain behaviours with a sense of regularity and habit. These rituals control behaviours and are less abstract or formal than are collective rules or laws. They are often indicative of affective-conatative strivings. At times they may involve self-obligations having no conscious necessity to be codified and communicated to others. Feeling that one ought to brush one's hair fifty times before walking to school is an example of a childish ritual which is individual and particularistic; feeling that one ought, on some particular occasion, to be an early riser, without obliging others to do the same, is one approximate adult equivalent.

By contrast,

> we must distinguish carefully between the behaviour into which there enters only the pleasure of regularity, and that into which there enters an element of obligation. It is this consciousness of obligation which seems . . . to distinguish a rule in the true sense from mere regularity.
>
> (Piaget, 1932/1977, p.29)

Such collective rules are generally applicable and inter-subjective; these operate as component features of more co-ordinated systems of obligations (such as a code of classroom behaviour or of criminal justice). As features of larger systems, some such collective rules may co-exist, while others should contradict and make logical impossibilities of their opposites. By this account, the attainment of the rule-oriented state of concrete operations should be an intellectual prerequisite for the conscious following of collective rules. Finally, principles (or "meta-rules") represent statements about relationships between rules. They pertain to still more general abstract and formal value schemes for arbitrating conflicts involving other principles, rules, or rituals. According to Piaget, the attainment of formal operations is an intellectual prerequisite for the comprehension of principles which by definition are abstract and propositional in structure. The advent of formal operations usually occurs early in adolescence. At this time, the adolescent becomes capable of hypothetical, future-oriented thinking. He is able to evaluate the rules as they are in comparison to utopian possibilities.

Given this tripartite description for characterizing the range of possible moral obligations, conflicts between these different sorts of obligations can include those between rituals and rules, rituals and principles, and rules and principles. By this account, there should be a structural "match" between a child's level of cognitive development and the complexity of the conflict. Preoperational children should prefer rituals to rules and principles, concrete operational children should prefer rules to principles and rituals, and formal operational children should prefer principles over rules and rules over rituals. But this is all too simplistic since cases of regression are by no means infrequent in such stage-structural models, and these may be attributed to the acute or chronic debilitating effects relating to adult influence.

It is for this reason that the strength of parent–child identification is of importance and cannot be neglected in any comprehensive study of moral development. The notion of identification originated with Sigmund Freud (1923/1961) and has occupied the writings of psychologists ever since (Bandura, 1971; Kagan, 1958; Kohlberg, 1969). There are many different facets to the hot cognition of identification. For example, a child may identify with a parent out of empathy and admiration or out of envy for the adult's power and status. But regardless of the source of identification, its outcome can be defined as the child's adoption of the parent's own standards for rules of behaviour. If the concept is a viable one, it can be expected that the stronger the identification the more likely will the child adhere to his or her perceptions of parental values rather than to idiosyncratic rituals. Even a preoperational child with little comprehension of collective rules might in practice display rule-following behaviour, provided the child has come to identify with adults who have given their assent to these rules. Thus the "shell" of morality may be acquired through formal adult instruction.

In a similar way, those who act on the basis of principles can be differentiated from others who prefer to follow rules by their adoption of a parental moral-political ideology and a low-level of conflict associated with

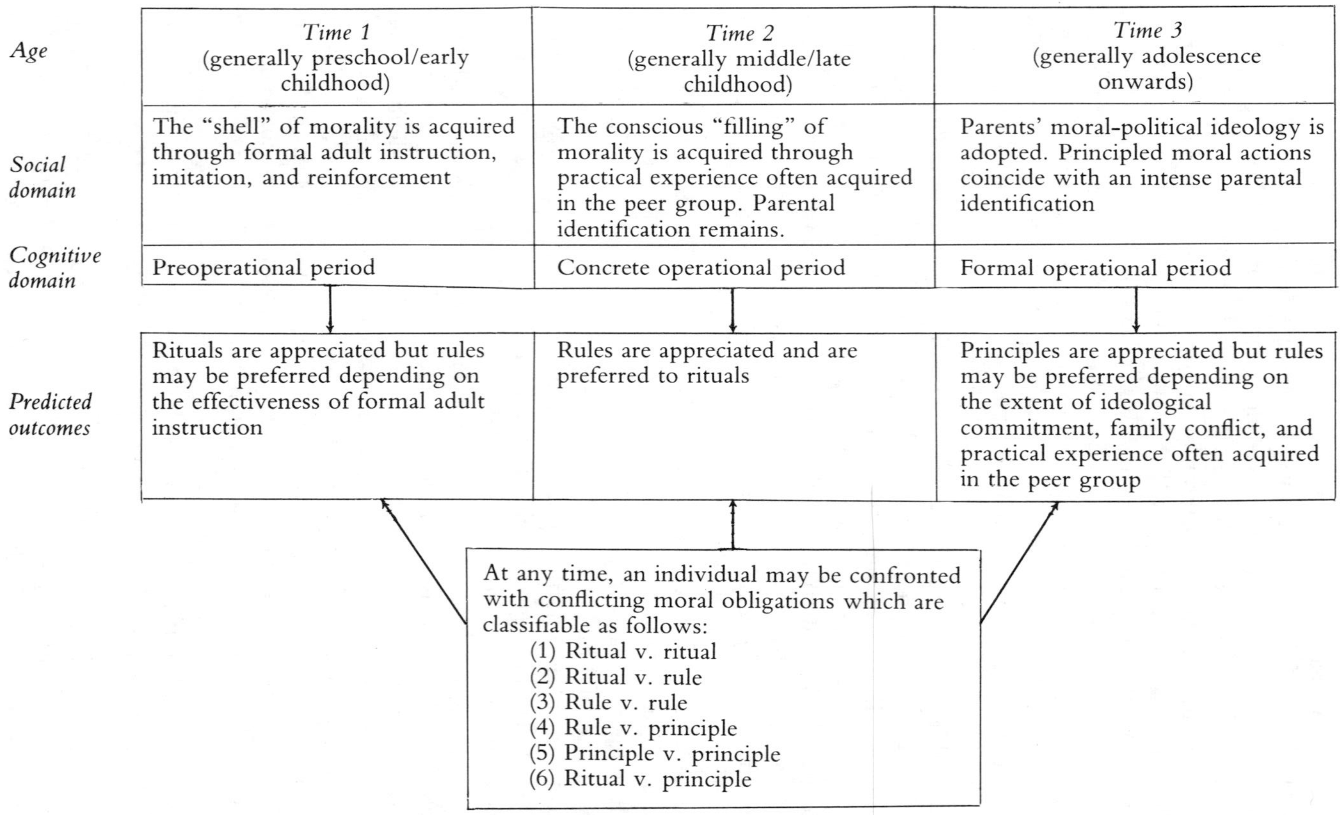

Age	*Time 1* (generally preschool/early childhood)	*Time 2* (generally middle/late childhood)	*Time 3* (generally adolescence onwards)
Social domain	The "shell" of morality is acquired through formal adult instruction, imitation, and reinforcement	The conscious "filling" of morality is acquired through practical experience often acquired in the peer group. Parental identification remains.	Parents' moral-political ideology is adopted. Principled moral actions coincide with an intense parental identification
Cognitive domain	Preoperational period	Concrete operational period	Formal operational period
Predicted outcomes	Rituals are appreciated but rules may be preferred depending on the effectiveness of formal adult instruction	Rules are appreciated and are preferred to rituals	Principles are appreciated but rules may be preferred depending on the extent of ideological commitment, family conflict, and practical experience often acquired in the peer group

At any time, an individual may be confronted with conflicting moral obligations which are classifiable as follows:

(1) Ritual v. ritual
(2) Ritual v. rule
(3) Rule v. rule
(4) Rule v. principle
(5) Principle v. principle
(6) Ritual v. principle

Fig. 3. *Model of the social-cognitive approach*

an intense identification with one or both parents. An individual may adopt the political-moral ideology of his or her parents, and identification may be associated with the generation and following of a principled course of behaviour in striving to uphold human rights.

In this fashion, the hot cognition of identification provides an affective and motivational force underlying moral behaviour. Against the background of a "cool" and general stage of cognitive development, it gives a systematic meaning to moral rules and principles and is an integral part of a person's self-definition with respect to others.

The full model is shown in Fig. 3. The theory will be elaborated much further in what is to follow—in providing detailed evidence for these claims concerning the respective roles of adult and peer-group influence, intellectual development, and the difficulty of the moral problems which the child confronts (Chapter 4). From this approach, identification and peer group influence will be discussed in a socioeconomic and crosscultural context; and implications for childrearing and education will be considered.

1.3 *The Issue of Ideology*

In assembling support for this approach, only one type of evidence will be cited: experimental and naturalistic studies in which samples of children have been systematically tested or observed. Only by use of such evidence can we claim, for example, that a particular childrearing effect is statistically associated with children's behaviour. Significant findings from the studies cited here will recur by chance alone not more than five times out of a hundred.

Unfortunately, much of the most heralded writing on child psychology has made little or no reference to this type of evidence. There are writers who have, for example, based their childrearing recommendations on impressions or case histories. Possibly, these speculations will later spur some empirical studies. But as practical recipes for developing a sense of fairness in children, they are often weakly founded on the unsystematically observed behaviour of one or two subjects.

It is small wonder that such ideas have coincided with fads in childrearing methods. Speculations have spawned appealing prescriptions for the parent to follow; certainly some of these have not led to the best of outcomes. To adhere to the experimental evidence may be an arduous and at times even counter-intuitive path to follow, but it is the sole means for securing reliable results.

Methodological and statistical scrutiny is, of course, a very important criterion for accepting the results of experimental studies. An equally important aim is to interpret and synthesize results in a fashion which is not prejudged by an inflexible ideology. According to Karl Popper (1974), a theory must be capable of falsification or else it cannot be called scientific. Psychological theories must also be capable of falsification. Often it is only possible to verify or falsify one small corner of a grand overarching theory. If this is so, only that theoretical component can at that point in time be deemed scientific. Unfortunately, psychology has at times been vulnerable to an ideology which is more a handmaiden to mythology than to science. Perhaps this is not altogether a bad thing. Alongside a myth can come the youthful idealism and vision so essential in the building of elegant theoretical constructs. But too often this situation has led to the proliferation of ideologically pure but untestable ideas, or of relatively impure ideas left untested (Riegel, 1972; Rose and Rose, 1973). According to one relatively detached observer, the philosopher Michael Scriven (1969), within the ideological sub-groups of psychology there is a powerful pressure toward conformism, so much so that it may sometimes be extremely difficult for one generation of junior researchers to reject the ideology of their seniors without seeking haven from the secure base of a rival. Nevertheless, without challenging the accuracy of Scriven's remarks, it is clear that the ideology of a school of psychology can define researchable problems and mould the interpretation of experimental results.

To some considerable extent, theory and research are also influenced by the contemporary and changing ideologies of society in general. This may be particularly characteristic of developmental psychology, which came about to some considerable extent as a result of strong outside pressure from parents and non-psychologists (such as educators, physicians, and social workers) for answers to questions about children (White, 1979). For better or worse, areas of need are established by policy makers and researchers strive to meet these priorities. Resources are often allocated to those thought best able to answer questions of relevance to societal problems. For example, Brodbeck (1969, pp.274–275) among others has observed how trends in American psychology have paralleled current events:

> When one studies the "fads" in motivational analysis in social science, one notices how each type of drive has arisen at a time when it was a major component of public issue. Thus, the *hunger* drive was emphasized during the depression; the *aggressive* drive during the rise of fascism; the *anxiety* drive as America was drawn into World War II; the *dependency* drive with prolonged separation of families during the war; the *conformity* drive during the McCarthy period; the *achievement* drive during the space race with Russia. In short, all of this nonpolicy and detached, academic research interest is unwittingly responding to larger public events of immense policy significance. The "unconscious" of social scientists is much more policy-oriented than their theories would like to honor.

Brodbeck's conviction is that there is a subliminal "click of the heels" both to ideology and societal needs. He aims to be prophetic in his claims that we are ready for some new fashionable research area. Without much doubt one of these areas has become moral development. At one time, interest in moral development was almost totally eclipsed by the traditional fields of study in psychology, such as memory, language, and perception. Such is not the case at the close of the twentieth century. In these days of scandal touching those holding the highest of public office, of collusion among those marketing scarce but essential commodities, and of famine and even genocide in several parts of the globe, morality has resurfaced as an issue. It is one that permeates the mass media (for one controversial account see Chomsky and Herman, 1980, and the critique by Lukes, 1980). In the Western world, there is a greater concern for defining moral behaviour and for enacting codes of fairness both for children at school and adults at work. The preservation and the disintegration of the family unit have become the focus of much heated debate. These concerns have come to be shared by more and more developmental psychologists. In this respect, it has been recognized that an ideology which is so cognitive as to exclude historical and socioeconomic influences provides an inaccurate account of children's fairness (cf. Sampson, 1981).

But unlike other disciplines of observation and experimentation, psychology has not yet produced one commonly shared paradigm for pursuing scientific advances. There is no thoroughly recognized approach to research. Instead there are a number of competing mini-paradigms, each propagating their own theories and schools of thought. Perhaps for this reason, psychology must be considered apart from the older biological and natural sciences which have normally (though not exclusively) worked within paradigms. Thomas S. Kuhn writes in *The Structure of Scientific Revolutions* (1970, pp.64–65) that

> In the development of any science, the first received paradigm is usually felt to account quite successfully for most of the observations and experiments easily accessible to that science's practitioners...professionalization leads, on the one hand, to an immense restriction of the scientist's vision and to a considerable resistance to paradigm change. The science has become increasingly rigid. On the other hand, within those areas to which the paradigm diverts the attention of the group, normal science leads to a detail of information and to a precision of the observation-theory match that could be achieved in no other way...novelty ordinarily emerges only for the man who, knowing *with precision* what he should expect, is able to recognize that something has gone wrong. Anomaly appears only against the background provided by the paradigm.

According to Kuhn, a paradigm whose features are precise, wide in scope, entrenched and resistant to change is a paradigm which will be sensitive to anomalous findings. Discrepancy from what is expected will be sharpened by these features. Against a monolithic background of "normal science", anomaly will be poised to strike at the core of what has been acknowledged to be factual information. Hard on the heels of novelty comes scientific progress. But what if the background itself is as fragmented and imprecise as in the case of psychology? It follows that anomalous evidence should be more difficult to detect and will be less likely to penetrate established thinking.

Perhaps psychology is in a preparadigmatic phase in its history. Out of the contemporary competing mini-paradigms will eventually emerge one generally received paradigm. One sensible way to surmount the problem has involved efforts to weld together knowledge from disparate areas of study. This has been attempted with a variable degree of success in the area of cognitive development (e.g., Berlyne, 1965; Halford, 1982; Russell, 1978; White, 1965). It is also surely the sanest approach to advances in the study of moral development.

Particularly in any examination of behaviour which can be defined in terms of rational properties such as that of fairness, there is a need to steer between two signposts: that represented by the staunch behaviourist and the staunch cognitivist. A spectrum of ideas have spanned these posts and have come from the work of many writers (including J.B. Watson, B.F. Skinner, Neal Miller and John Dollard, Albert Bandura, James Mark Baldwin, L.S. Vygotsky, Jean Piaget, and Lawrence Kohlberg). From the outset it must be stressed that all of these figures have made colossal and enduring contributions to psychology. Yet the objective here is not one of deification. Since the theories of any writer inevitably must grapple with anomalous evidence, the task is to chisel out, connect, knit together, and synthesize the strengths of many different studies. In the absence of one received paradigm, this undertaking will not be a smooth one. Moreover, without the uniform shield of a paradigm, anomalous evidence will not quickly pierce the core of established knowledge. But if Kuhn can be believed, and one of science's aims is to account for anomaly, this is one path towards novelty and progress.

In my opinion, the task here seriously has some affinity to the study of ornithology. As a trusted colleague once assured me, species of psychologists can be spotted like blue jays and robins. A blue jay is a bird which likes to display its features and restricts its movements to a limited range of familiar locations; by contrast, a robin surreptitiously hides its colours in seeking to explore new and unfamiliar turf. Similarly, blue-jay psychologists restrict their efforts to what have been acclaimed as researchable problems, flashily displaying their methodological tools. Others, like robins, attempt to explore new and more wide-ranging problems with a less adequate methodology; their efforts often remain inconspicuous and unobtrusive. There are king blue jays and king robins, although there is probably a bit of both in every psychologist, be he behaviourist or cognitivist. Those who aim to be both birds at once are certainly not necessarily whimsical chameleons, changing their colours at every opportunity. But it is the rare virtuoso bird indeed who can employ both inclinations in worthwhile ways.

1.4 *The Issue of Ecological Validity*

Psychology today, as most who have studied the subject will admit, is plagued by a network of terms which are less than precisely defined. Consequently, many writers—psychologists and non-psychologists alike—have been commissioned to impart a real-life elegance to incisive ideas which were originally set down in an obtuse, perplexing manner (for a documented and penetrating analysis of this matter see Kadushin, 1979). Part of the problem might be attributed to the notion that psychological questions are so involved that it is not easy to formulate answers in clear simple language. But sad to say, part of the problem can also be attributed to the quandary faced by modern authors in a great variety of fields having to compete for the reader's attention with television, radio, magazines and the mass media in general. This state of affairs has been neatly expressed by Cogswell (1979, p.192):

> One of the misfortunes of the English-speaking world during the past century has been the ever-growing separation between the potential audience and the serious writer. Both parties have suffered by this rift. The audience has been left to the tender mercies of the mass media, with the result that wherever English is read, "junk food" is as much a part of the diet of the eye as it is of the stomach. At the same time, the writer, deprived of a large source of revenue and prestige and compelled to spend a good deal of energy earning a living apart from writing, has been equally unfortunate. The rift has deepened normal feelings of individual alienation and difference and forced him to greater extremes of esotericism in form and theme to show the degree of his separation from the average man. He has, therefore, tended to emphasize expression rather than communication and to abandon as platitudinous a good many of the concepts and forms devised by his predecessors which had been a source of wisdom and pleasure to mankind for ages. He has, in fact, become more revolutionary and less humanistic even than circumstances have warranted.

Those who write on child development issues certainly cannot be expected to be immune to this pervasive defect of aloofness and uncommunicative "expression"; and it is one which must be consciously recognized in the formulation of any viable theory in the area. For this reason, modern approaches to the study of fairness in children can be traced to an outline of historical events which have been associated with the abandonment (or for that matter the retention) of ancient and common-sense sources of wisdom and knowledge. Here again, an historical background can contribute importantly to understanding the origin and spread of ideas on child development. The objective is to understand historical events in their own context while searching for any lessons history may offer for the present (Henle, 1976).

With reference to historical trends, a constant watch must be made over the real-life relevance or "ecological validity" of the research settings. The criticism that an experiment lacks ecological validity is not an empty one, a convenient "catch-all" or throwaway line. To gain any worthwhile information from experimental studies, some variables must be controlled while others are varied systematically. This can be done in trivial situations which are hardly generalizable to other settings and have little bearing on actual behaviour, and indeed there have been studies conducted in experimental settings so divergent from real life that they have shed only the minutest sliver of light on psychological processes. Ideally the task is to conceive of down-to-earth situations which are capable of providing a sensible analogue to occurrences in everyday life. Thus "ecological validity" can be defined as "the extent to which the environment experienced by the subjects in a scientific investigation has the properties it is supposed or assumed to have by the investigator" (Bronfenbrenner, 1977, p.516). Accurate predictions and explanations of real-life behaviour can be generated from experiments with a high ecological validity.

But in practice, the extent to which a situation possesses such ecological validity may not be easy to discern at the outset of an experiment. An outstanding case in point comes from the work of Kahneman and Tversky (1973) in the field of adult cognitive psychology. University students, the subjects in these studies, were given hypothetical base-rate information about the distribution of persons in a population, e.g., 70% lawyers and 30% engineers. Then they were presented with a character sketch of an individual and were asked to predict the probability that he is a member of the engineer group. According to Kahneman and Tversky, subjects in such situations prevalently and commonly commit a fallacy. They mostly ignore the prior probabilities and predict on the basis of a representation conveyed in the sketch. A person described as showing no interests in politics and whose hobby is carpentry, is assigned about a 50–50 chance of being an engineer. This is a higher probability than is warranted by the original 30% base-rates supplied by the experimenter.

If Kahneman and Tversky are correct in claiming substantial generalizability of their results outside the experimental situation, their studies would be most impressive in demonstrating the fallaciousness of intuitive judgments. However, as Gillian Cohen (1977, p.69) points out, unlike in the Kahneman and Tversky experiments the prior probabilities in everyday life may approximate an even toss-up or be unknown altogether. This lack of information is so common that experimental subjects may discount probability even when obtainable. There are also many cases when it is quite apparent that people do predict on the basis of prior probabilities: insurance salesmen quoting life-insurance policy premium rates, gamblers using the racetrack odds quoted by bookies, stockbrokers advising clients on investments, pilots following a flight path to avoid weather turbulence, standby passengers hoping to board an aeroplane. The list is virtually endless.

Not only may persons ably and prudently use prior probability information when available but, in opposition to the assumption made by Kahneman and Tversky, there are often extremely good reasons for ignoring such prior probabilities when judging individuals. As L. Jonathan Cohen (1979, 1980) points out in an article entitled "On the psychology of prediction: whose is the fallacy?" the legal system would certainly be a travesty if defendants were judged on prior probability. While 90% of convicted criminals may come from ethnic group A and 10% from ethnic group B, it does not follow that jurors should then assign a 90% chance to finding an A defendant guilty in contrast to a 10% chance for the B defendant. Since all are presumed to be equal before the law, the representativeness of the defendant's character sketch should count rather than the prior probabilities. In this respect, Kahneman and Tversky's subjects were correct in rejecting probability and judging individuals as engineers or lawyers without a presumed opinion.

Therefore the extent to which these studies have an ecological validity and are indicative of widespread fallaciousness in the reasoning of adult subject populations is left dangling in mid-air (see Kahneman and Tversky, 1979, for a contrary view). While further research could clarify these issues, here is an illustration of how the results from experimental settings must be closely scrutinized for their relevance to everyday occurrences. In the presentation of studies on fairness in children the evidence will be surveyed with an eye toward uncovering possible illusions of ecological validity.

1.5 *Overview*

The aims of this book, then, are to show in what ways cognitive development, problem complexity, and adult and peer-group influences can combine to develop a sense of fairness; and to chart the course of this development through piecing together the findings of experimental studies which can be entrusted with a reasonable degree of ecological validity. The contents consist primarily of the research which speaks most directly to the subject of fairness and not necessarily to the related constructs of altruism and empathy. But even so, there remains a very broad terrain to explore here, one which encompasses theoretical and methodological problems as well as issues in childrearing and education. For this reason, there is no attempt at a full, comprehensive review of all aspects of social and personality development. Naturally such an undertaking would fill several tightly written volumes, and here some excellent reviews have appeared (e.g., Cairns, 1979; Hoffman, 1977a; Lamb, 1976; Lee, 1976; Maccoby, 1980; Mussen and Eisenberg, 1977; Shaffer, 1979; Staub, 1979). This is not such a review. There is much important work which is only tangentially relevant here and will not be pursued in detail. Included in this residual category are numerous studies on topics as diverse as birth-order effects and physical attractiveness.

Initially no better case for the social-cognitive theory can be assembled than through a detailed examination of the broad research approaches which have each generated a multitude of studies. The effects of adult influence will be examined first in terms of a social-learning viewpoint (Chapter 2). The strengths and weaknesses of this approach are explored as well as the relationship between imitation and identification. It is concluded that the adult's behaviour can serve as a model for the child's; the adult can reinforce what children say and do by verbal praise or physical rewards, and can direct children to control their own behaviour by their verbalizing of what is right or wrong.

But to encourage children to act fairly in considering the interests and intentions of the disadvantaged, peer-group experience is often important if not essential. This notion follows from the classic pioneering work of Jean Piaget. The course and causes of moral development according to Piaget are outlined (Chapter 3). He proposes a transition from a morality of adult constraint to one of mutual respect and co-operation among peers. This transition is to a large extent said to be the result of an increasing peer-group contact which widens children's cognitive capacities and liberates children from the moral rules externally imposed by adults. But though Piaget often casts adult influence in a less than positive role, findings from subsequent studies have questioned this assumption.

In short, one simple implication which is drawn from these experimental studies is that both adult and peer-group influences are complementary contributions to the development of fairness. It is proposed that a hot cognition is embodied within identification, a motivation to want to be like others. This identification may reveal the affect and motivation underlying moral behaviour. Theories and evidence for identification processes are discussed, and on this basis a four-component model of development is constructed; it is assumed that four key factors converge to encourage a sense of fairness in children: children's level of intellectual development, the complexity of the problems with which they are confronted, and the influence unleashed by the forces of hot cognition, which can originate from adults or peers (Chapter 4). To prefigure, particular attention is focused on the relationship between hot cognition and fair behaviour. Research bearing on the model is examined, particularly that pertaining to the rule-following behaviour of children in the classroom and to the behaviour of civil rights demonstrators acting on the grounds of principles. The first case is representative of a clash between a rule and a ritual, the second of a clash between a principle and a rule. In either case, children's identifications with their mothers are found to be predictive of their moral actions. Limitations to the model are then examined. The findings are discussed both in terms of the interpretation of the direction of effects in correlational studies of moral development, and in terms of the predictability of children's behaviour across different situations.

These conclusions operate under the assumption that there is no particular critical period in children's development, and that even though adult and peer-group influence may be especially important in children's early years, it can also be effective later. A detailed consideration is devoted to the idea that attempts at encouraging fairness may be doomed to failure if children are not reached when they are very young, when the doors of understanding are flung open (Chapter 5). The evidence which must be regarded as tentative is found to be consistent with the assumption that the existence of a particular critical period has not yet been established. Moreover, there appears to be little support for Piaget's claim that the primary schooler's respect for adult authority crumbles in middle childhood beneath the onslaught of peer-group contact. On the contrary, it seems that children's respect for adults may, if anything, deepen with age at least in the case of the development of moral judgments.

Having examined the role of parent–child relations from a social-cognitive approach, ways are discussed in which peer-group influence can complement adult influence (Chapter 6). To this end, it is suggested that adult influence is not limited to direct adult–child exchanges but can extend to peer–child exchanges as well. The adults' impact on peer-group relations can take several forms. Through adult intervention, children can be encouraged to consider others' interests and intentions. Experiences involving unjust privilege and deprivation can be prevented and control and self-direction in children's actions can be prompted. Examples will be given to illustrate how experience gained through peer-group contact can encourage children to act fairly without the benefit of a superior authority.

No discussion of these issues can be complete without a discussion of Kohlberg's provocative and controversial stages of moral development. The pertinent research is reviewed and discussed with respect to the present social-cognitive approach. The difficulties in scoring for principled moral reasoning and in establishing an invariant, irreversible stage sequence are noted, as well as the paramount goal of investigating moral action along with moral reasoning (Chapter 7). The importance of emphasizing normative influences on development is asserted.

The final chapter (Chapter 8) is addressed to the thorny area of moral education and childrearing. It is here that the socioeconomic and crosscultural context of identification and peer-group influence will be discussed. In the light of alternative pedagogical approaches, practical applications of the social-cognitive approach are suggested. It is hoped that these will strike a blow—even if it is a very mild one—at the solar plexus of the age-old problem of how children should be morally educated.

Chapter Two

SOCIAL LEARNING: COGNITION, IMITATION AND REINFORCEMENT

2.1 *Psychology and Positivism*

TO UNDERSTAND HOW the enormously influential social learning approach has evolved, it is necessary to turn to its historical beginnings. The emergence of social learning theory can be traced back to an American-centred revolt and then to a sort of revolution in psychology which occurred just after the First World War. This was the beginning of the now-famed movement of "behaviourism" which took its cue from a then-fashionable ideology of positivism: that psychology as a science should be solely concerned with observable behaviour amenable to experimentation. Since cognitive processes such as thinking and imagery are not directly observable to the experimental psychologist and must be indirectly inferred from other behaviour such as verbal reports and introspection, these processes were swept under the carpet and disowned as researchable topics, for the time being at least. The hardened edge of the viewpoint which emerged from this positivistic ideology was eventually to obstruct the study of social and personality development for many years to come. For how could a study be made of children's abilities to consider and imagine others' interests and intentions if such cognitive processes are not researchable?

Yet it may be conjectured that this pragmatic philosophy was one in keeping with the optimistic winds which swept through American society during the 1920s. Following the war, the United States became the world's undisputed industrial leader. Optimism and pragmatism became the bywords, invention and production the watchwords. For it was during the 1920s that the first assembly lines produced goods in massive, purchasable quantities. The value of labour-saving devices went unquestioned: the automobile above all was the machine which transformed society.

But this take-off in the economic sphere was accompanied by changes and even disruptions in the fabric of social and family life. In short, to produce massive amounts of goods available to the general public, it was necessary to build huge factories employing great numbers of workers. This meant that an individual who was once the sole owner or one of the few workers in a small enterprise was now often rendered inefficient and unproductive. For the purpose of smooth, competitive production, these small enterprises were compelled to merge into larger ones. Thus economic viability was maintained, but at a price. According to the account offered by the anthropologist Karl Polanyi (1947/1968), once the individual's "place at the campfire, his share in the common resources, was secure to him" and he himself was not endangered with starvation unless the entire community was faced with famine. But the market mechanism of the Machine Age reversed the predominance of social relations with regard to the economic system (for an illuminating discussion of this matter see Habermas, 1975). Now, within the enormous and sometimes impersonal corporation or union, the worker in reaping the benefits of technology also lost some of the social relationships he used to have in the small under-industrialized community where every worker could be known and respected individually. To no small extent much of the factory work necessary to produce innovative goods was demeaning and impersonal, giving rise to a chronic sense of alienation (for a thorough review of the evidence on the issue, see M. Jahoda, 1979). Yet the value of technological advancement in the consumer-oriented society seemed so overwhelming that these drawbacks tended to be overlooked. Nowhere perhaps was this more the case than in a postwar America favoured by geography, raw materials, and a seemingly insatiable market for goods.

These socioeconomic conditions were accompanied by a psychology of "more": of future economic growth spawned by unlimited natural resources, competitiveness and acquisitiveness (Looft, 1971). Success was judged not only in terms of family and friendship but also by the acquisition of material rewards of money, cars and clothes. This sense of alienation from social relationships in favour of the materially productive has been explored extensively in the writings of the erudite Harvard economic historian, Joseph Schumpeter (1950). Schumpeter pulled no punches in denouncing the blindly acquiescent "rational" attitude to technology, mass production and efficiency. He believed that the attitude of "economic man" served to "blot out personality". Arm-in-arm with the rational pursuit of glamorous mass-assembled cars and labour-saving devices came the disintegration of the traditional family (Schumpeter, 1950, pp.157–163). For example, where once wives and children were valuable assets in running the family business or farm, the inefficiency of these small-scale enterprises meant that this was no longer the case. Also, the support of children during the long years of schooling required for entry into a well-paying position in technology conflicted with the breadwinner's own desire for material success.

Schumpeter also saw the disintegration of the family home as the focus of social life. It was much more efficient for the purpose of facilitating business meetings to reside near boardrooms and restaurants, and to move out of traditional neighbourhoods so as to be closer to one's financial connections. With the growth of Western industrialization came urbanization and a drastic decrease in the population living in small towns. Before the urban sprawl, everyone tended to know his or her neighbour personally and the home was the centre of entertainment and social relations. In contrast, the anonymity of the large city provided many varied opportunities to work, eat, and shop. Yet paradoxically, for efficiency's sake, suburban housing areas were often located an inaccessible walking distance from community shops and services. At the same time, much social life was transplanted from the home to large office blocks, industrial parks, and shopping centres.

It is worthy to note that an influential school of economists has accepted this characterization of economic man in assuming that personal material gain is the highest and most rational goal of the individual, whose social responsibility should be subordinated to the financial growth of his firm (cf. Friedman, 1962, pp.119–136). A widely shared adherence to this assumption in sections of Western society carries ramifications for the relationship between adult economic arrangements and children's identification processes (Section 8.1).

In this historical setting, as Riegel (1972) has written, ideology was consistent with the notion that methods of introspection and self report which attempted to examine cognitive determinants of behaviour, such as the thinking and imagery involved in social relationships, were hopelessly inefficient. Coincidental with the prevalent model of economic man, little objection was raised to proposals which de-emphasized the study of individual qualities of thinking and reasoning. The state of the organism was to be tabled as a subject of inquiry; instead, one of the most important questions should revolve around "learning", defined as a permanent change in an organism's behaviour that occurred as a response to an observable stimulus, the existence of which need not be inferred but be subject to manipulation in the laboratory. There was no need to posit the existence of innate mechanisms or the occurrence of a behaviour, unmatched to a stimulus, for its own sake. The human organism from birth was a "blank slate", a "white paper", an "empty cabinet", to be shaped and moulded by environmental forces and contingencies. This argument neatly followed from the writings of the British empiricists such as John Locke who in the seventeenth century argued that all knowledge is acquired through environmental experience:

> The knowledge of some truths, I confess, is very early in the mind; but in a way that shows them not to be innate. For, if we will observe, we shall find it still to be about ideas, not innate, but acquired: it being about those first, which are imprinted by external things, with which infants have earliest to do, and which make the most frequent impressions on their senses.
>
> (Locke, 1690, Bk.I, Ch.II, Sec.15)

If behaviour is learned rather than innately present, its acquisition should be empirically verifiable through observation and experimentation. While this positivist assumption had wide appeal for scientists who sought to confine their attention to what they regarded as researchable problems, it was also enthusiastically welcomed by metaphysicians and theologians. The acceptance of positivism may have been sufficiently ensured by this event alone. Since cognitive processes were deemed to be in the realm of the unobservable and hence not researchable, science could not threaten to examine a subject which had up to now only been studied in religious contexts. It was even said approvingly that the aim of positivism is "to disontologize science" (McKenzie, 1977, p.36). A clear demarcation was greeted by psychologists and theologians alike: psychologists would study only observable changes in behaviour, as would any other *bona fide* scientists, while theologians would continue to study what they regarded as the more important issues (involving goodness and fairness) relating to the mental state of the individual.

2.2 *The Movement Toward Behaviourism*

Against the background of these historical events, American psychology's movement toward behaviourism was armed with a positivist scientific philosophy; with a few important exceptions, this flourished and almost culminated in a stampede. It was noted that advances made in the natural sciences of physics and chemistry with their household and industrial applications were not paralleled by advances in the field of psychology. Alarm spread that psychology was falling behind. According to behaviourists such as John B. Watson (1931), the culprit was introspection and psychoanalysis. Such methodological techniques aimed to discover facts about sensations, dreams, images, fixations, complexes, and the like were derogated as unscientific; and to the behaviourist these phenomena ought to be exorcised as if bewitched pariahs. No doubt they exist but are "subjective", are given different labels by different self-reporting subjects, and hence defy accurate description. No common scientific language, the argument went, could ever be found to give these mentalistic processes a meaningful interpretation. The concept of "instinct" itself was relegated to the undescribable and thus unresearchable. Instead, human behaviour was very simplistically likened to that of the course of a boomerang shaped to follow a trajectory and return to the thrower. In the same way, humans, like the boomerang, have no instincts. They are merely hurled into actions ("responses") as a result of shaping and stimulation. According to the behaviourist, man's actions are "just as peculiar (but no more mysterious)" than those of the boomerang (Watson, 1931, p.112). Such remarks served to define a position more extreme than that of writers such as Locke who believed that the mind can actively manipulate ideas once experience has furnished the "empty cabinet".

In fact, for Watson, every emotion as well as every physical movement could be explained through stimulus-response psychology. Emotions were equated with observable behavioural habits; the following, for example, was Watson's account of "love" (1931, p.57): this consisted of a stimulus ("stroking skin and sex organs, rocking, riding on foot, etc.") paired with a response ("cessation of crying; gurgling, cooing and many others not determined ... changes in circulation and in respiration, erection of penis, etc."). Indeed the "father of behaviourism" in elucidating the potential of his approach went so far as to claim:

> Give me a dozen healthy infants, well-formed, and with my own specified world to bring them up in and I'll guarantee to take any one at random and train him to become any type of specialist I might select—doctor, lawyer, artist, merchant-chief and, yes, even beggar-man and thief, regardless of his talents, penchants, tendencies, abilities, vocations, and race of his ancestors.
> (Watson, 1931, p.104)

The behaviourist's prescription for childrearing was to treat children as if they were little adults. It was a matter of choosing a stimulus to elicit a socially acceptable response. Since most faults in socialization allegedly arise from hugging and kissing, Watson's advice (1928) was to de-emphasize the emotional side of parent–child relationships. Childrearing should be firm and objective. Children should never be hugged, kissed, or cuddled on one's lap. A pat on the head is sufficient reward for achievement. If the adult cannot resist, children may be kissed once on the forehead before bedtime; the parent and child can shake hands in the morning. For children to master the demands of society, they should be trained strictly much as one trains a watch dog. According to Watson, the end result will be a "happy child free as air".

Because of what was seen at the time to be a scandal in his personal life, Watson was forced to leave the formal study of behaviourism in 1920 at the age of 42. He soon became an advertising salesman, eventually rising by 1936 to the status of vice-president of the Madison Avenue firm of William Estay and Company (a book by Cohen, 1979, gives a good biography of Watson's career). But his comparatively short academic career, from its beginnings in South Carolina to his last academic appointment at Johns Hopkins, had a lasting impact on American psychology. As Kessen (1965, pp.229–231) observes,

> The war marked a turn in American culture, and Watson's simple dogma of the limitless power of man to change his fellow man was met with the unreasoning support and unreasoning opposition that builds cults and newspaper copy . . .. The result, as Watson's doctrines became models for research on the behavior of the child, was a theoretical language and range of method too narrow to contain the child's variety and almost prohibitive of sensitive investigation of emotion and thinking in the child.

Behaviourism was strong stuff but it converted much of the US mainstream. Its ahistorical nature appealed to the democratic ideals of a society in which every child is assumed to have an equal chance for successful development regardless of prevailing socioeconomic conditions (Brandt, 1979). As Kurt Danziger (1979) notes, Watson's brand of behaviourism was also appealing to those in positions of social power. It was looked upon to supply answers to problems faced by technologists, administrators, and educators concerned with the prediction and control of behaviour. For these reasons, it has been said that behaviourism was intertwined with an ideology which served to assist in maintaining the existing social order (Sampson, 1981).

Today the philosophy and methods of behaviourism are most strongly associated with the name of B.F. Skinner whose controversial views continue to attract comment from critics, most prominently from the linguist Noam Chomsky (1958). However, parenthetically, it must be noted that even at its crest in the pre-Second World War era, the movement towards behaviourism was not a solid monolithic one. While disenchantment with introspection was pervasive, other viewpoints were forcefully expressed. Most notable were those of James Mark Baldwin (1906).

For Baldwin, behaviourism was a "philistinism" in that it refused to consider the importance of consciousness and cognitive processes. In stark contrast to Watson, Baldwin described children's development in terms of mental principles. The two major ones were: habit ("assimilation") and accommodation, the learning of adjustments to habits as a result of experience and stimulation. Baldwin's theory of moral development was a unique hybrid of philosophy and psychology and was somewhat less than precisely stated; but what is clear is that it was a characterization stated in terms of three consecutive "refinements" in the relationship between self and others.

Children initially have a *projective* sense of self in which they are stimulated to deny their asocial impulses and desires to accommodate themselves to an ideal self, exemplified in the behaviour of good others. This process at first is non-cognitive and occurs through affective-conative strivings. According to Baldwin (1906, p.327) it then shapes into a *subjective* sense of self in which the child develops a conscious awareness of this ideal and says to himself:

> Here is my ideal self, my final pattern, my "ought" set before me. My parents and teachers are good because, with all their differences from one another, they yet seem to be alike in their acquiescence to this law. Only in so far as I get into the habit of being and doing like them in reference to it, get my character moulded into conformity with it, only so far am I good.

The child's strivings to "identify" with the parents' rules and standards for behaviour now take on a cognitive element. Then this process gradually culminates in an *ejective* sense of self, which involves reflections upon the discrepancies between actual and ideal selves, producing dialectically based courses of action.

Baldwin's work was much honoured in its day and later was influential in the prolific writings of George Herbert Mead (1936). Yet its esoteric nature was largely devoid of concrete research proposals and could not compete with the brass-tacks approach of behaviourism. Nevertheless, Baldwin's contribution seems no longer doomed to remain a mere "hiccup" in the history of psychology. Efforts are afoot to resurrect Baldwin from oblivion (cf. Russell, 1978). As will be seen (Sections 2.5; 3.6), his theory has profound contemporary implications.

2.3 *The Work of Miller and Dollard*

The faith of behaviourism was that all behaviour could be explained through the application of S-R principles. This mandate was all-encompassing and it was necessary for those following a behaviouristic approach to engage in the study of specific problems of animal and human learning. Working in the field of social and personality development, there was no shortage of researchers. Miller and Dollard (1941), the best known of all those who followed in the behaviourist tradition, attempted to set out principles of "social" learning. They acknowledged their debt to Watson as well as Pavlov (1927). But following the "neo-behaviouristic" writings of Clark Hull (1943), they also incorporated in their account a class of stimuli or "primary drives" such as hunger, cold, and sex, besides others smacking of a more intellectual or higher mental quality. These were "acquired secondary drives" such as pride, ambition, and rivalry. At the time, it had become widely recognized that a reinforcement such as food may be inconsequential if the behaviour becomes weakly motivated. To cite one example given, eating behaviour cannot be reinforced by a dessert unless the diner is hungry in the first place. Once the hunger is abated, the reinforcement associated with eating may lose its strength. In this light the introduction of a mentalistic concept of "drive" seemed appropriate.

Miller and Dollard aimed to apply this neo-behaviouristic learning theory to problems of socialization and social behaviour. They lead off their analysis by taking an example from the world of business (1941, p.6). "Aggressive individuals" it is observed,

> have competed in business with cut-throat severity, but have been rewarded by success. They have boldly copied the manners and habits of those above them in social position, and though often ridiculed, have often succeeded in achieving higher status . . . since competitive and aggressive habits have been so highly and consistently rewarded, it is not surprising to find such persons displaying aggression in a great variety of situations . . .. The social structure of our society is so designed that it grants rewards to those who fight for them; in the course of so doing, it creates combative individuals.

Miller and Dollard then extended their discussion to all forms of social pathologies from alcoholism to lynchings. They minimized the possibilities that aggression, for example, may occur in the absence of environmental stimuli or that aggression may be rewarding in itself despite the fact that it meets with punishment rather than reward.

But Miller and Dollard's contribution rests on their analysis not of the social learning processes of reward and punishment but of imitation. They noticed that children in particular tend to exhibit "matched dependent behaviour" which tends to occur whenever one person is older, shrewder, or more powerful or more skilled than another. In this case, especially, a young child imitates the behaviour of an older one or an adult because the "leader" is cleverer and more experienced. Social learning occurs when the child is rewarded for imitating the leader's behaviour. For example, two brothers may be playing in their bedroom. The older one, the "leader", hears the footsteps of the father; runs to meet him, and is rewarded by candy. By chance, the younger one is running in the same direction as his brother and he also is rewarded with candy. In this way, the younger brother has learned to imitate the older one's behaviour and acquires socially acceptable responses. It is claimed that a drive—hunger for candy—has produced learning. Without hunger, the candy reinforcement would be ineffectual and there would be no such subsequent learned imitation.

As Miller and Dollard point out, simplistic as it may seem, this neo-behaviouristic social learning account of the development of social behaviour fits aptly into the ethos of a wartime effort which demanded conformity and discipline. Novel, protest behaviour of the unmodelled civil rights variety was largely de-emphasized. The overwhelming majority of social behaviour—from crying in babies to the growth of political movements—could be explained through principles of social learning and imitation.

2.4 Contemporary Social Learning Theory

Following the publication of Miller and Dollard's *Social Learning and Imitation* (1941), little work in the area was done for over 15 years. All in all, from the standpoint of those presently engaged in modelling research, "it was an era of famine" (Rosenthal and Zimmerman, 1978, p.58). But at last the torch of social learning theory was ardently taken up by many American psychologists during the early 1960s. Most prominent among the research generated by this approach has been the work of Albert Bandura at Stanford University in California. Bandura and his co-workers have designed numerous experiments in order to present formal evidence for the validity of social learning theory. In addition, they have been concerned with the cognitive determinants of a social learning which does not require reinforcement of either model or imitator for the acquisition of a behaviour.

An early formulation (1969) of Bandura's social learning theory is shown schematically in Fig. 4. Children learn their social behaviour by observing and recognizing distinctive features of a model's actions. This "vicarious reinforcement" may be all that is needed if the model is physically attractive. In such cases, learning may take place without verbal praise, prizes or rewards, though such reinforcements may speed up the process. Learning is also enhanced through a number of sub-processes such as the prestige and distinctiveness of the model, as well as the observer's arousal level, motivation, memory abilities, intelligence, physical capabilities, and self-observation capacities for accurately reproducing the model's behaviour. Yet even this initial improvement on Miller and Dollard's theory still fell short of avoiding the pitfall which had plagued earlier accounts: it still generally assumed that children can develop a sense of fairness without imagining others' interests and intentions.

The Bandura account of social learning processes has generated so many studies that it is difficult to give an exhaustive review. But because these studies have been cut from the same cloth, they mostly share a common procedure which can be easily characterized. Children are shown different types of models (e.g., adults, other children, males, females). The models perform distinctive prosocial or antisocial behaviour. Afterwards the children are placed in situations conducive to imitating this behaviour. If they

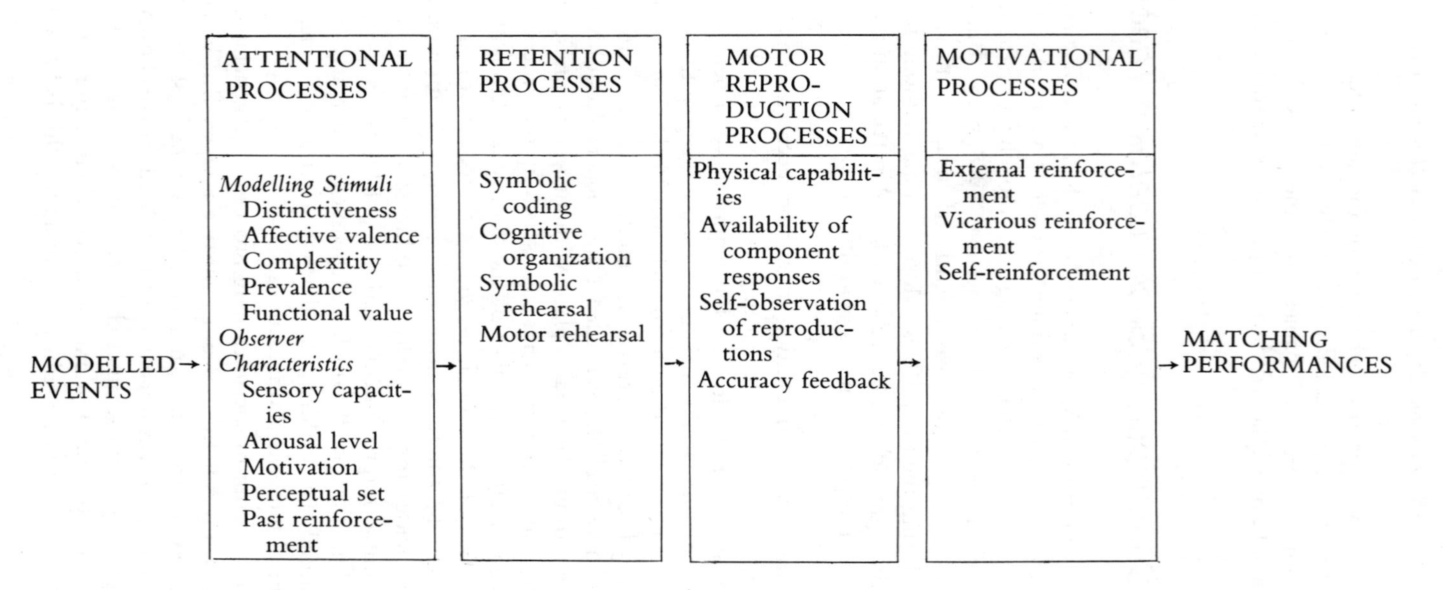

Fig. 4. *Sub-processes in the social learning view of observational learning. (From Bandura, 1971.)*

imitate, it is concluded that this behaviour has been learned and the child has identified with the model in adopting his rules and standards for behaviour.

For example, in one of the earliest studies (Bandura, Ross and Ross, 1961), the subjects were preschool children aged 3 to 5 years. In the first phase of the experiment, the children were all seated in the corner of a room. An experimenter instructed them how to make pictures from potato prints and picture stickers. The experimenter then escorted the model (an adult male or female) to the other side of the room. This had a small table and chair, a tinker toy set, a mallet and an inflated plastic doll named "Bobo" standing five feet high. Some of the children were placed in the non-aggressive condition in which the model put the tinker toys together and completely ignored the doll. The model's actions lasted for ten minutes.

The rest of the children witnessed the model's behaviour under an aggressive condition. For the first minute, the model again started to put the tinker toys together but in the remaining nine minutes the model acted very aggressively and exhibited some novel and astonishing behaviours. For example, she put Bobo on its side, sat on it, and kept punching it in the nose. She picked Bobo up, took the mallet and hit Bobo over the head. She then picked Bobo up again, threw it around the room, and shouted verbal abuse such as "Sock 'em in the nose. Kick 'em. He keeps coming back for more. He sure is a tough fella."

Then all the subjects were led to an experimental room which contained another Bobo doll, as well as a toy dart gun, and other such objects classified as aggressive toys which were not used by the model. There were also a number of non-aggressive toys present (e.g., a tea chest, crayons and colouring paper). The results of the study are not surprising: the children exposed to the aggressive model behaved more aggressively in playing with the aggressive toys than those exposed to the non-aggressive model.

Yet there is reasonable doubt that the children *learned* to be aggressive by watching the model. They may have knocked the Bobo doll around because it was the socially acceptable thing to do, because they felt that this behaviour would be accompanied by a reward, or because they felt it was merely another harmless, interesting way to play. There is no proof here that learning, as a permanent change in behaviour, has occurred. In fact even the posttest imitation effects may be very specific to the experimental treatment. Had the children as in real life witnessed somewhat less astonishing and bizarre behaviour, they might never have imitated. Nor might they have been aggressive outside the confines of the experimental room. Whether they would have imitated the model's behaviour at home, on the playing field or in the sandbox is very dubious (cf. Kuhn, 1973).

There is, then, a problem which looms very large on this horizon: the certainly unreal quality to generalizations based on the results of social learning experiments. To claim that processes extending through years of childhood are aptly analogued by the imitative responses which follow a five- or ten-minute modelling session is plainly artificial. How much so is hard to determine. Such experiments have an inbuilt assumption of "as if"—as if behaviours such as altruism and aggression can be studied using brief and fleeting exposures to models (Staub, 1979, pp.37–38). This involves the issue of ecological validity. To establish the generality of effects arising from imitation experiments would require children's behaviour to be examined in a wide variety of *highly dissimilar* situations. Yet in general, only minor changes have been made to the test situations in studies which have been interpreted to suggest a significant degree of generalizability.

Beyond this objection to the assumption of ecological validity, there are still others (cf. Hoffman, 1970). Experiments generated from the social learning paradigm have often treated the child in isolation either from other peer models or other adult models. Frequently, the child is studied in a two-person situation, the other participant being a strange model who is usually a postgraduate student.

But perhaps the most piercing criticism comes from Robert White (1963). The interpretation of social learning experiments, according to White, is limited because imitation cannot be regarded as synonomous with identification. The former involves "wanting to do something someone else has done" while the latter involves "wanting to be like someone else". For example, a customer who imitates a salesman's demonstration of a gadget's use does so because he wants to learn how to use it himself, and not because he admires and strives to emulate the salesman, or because he envies the salesman's power and status. Likewise, it would be a mistake to maintain that a child who has imitated a model's behaviour wants to be like him. To cite two examples, a child who imitates an aggressive model may do so simply to develop his own muscles, not because of a desire to use these muscles in a fight. A child who imitates an act of generosity originally performed by a self-sacrificing model may follow suit out of a very different motive: to ingratiate himself to his or her peers. In neither case does the child identify and want to be like the model in adopting his behavioural standards. Consequently, it is important to understand the perceptions underlying the child's own overt behaviour in order to infer identification from imitation.

The thrust of these troubling difficulties is illustrated in studies of the effects of modelling on children's learning of altruism or generosity. For example, in one experiment (Rosenhan and G. White, 1967) Grade 4 and 5 children were given the opportunity to watch an adult model play a bowling game and donate half his winnings to charity. When allowed to play the game themselves without the adult present, the children tended to model his behaviour. They gave significantly more of their winnings to charity than a control group of children who had not observed the model.

However, it would be erroneous to label the children's behaviour as altruistic, let alone fair, just because the children gave up rewards at their own expense. Rather than donating their winnings for the good of others, they may have felt under some pressure to give generously from the now absent model. Perhaps they expected that on his return, the model would ask them how much they gave to charity and would appreciate a favourable response. Should this in fact be the case, the children's "altruism" may have been only to please the experimenter. Thus, such "generosity" may be unaccompanied by a consideration of others' interests and intentions and the effects of viewing the model might be of questionable durability. The point is vividly demonstrated by the unanticipated results of an important later experiment (G. White, 1972). Boys and girls aged 10 and 11 played a miniature bowling game. For every score of 20, they could win two 5c gift certificates. Near the game was an open charity box in which certificates could be donated to orphans. One group of children was assigned to a "guided rehearsal condition" in which they practised giving to charity; they were prompted to donate one of the two certificates on winning trials. A second group took turns playing with an adult model and observing him donating. A third group merely observed the model. Finally, a control group was simply told about the charity box. Following these treatments, half the children played alone both immediately and in a second session several days later. The other half played only in the second session. Results indicated that, during the immediately played session, those in the rehearsal conditions donated more certificates than those in the observation and control conditions. However, in the second session there was a significant decrease in altruism and an unexpected and quite spontaneous increase in stealing gift certificates. This was most evident in the guided rehearsal group. Their practice in donating apparently became practice in stealing for a competition seems to have emerged in the interval between the two sessions as to who could obtain the most certificates.

Such results suggest that "observational learning" cannot be granted the linchpin role in all aspects of social and personality development and, in particular, that it does not provide a wholly adequate account of fairness in children. For imitation, as operationally defined in such experiments, is not the same as understanding. In the first session of the White experiment, donations may have been made thoughtlessly without any concern for others and without any desire to be like the model. In the second, it is clear that a "learned concern for others" if this had been achieved previously was overridden by other considerations. Either an immature intellectual orientation or intense competition from peers may have been a more important determinant of social behaviour than observational learning (Section 3.1).

But even if the results accurately reflected the learning of the behaviour of a purely consistent model in an experimental setting, the ecological validity of many imitation studies remains problematic. For models are often inconsistent in what they portray to children. Adults may preach the importance of imagining the interests and intentions of others; but there are certainly times when they practise the opposite to what they preach. In such circumstances, as deftly shown in experiments using inconsistent models, the impact of observational learning may be weakened significantly (Staub, 1979, p.124). In fact, adults who hypocritically exhort children to share generously when they themselves act greedily may make matters worse if encouraging charity (let alone a motivated disposition toward fairness) is their aim (Bryan, 1975).

Studies comparing the influence of consistent and inconsistent models have shown that imitation effects of a model's generosity can persist over some weeks (e.g., Rushton, 1975). But the "altruism" acquired through such observational learning again seems to have been unaccompanied by an increased concern for others. Far and away the lion's share of the evidence has revealed no significant relationship between the altruism displayed in imitation experiments and children's level of cognitive development as indicated, for example, on measures of the ability to understand other's interests and intentions (see Rushton, 1976, for a review of the pertinent research). In sharp contrast, such relationships have been found in experiments on altruism conducted outside the context of imitation (Buckley, Siegal and Ness, 1979).

Moreover, imitation studies lack the stringent, albeit serendipitous, test for observational learning effects used in the White study. Giving children the opportunity to steal as well as to donate provides a clearer indication of whether or not they have learned a concern for others. Without allowing for this possibility, there is no way of ascertaining whether children exposed to a generous model might steal rather than donate if given the choice.

For these types of reasons, social learning theorists have come to link observational learning to cognition or personal experience. For example, "seeing inequitable punishment may free incensed observers from self-censure of their own actions, rather than prompting compliance and thus increase transgressive behaviour" (Bandura, 1974, p.51). And the latest thrust of social learning theory is to place more emphasis on cognition and less on modelling to the extent that the earlier social learning concept is recast towards a rapprochement with Robert White. This account explicitly breaks with the behaviourist proposition that an individual's behaviour is controlled by the environment, and asserts that the "environment is partly of the person's own making" (Bandura, 1978). It thus provides a rationale for studying people's perceptions of themselves and others within a theory of self-efficacy.

According to Bandura (1977a; 1981), self-efficacy refers to judgments about oneself, about how well one can cope with the demands of situations. This self-knowledge is gained from four sources. Three of these can be categorized, roughly speaking, as knowledge gained from the observation of the behaviour of similar people ("vicarious reinforcement"), from verbal persuasion by others, and from the degree to which situations elicit aversive or stressful emotional arousal. But the most important basis for such judgments is obvious to the layman and that is actual practical experience in coping with situations (labelled "performance accomplishments", "enactive attainments" and "enactive mastery").

A test of the self-efficacy notion is reported in a study designed to alleviate adults' fears of snakes and thus does not bear on the issue of identification (Bandura, Adams and Beyer, 1977). Advertisements were placed in community newspapers to recruit subjects who suffered from chronic snake phobias. Those who answered the advertisement (7 men and 26 women) and who were included in the experiment demonstrated substantial fear in an avoidance behaviour test. These subjects were unable to hold a red boa-constrictor with a gloved hand. At the same time, they indicated the magnitude, strength, and generality of their expected behaviour toward snakes on rating scales.

The subjects were then randomly assigned to one of three conditions. In a "participant modelling" condition, the modelling element was minimized. In effect, a female experimenter had subjects enact performances which were broken down into easily mastered steps which increased in difficulty following a pre-established sequence. The subjects first looked at, then touched and held another snake: a "rosy" boa-constrictor distinguishable from that used in the pretest. They were then induced into allowing the snake to crawl freely in their laps and retrieving the snake after it had been let loose in the room. It was reported that the treatment time varied from 40 minutes to 7 hours (median time = 90 minutes).

The second condition merely consisted of modelling. The subjects did not perform the behaviour itself but watched the model complete the same graduated steps of encountering snakes. Subjects in a third control condition received no treatment.

The participants were then retested on the red-tailed boa used in the pretest and a dissimilar 90 cm corn snake. The results are shown in Fig. 5 and these indicate that the actual practical experience of "participant modelling" was most effective in curing adult snake phobia. In this

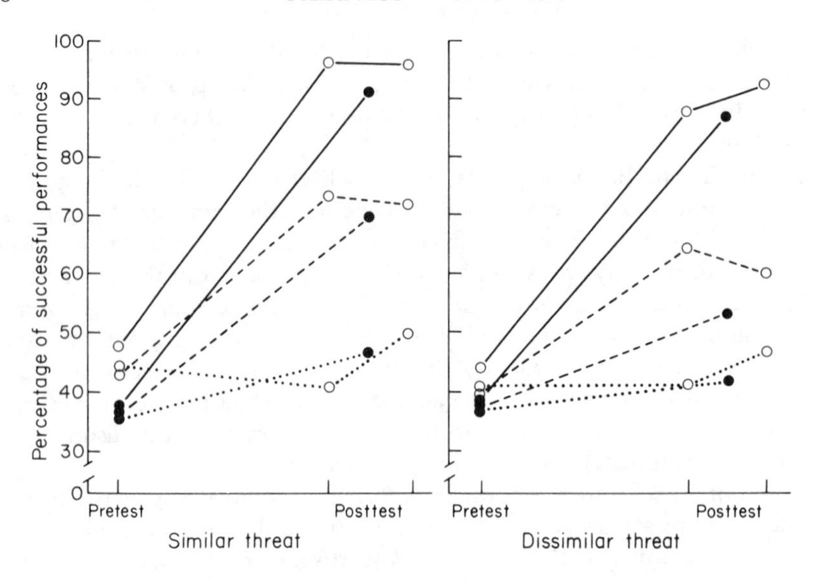

Fig. 5. *Level of self-efficacy and approach behaviour displayed by subjects toward different threats after receiving modelling, participant modelling, or no treatment. In the posttest phase of the experiment, level of self-efficacy was measured prior to and after the behavioural avoidance tests with the two snakes.* Participant modelling: (○——○)*efficacy*; (●——●) *behaviour.* Modelling: (○– –○) *efficacy*: (●– –●) *behaviour.* Control: (○· · ·○) *efficacy*: (●· · ·●) *behaviour.* (From Bandura, Adams and Beyer, 1977.)

condition, self-judgments of the ability to cope with snakes were altered and subjects' rated expectations of personal efficacy rose. Modelling without this practical experience was not nearly as effective in reducing the subjects' fears, though those in the modelling condition outperformed those in the control condition.

All this serves to underscore an important facet of everyday learning that much, if not a very large part, of behaviour cannot be successfully acquired by observation alone. Watching a model may be but one way of developing an interest in eventually performing an overt behaviour. Practical experience is necessary for the acquisition of many skills and, as will be seen in the next chapter, the one psychologist who has been most successful in specifying the nature of this experience is Jean Piaget.

An important part of moral development involves the encouragement of self-efficacy. In establishing this type of cognitive link, social learning theory becomes more sensibly real, more ecologically valid. And it is almost a truism to assert that a theory without this cognitive link provides a less than adequate account of children's social and personality development.

Nevertheless, imitation and reinforcement processes do play some role here even if it is not clear just what this role is. These processes cannot be so readily criticized as a primary source of aggressive or destructive behaviour. To behave aggressively does not require highly developed information-processing skills or mental gymnastics. Unlike the case of altruism and fairness, there is evidence to suggest parallels in the aggressive behaviour of man and sub-human species (Hinde, 1974, p.278). Therefore, in some circumstances a simple imitation explanation of aggression might suffice and for decades has been invoked:

> the imitative tendency which . . . produces frenzies of violence . . . is possessed by man in common with other gregarious animals . . . being a blind impulse to act as soon as a certain perception occurs. (James, 1890, p.408)

Leaving the valuable "self-efficacy" notion aside for the moment (cf. Section 6.2), it is important here to delimit to what extent the imitation and reinforcement analysis does apply in the development of children's sense of fairness.

2.5 The Role of Imitation and Reinforcement in Identification

To this end, social learning processes can be examined as they pertain to the learning of concepts or generalized ideas, for an understanding of the relevant concepts is an essential part of the acquisition of any subject matter, including morality. In the study of history, for example, "government" and "economy" are important concepts; among those in the area of morality is the concept of "fairness". In this respect, there is good reason to believe that children learn "fairness" much as they learn other abstract concepts such as "gravity" or "slavery".

Of special significance here is the work of Lev Vygotsky (1962, 1967), a Soviet psychologist who wrote during the 1920s, whose work bears an affinity to that of Baldwin and whose thoughts on child development have been amplified in the writings of many other Western psychologists (e.g., Beaudichon, 1973; Bruner, 1964; Damon, 1979; Piaget, 1962). In discussing the implications of imitation and reinforcement for concept-learning Vygotsky claimed that the child acquires two types of concepts: the spontaneous concepts which he develops "mainly through his own mental efforts" (1962, p.84) and the non-spontaneous concepts imposed on the child in the course of formal instruction from adults. The concept "brother" is given as an example of a spontaneous concept. The preschool child knows often through his own efforts during play that he has a brother, but it is not until much later through adult instruction that he can generalize the term "brother" to other precisely similar situations. Only later does he acquire the mature meaning of the word and gain the ability to classify new instances systematically, e.g., that his brother also has a brother and that the child himself is his brother's brother.

Yet not all concepts can be regarded as spontaneously developed. In a complementary process, some layer of sophisticated meaning is *immediately* attached to non-spontaneous and particularly scientific concepts. Children first learn these by reinforcement and imitation as associations tied to particular situations and unidentified with other precisely similar ones. For example, the meanings of social science concepts such as "slavery" and "exploitation" initially "lack the rich content derived from personal experience" (1962, p.108). As this experience is gained, the full mature meanings gradually evolve, for "scientific concepts . . . supply structures for the upward development of the child's spontaneous concepts towards consciousness and deliberate use" (1962, p.109).

Thus the child's spontaneous and non-spontaneous concepts merge to be used in a systematic way. Words and actions indicative of concepts can be generalized without contradiction to precisely or relevantly similar situations. The child comes to know that he is his brother's brother, or that slavery is slavery whether it is building pyramids in Pharaoh's Egypt or doing forced labour in a twentieth-century concentration camp. He comes to understand and identify with the adult's standards of fairness.

Now the critical question here concerns moral concepts such as "fairness", "right" and "good", "helping" and "lying". Are these first learned spontaneously through the child's own mental efforts and personal experience or non-spontaneously through formal adult instruction? There are grounds to believe that moral concepts are non-spontaneous ones, normally first learned through adult instruction (cf. Hare, 1952). For young children are not congenitally moral, and often do not imagine the interests of others unless adults prompt them to do so (Bearison and Isaacs, 1975). Adult instruction through imitation and reinforcement conveys the necessity of acting fairly to children who have little or no personal experience of others' interests and intentions. This instruction must be short and simple for children to follow. For

> it is easier to teach a child that he must never lie . . . than to teach him that he must not lie unless to tell the truth would do such injury to another person that the child would be justified in lying in order to spare the person that injury, despite the losses in mutual trust that might ensue from the lie. To perceive and balance different values which are not together compatible in a given situation ought to require more cognitive maturity than the application of a single, simple rule. (Maccoby, 1968, pp.256–257)

No wonder young children often first meet concepts such as "lying" through social learning processes as associations tied to particular circumstances, circumstances which admit no exceptions.

The analysis can be restated using Baldwin's terminology. The child first "projects" his or her self to conform with adult rules through affective-conative strivings. Only later does the child become stimulated and experienced enough to develop a cognitive, subjective or ejective sense of self in relation to others.

So the moral concepts learned through adult instruction later supply the structure of "cognitive maturity" for personal experience. Provided children have a respect for adult instruction, there are several ways in which the adult might affect their sense of fairness and cultivate their identification with adult rules and standards. The adult is a model for children's behaviour; but as we have seen before, the effects of modelling *alone* are rather limited without personal, practical experience. Just how limited is illustrated by a look at some of the contemporary representative work on the three motivational sub-processes in observational learning which are singled out by Bandura: external reinforcement, vicarious reinforcement, and self-reinforcement.

External reinforcement

Perhaps social learning experiments are on the solidest ground when their interpretations are limited to the immediate effects of external reinforcement. It is hardly surprising that reinforcement of children's verbal responses can affect their moral behaviour. Two early well-conceived experiments are useful as illustrations. For example, in one study (Lovaas, 1961), 3- and 4-year-old children were pretested on two types of equipment. Both were operated by pressing a bar. In one case, the bar pushed a ball on the top of a cage. In the other, the bar caused a doll to hit another doll over the head with a stick. The subjects then underwent a verbal conditioning session. They were asked to speak into a "talk-box" on the top of which were seated a clean doll and a dirty doll. Half the children were reinforced for giving verbal responses such as "bad doll", "doll should be spanked", and "dirty doll"; the other half were reinforced for non-aggressive responses such as "clean doll" and "good doll". In a posttest, the children reinforced for bad-type verbal responses made a significantly greater number of responses on the aggressive doll equipment than did the children reinforced for good-type responses. Similar results were reported in a study by Slaby (1974). Elementary school children were trained to speak either helpful or aggressive words. Compared to children trained to speak aggressive words, those in the helpful condition were less aggressive and more "altruistic" in that they gave more pennies to a non-existent peer for making mistakes on arithmetic problems.

In another study designed to examine the effects of reinforcement on children's self-control processes (Liebert and Allen, 1967), third- and fourth-graders played a bowling game in which they could score 5, 10, 15 or 20 points. The children were reinforced by an adult for scores of 20, either by token rewards or by token rewards and a verbal "rule structure". For a score of 20, the adult said, "20, that's a good score that deserves a chip." For a score of 15, he said, "15, that's not a very good score . . . that doesn't deserve a chip." Children who were trained by this rule structure later deviated less from the rule that only a score of 20 merited a reward than those children reinforced by tokens alone. At the same time, the children in the rule-structure condition also made significantly more self-critical comments in describing their performance as good or bad.

Such studies demonstrate how reinforcement can affect aggressive and self-controlled behaviour in the short-term, though the explanation for these effects is not clearly specifiable using these types of experimental situations. Again, it is certainly far-fetched to conclude that the children have learned to identify with the experimenter's rules and standards for behaviour.

Vicarious reinforcement

Especially in the case of vicarious reinforcement, some of the claims made by social learning theorists can be regarded as loose or imprecise statements at best, the evidence falling drastically short of what would be required to verify or falsify these propositions against rival ones. For example, it has been maintained that processes in creativity and enculturation can be fostered by observational learning and that a significant portion of novel behaviour is best explainable in terms of vicarious modelled responses. For example,

> Modeling probably contributes most to creative developments in the inception of new styles. Once initiated, experiences with the new forms create further evolutionary changes. A partial departure from tradition thus eventually becomes a new direction. The procession of creative careers through distinct periods provides notable examples of this process. In his earliest works, Beethoven adopted the classical forms of Haydn and Mozart, though with greater emotional expressiveness which foreshadowed the direction of his artistic development. Wagner fused Beethoven's symphonic mode with Weber's naturalistic enchantment and Meyerbeer's dramatic virtuosity to evolve a new operatic form. Innovators in other endeavors in the same manner initially draw upon the contributions of others and build from their experiences something new. (Bandura, 1977b, p.48)

Whatever is meant by "experience", "evolution", and "emotional expressiveness", to substantiate definitively how Beethoven arrived at his compositions is not an easy task. Many other alternative explanations can be proposed. Of these a biological, nativist one is perhaps the most popularly favoured: that Beethoven was born with the ability to write music brilliantly beyond what previous composers had achieved. Some of the similarity in style with other composers could be viewed as coincidental rather than purposely imitative. This explanation is compatible with the one advanced by D.O. Hebb (1974) who regards the social aspects of psychology to be part of a biological science. Hebb proposes that creative ideas can be explained by separate ideational components which are stored in the mind. Each separate element, which contains a possible component of the new idea, fires and subsides continually and independently until the critical combination gels in the correct sequence.

Hebb's explanation is a mechanistic one and, as he himself points out, that some are able to recognize and profitably use new ideas whereas others are not remains problematic. Hebb's account does not detail any better than Bandura's why Beethoven and no one else exposed to the same musical stimuli could compose in a novel way; nor does it explain why no one since has been able to imitate with precision the distinctive style of Beethoven's music. (The same applies to the many attempts which have been made to imitate the music of more contemporary rock-and-roll stars such as the Beatles.)

Still another explanation of creativity has been suggested by Jean Piaget (1962). In contrast to Bandura, Piaget claims that individuals may initially draw on their previous knowledge or schema of behaviour and then build on this knowledge by accommodating to the contributions of others: hence "imitation always depends on intelligence" (Piaget, 1962, p.85), rather than vice versa. This process is characteristic of those who create strategies for adapting to novel situations. Piaget's version has the strength of integrating what the individual brings to bear on the situation with what the situation itself consists of. Suppose a letter-sorter has been sorting mail into pigeon-holes. He "assimilates" this information into preformed categories: mail bound for Australia, Britain, Canada, etc. One day he comes across a letter for a novel and previously uncategorized destination, e.g., Zimbabwe. He accommodates his system to fit novel information by creating a new pigeon-hole and sorting category.

But at least with respect to the Beethoven example, it is exceedingly difficult to substantiate any explanation, including Piaget's. For this reason, there is plenty of room for rival theories to co-exist and certainly it would be premature to place all the money on one theoretical horse by assigning a pre-eminent role in creativity to social learning.

The same intractable problem of interpretability plagues social learning experiments on vicarious reinforcement in parent–child relations. For example, in one cleverly designed study aimed to show the relationship of identification to parental dominance, warmth and conflict (Hetherington and Frankie, 1967), the subjects were 80 preschoolers and their parents. This experiment consisted of four phases. (1) Each parent was given a Structured Family Interaction Test which involved 12 hypothetical situations in which the child has misbehaved (e.g., a neighbour calls up and complains that your son/daughter has been throwing rocks at her child). (2) The parents were brought together and asked to come to an agreement on how to handle the situations. (3) The parents were each asked to perform a sequence of distinctive behaviour in view of their child. (4) The child was tested for imitative responses during a play session. Phase 1 and 2 measures of warmth and hostility shown toward the child and of conflict and dominance in coming to a solution were related to the child's imitation in Phase 4. The results indicated that both warmth and dominance increased imitation. Boys tended to imitate a powerful father and girls a warm mother. But when there was conflict and hostility in both parents, the dominant one tended to be imitated. Indeed subsequent research has demonstrated that children are likely to imitate a powerful model who controls economic resources (Section 8.1).

As revealing as such results are for imitation, they unfortunately say little about identification. It is unknown whether any of the children in the study actually wanted to be like their mother or father. For example, in an experimental situation in which others are not present, a boy may imitate his father. But this is a far cry from saying that he actually wants to be like his father in adopting his behavioural rules and standards, a test of which necessitates a measure of children's behaviour toward others. Indeed, in a naturalistic peer-group situation children may display a sense of fairness imparted by their mothers. What is needed is a clearer, more ecologically valid measure of identification (Section 4.1).

Self-reinforcement

The third of Bandura's motivational sub-processes involves self-reinforcement, about which it has been claimed (Luria, 1961) that not only does self-reinforcement through language help to promote certain behaviours, but that it also helps to regulate them. So far there is little consistent evidence to support this claim in the case of motor tasks (Bloor, 1977; Bronckart, 1973; Jarvis, 1968; Meacham, 1978; Miller *et al.*, 1970; O'Connor and Hermelin, 1971). Here the object typically is to instruct oneself verbally to squeeze a ball when a light appears. The purpose is to direct motor behaviour.

Yet in the area of social and personality development, there is a consistent pattern of exceptions suggesting that moral behaviour can be guided by verbal self-reinforcement. Two of the earlier studies are especially worthy of mention. O'Leary (1968) taught 48 first-grade boys what was "right" or "wrong". They learned to press a key when shown the "right" shapes (i.e., triangles) and not to press a key when shown the "wrong" ones (i.e., circles). Then the boys were told that they would now have the chance to win 5c, 10c or big prizes such as a toy fire truck if they continued to earn tokens by responding *only* to the right shapes. However, they were told that tokens could be gained from responding to the wrong shapes as well. Half the subjects were told to instruct themselves out loud with the labels "right" or "wrong" whether or not they could respond to the stimulus; the remainder were told to respond silently. Results indicated that the self-instruct group cheated significantly less than the silent group. Thus the labels "right" and "wrong" helped to regulate moral behaviour.

In another study (Hartig and Kanfer, 1968), children aged 3 to 7 were told that they were to see attractive toys. The experimenter then asked them to turn away from the expected location of the toys or the "surprise" would be spoiled. For the experimental manipulation, the children were divided into five groups. One group was told to self-reinforce by repeating the words, "I must not turn around and look at the toy". The second group was told to do the same but to follow these words with "If I do not look at the toy, I will be a good girl (boy)". The third group was told to follow with "If I look at the toy, I will be a bad girl (boy)". The fourth group was to repeat an irrelevant verbalization, "Hickory, dickory, dock, the mouse went up the clock", and the fifth, a control group, was not told to verbalize. The experimenter went out of the room for a maximum of ten minutes and surreptitiously recorded the number of seconds before the subject transgressed in turning around to look at the toys. Findings were that the three self-instruct groups showed significantly greater self-control than the fourth and fifth groups. There were no significant differences among the first three or the last two groups.

Other studies have also obtained results that support the effectiveness of verbal self-instruction in regulating moral behaviour (Masters and Santrock, 1976; Meichenbaum and Goodman, 1971; Monahan and O'Leary, 1971). Moreover, it is possible that verbalizations can enhance the observational learning of a model's behaviour (cf. Bandura, Grusec and Menlove, 1966) though this is far from conclusive (Coates and Hartup, 1969; Zimmerman and Bell, 1972).

Hence verbalizations may both promote and regulate certain kinds of moral behaviour. Then what are the mechanisms that determine the acquisition and usage of verbalizations from the standpoint of adult instruction?

According to one line of research (Aronfreed, 1963, 1964; Aronfreed, Cutick and Fagan, 1963; Grusec, 1966; Grusec and Ezrin, 1972; Herbert, Gelfand and Hartman, 1969), such verbalizations can be equated with the development of self-critical comments. These have been learned from adults' descriptions of prohibited acts. Their function is to indicate to the child the appropriateness and potential consequences of his moral behaviour (Aronfreed, 1969, p.288).

In this type of experiment, the subjects have been primary school children. They have participated in tasks designed to examine the conditions which elicit self-criticism. For example, in two studies (Aronfreed, 1963; Aronfreed, Cutick and Fagan, 1963) the object was to shove a toy nurse into a protective box. This could only be done by knocking down some toy soldiers. At the start of the experiment, the children were given a supply of sweets. These were gradually removed by the experimenter as "punishment" when toy soldiers were knocked down. For some of the children, the punishment was associated with the experimenter's commenting "how careless and rough you've been". For others, these comments were omitted. On a test trial, it was made to seem that the child had broken the toy nurse. He was then asked, "I wonder what happened?" or "Why did this happen?". The general result of both experiments was that the children learned through "observation". Those provided with the experimenter's self-critical comments were more self-critical in mentioning their "roughness" or "carelessness" than those for whom the comments were omitted.

A common claim is that these children appeared to hold their own behaviour responsible for the mishaps in the test situation. But there is a strong drawback to this interpretation. It is likely that the self-critical responses were never the result of the child spontaneously describing his action as careless and rough without the experimenter's probing. As Hoffman (1970, p.305) has written, "it seems from the descriptions given in the research reports that the child may merely reproduce the labels used by the experimenter and apply them in a parrot-like fashion to his own behaviour". This is the very antithesis of wanting to be like (i.e., to identify with) the experimenter. Furthermore, the children in these experiments were given either the proper self-critical labels or none at all. So it is not surprising that they chose "self-criticism" rather than some inappropriate comment typical of primary school boys such as "I don't like dolls anyway". Difficulties in substantiating the generalizability of self-instruction have been acknowledged by Meichenbaum and Asarnow (1980), and these remain to be overcome in further research.

In summary, formal adult instruction through external, vicarious and self-reinforcement may be a first step toward identification with adult behaviour. But for children to acquire a more complete concept of "fairness" involving the consideration of others' interests and intentions, personal, practical experience is often necessary involving elements of mutual respect, cooperation, and responsibility; and it may be that imitation experiments can be more profitably conducted in conjunction with such cognitively based features of moral development related to "self-efficacy" (Section 6.2). As one who has written extensively on the history of the learning-theory approach, Sheldon White (1970, p.678) has pointed out that the introduction of an unreinforced imitation to the social learning tradition is tantamount to a virtual upheaval in the field. No longer is it necessary to posit a hypothetical reinforcement schedule which shapes the child's behaviour. We now have a history of unreinforced observation and, from outward imitative behaviours, an inward "central processor" of cognitive operations such as "symbolic coding" and the like is implied. The force of this radical reformulation is to move away from a psychology influenced by an ahistorical ideology of positivism. It serves to create a tenuous bridge between social learning theory and the constructivist, experiential theory of Piaget, a provocative theory which lays great emphasis on the experience gained through peer-group contact.

Chapter Three

PIAGET'S THEORY: COGNITION AND PEER-GROUP CONTACT

3.1 *Psychology and Rationalism*

PIAGET'S BIOGRAPHICAL DETAILS are unusual to say the least. In characterizing his approach to child psychology in general and to the study of moral development and fairness in particular, let us begin by outlining some landmarks in Piaget's own intellectual history.

Jean Piaget (1896–1980) was born and spent his childhood in Neuchâtel, Switzerland. In his autobiography (1952), Piaget writes that he was strongly influenced by both his parents. His mother suffered under the stress of a mental disturbance and this contributed to his later interest in problems of reality and the unconscious. From the earliest age he sought to imitate his father, a scholar of medieval literature. The young Piaget sensed that, for his father, religious faith and historical criticism were "incompatible". From reading in his father's library, Piaget came to develop an interest in philosophy which he maintained throughout his career.

But Piaget first began as a student of natural history. Between the ages of 7 and 10 he studied fossils, birds, and sea shells. As a 10-year-old, he published his first scientific paper in a natural history journal of Neuchâtel. It was on the sighting of a partly albino sparrow in a public park. Piaget then started to spend his free time in studying the collection of the local museum and became very interested in molluscs. He published several more articles on wildlife, sight unseen, and at the age of 15 years, was offered the position of curator of the mollusc collection at the Geneva National History Museum. This he had to decline because of his age and, as he was still a schoolboy, Piaget was afraid to meet other colleagues working in the field of zoology.

However, Piaget did not become a professional naturalist because, as he writes, during his late teens he suffered a series of emotional and intellectual crises over the meaning of life. He wanted to discover from the scope of the mind itself, between the scope of biology and philosophy, a solution to problems of epistemology. For Piaget, this became an intellectual need which could only be met through the intensive and serious study of experimental psychology.

Piaget approached psychology with a very different philosophical orientation than that held by the American school of behaviourism. This philosophy was wholly consistent with the traditions of continental Western Europe and it arose from a different set of social and economic conditions than those which existed in the United States. Nowhere, perhaps, was the distinction more striking than in Piaget's native Switzerland, particularly in Geneva located within a stone's throw of the three great continental powers of France, Germany, and Italy (Riegel, 1972). The coming of the Machine Age had very different effects on Switzerland than on America. There, as in the United States, industrialization created huge corporations and unions which tended to change the pattern of family and community life. But at the same time it has been observed that industrialization and the social changes that went with it tended to bring the Swiss closer together. According to at least one partisan account, "With the coming of the machine age, people moved their homes and jobs regardless of religious and political barriers, which had hitherto divided the Confederation" (Thurer, 1970, pp.130–131).

Rather than the American "melting pot" with all individuals judged against single standards of language, scholastic and economic achievement, continental Europe to some considerable extent retained its class distinctions which prevented social mobility. But industrial progress in Switzerland also created a climate of preservation and toleration for different languages and cultures. It fostered a continued embrace with the rationalist philosophy of Descartes and Kant that reason and concepts are the primary source of knowledge. Moreover, it generated a tradition diametrically opposed to a psychology which sought to reduce behaviour to quantitively continuous stimulus-response processes. The tradition of continental European psychology was to view children's development as qualitatively discontinuous and hierarchically organized in sequences of *stages* (Looft, 1971).

3.2 *Piaget's Cognitive Stage Approach*

Piaget's research grew out of this rationalist tradition. Unlike the behaviourists who believed that knowledge can be characterized in terms of stimulus-response processes, psychologists such as Piaget came to work under the rationalist assumption that man constructs his reality or intellectual "structures" through an interaction between the oganism and its physical and social environment. Armed with this philosophical sword of "genetic epistemology", Piaget first took his doctorate in the natural sciences by writing a thesis on molluscs. He spent a year studying psychoanalysis in Zürich. Then at the age of 23 (in 1919 immediately following the war), Piaget left for Paris where he spent two years at the Sorbonne. In the French capital, he became involved with Theophile Simon and Alfred Binet who were interested in developing intelligence tests for the purpose of identifying and remediating children's educational handicaps. Piaget set himself the task of standardizing the reasoning tests of Cyril Burt (1909) on Parisian children, and found that the results were useful for diagnostic purposes. But Piaget became more interested in the reasons for children's failure to solve items on the test. He developed a "clinical method" for looking at the structure of children's reasoning by giving them an open-ended interview. For example, children were given problems such as: "Edith is fairer [or has fairer hair] than Suzanne; Edith is darker than Lili. Which is the darkest, Edith, Suzanne, or Lili?"

The children interviewed by Piaget responded with answers such as "Once Suzanne is the darkest and once Edith is, [therefore] Suzanne is the same as Edith, and Lili is the fairest" and "You can't tell, because it says Edith is the darkest and the fairest". For Piaget, this was evidence of the "egocentrism" which characterizes children's reasoning. That is, children are unable to make comparisons and to take account of the relativity of different persons because they are "shut in" according to their own point of view. Children cannot imagine that Edith at the same time is both fairer than Suzanne and still less fair than Lili (Piaget, 1928, pp.87–92). Like Baldwin and Vygotsky, Piaget came to believe that the child constructs the reality of these relations in the course of gaining practical personal experience. But, for Piaget, the co-ordination of different elements develops from intellectual structures interacting with the environment rather than directly from imitation and acculturation. This concept of egocentrism took on prime importance in Piaget's developmental theory.

In 1921, Piaget returned to Switzerland to initiate his research programme at the Maison des Petits of Geneva's Institut J. J. Rousseau. Over an 11-year span he published five books on child psychology, the fifth entitled *The Moral Judgment of the Child* (1932/1977). In this book, Piaget claims that there are stages of moral development which correspond to stages in children's intellectual development.

These moral stages develop in two separate but parallel sequences. The stages are highly susceptible to a peer-group influence which dissolves the child's initial egocentrism and fosters his consideration of others' interests. All children proceed through stages in an invariant order, but the rate of progression varies from child to child and the age-ranges corresponding to each are rough approximations only. One stage sequence involves the practice of moral rules in general, such as those against lying and stealing; the other involves the verbal comprehension of these rules. The origin of both sequences lies in Piaget's observation of the rules by which Swiss children from the poorer parts of Geneva and Neuchâtel play the game of marbles. For this purpose, the rules of the marble game are assumed to be representative of moral rules in general. We need to consider these before comparing the strong points of Piaget's theory with those of social learning theory.

The practical stages

The practice or overt application of rules, Piaget claims, progresses through four stages. In the first stage from birth to about 3 years, very young children do not play games in common with other persons, and therefore do not submit to rules of social play or "generalized collective rules". Instead they behave wholly "individually" and practice regularities only according to their own particular fantasies.

The second stage in the practice of rules is one midway between that of purely individual and socialized behaviour. This is the stage of "egocentrism". During the years 3 to 6, children attempt to imitate the behaviour implied by adults' rules. Yet they play "in an individualistic manner with material that is social" (Piaget, 1932/1977, p.33). For instance, in the game of marbles, children play with each other but do not follow common rules in order to establish a winner or loser. Their interest, as in the initial individualistic stage, lies in the development of their own skills. During this egocentric stage, there is a collective monologue in which children speak, but only to address themselves.

In the third practical stage (7 to 10 years), the child's interest becomes principally social. This is the stage of "incipient co-operation". Players now try to win at games but the rules they follow are completely contradictory.

Finally, in the fourth stage (11 to 13 years), children's interest lies in the "codification of rules", in anticipating all possible cases and codifying these within a juridico-moral system. The purpose is now to win games according to commonly accepted rules which cover all possible cases.

The verbal stages

These four practical stages in the child's overt behaviour overlap with three stages in his verbal comprehension of rules: a stage in which the child attaches no precise meaning to rules, a stage in which the child rigidly declares his adherence to the letter of the rules, and a stage in which rules are adopted and followed in a spirit of mutual respect and co-operation among peers.

This first verbal stage (3 to 4 years) overlaps the first part of the practical egocentric stage. Here the child comprehends and speaks of rules only as examples that are uncoercive in character. His play is "individual" and not governed by collective rules generalizable from examples. His speech is egocentric and not directed towards communicating with other players.

The second verbal stage (5 to 9 years), coincides with the latter part of the egocentric and the first part of the incipient co-operation stages. During this period, children cannot dissociate the old from the new; they attach no precise meaning to the words "before" and "after" (Piaget, 1932/1977, p. 52). For this reason, rules are rigidly understood as permanent and unchanging. But the most prominent characteristic of rule rigidity is the child's unilateral respect for adult authority. Because rules are the infallible product of adult authority, they are held to be sacred and inviolable. Thus the rules of the marble game cannot be changed by the mutual consent of the players. Rules are eternal creations imposed on young children by older children and adults.

The third and final stage (about 10 years onwards) of verbal comprehension overlaps the latter part of the incipient co-operation stage and the whole of the codification stage. Now children declare that rule changes are possible through the mutual consent of peers. Rules are products of lawful convention and mutual respect; they are not imposed by external authority; they are equally applicable to all concerned. There is no disagreement over the rules of marble games, for everyone plays in the same manner.

There are many borderline cases which fall in between each of these stages. Piaget (1932/1977, pp.58–59) gives the example of 10-year-old Ben who is midway between the second and third stages:

Interviewer: Invent a rule
Ben: I couldn't invent one straight away like that.
I: Yes you could. I can see you are cleverer than you make yourself out to be.
B: Well, let's say that you're not caught when you are in the square.
I: Good. Would that come off with the others?
B: Oh, yes, they'd like to do that.
I: Then people could play that way?
B: Oh, no, because it would be cheating.
I: But all your friends would like to, wouldn't they?
B: Yes, they all would.
I: Then why would it be cheating?

B: Because I invented it: it isn't a rule! It's a wrong rule because it's outside of the rules. A fair rule is one that is in the game.
I: How does one know if it is fair?
B: The good players know it.
I: And suppose the good players wanted to play with your rule?
B: It wouldn't work. Besides they would say it is cheating.
I: And if they all said that the rule was right, would it work?
B: Oh, yes, it would . . . . But it's a wrong rule.

Ben realizes that it is possible for children to change the rules. But nevertheless he still believes that they are imposed by an absolute and almost divine authority.

So in both the practical and verbal stage sequence, Piaget proposes a transition from a morality of adult constraint to one of mutual respect and co-operation among peers. The notion of an egocentrism which progressively erodes with age provides a cognitive basis for the development of moral judgments. It presumes that the young child cannot co-operate fully with his peers because he or she has an inadequate understanding of others' intentions and interests which may differ from his own. This inability to simultaneously consider two or more points of view is closely aligned to the child's general intellectual development, for the egocentric child is unable to take into account two aspects of a problem in coming to a logical solution. To take one of Piaget's well-known examples of children's conservation abilities, a child may acknowledge that two balls of clay are equal in size. But if one is rolled by an experimenter into the shape of a long sausage, the child will now claim that one of the two has more clay. According to Piaget, such responses are evidence of "centration" in the child's reasoning. He or she attends to only one aspect of the objects and ignores the other. A child may report that one of the two balls has more because it is taller or that the other has more because it is longer. Just as the young child cannot co-ordinate others' viewpoints, he or she does not understand that the rule of logic that changes on one dimension (e.g., length) can be compensated by that on another (e.g., height).

Piaget also goes to great trouble to clarify the role of imitation in moral development. Often he maintains that by itself imitation is indicative of egocentrism. The young child who simply imitates the judgments and behaviour of others does not dissociate his or her own interests and intentions from those of others. Such children lack "conscious minds that impose themselves in virtue of an inner law to which they themselves are subject" (1932/1977, p.88). They do not demonstrate genuine and deliberate co-operation but only behaviour which arises out of the inequality of relationships between the child and others. In stark contrast with social learning theory, Piaget (1962, p.73) is careful not to endow imitation with a pre-eminent role in development:

> imitation . . . is never more than a vehicle, and not a motive for inter-individual relations . . . the dynamic link is to be found either in compulsion, authority, and unilateral respect, which give rise to the imitation of the superior by the subordinate, or in mutual respect and intellectual and moral equality, which are the origin of imitation among equals.

Having described the place of egocentrism and imitation in a cognitive theory of moral development, Piaget makes two key assumptions. First, a distinction is drawn between mutual respect and what is termed to be "mutual consent". For Piaget a mutual respect morality is possible only within a framework of rules of justice which enable co-operation and reciprocal treatment between members of society. By contrast, mutual consent may be present in vice—it can occur in collective thievery and organized crime which operates outside of rules as the actions of a gang of outlaws may display mutual consent but not respect. Thus Piaget's characterization of mutual respect necessarily implies a sense of fairness which mutual consent may lack.

Second, according to Piaget, the relationship between verbal moral judgment and actual moral behaviour is indisputable. He alleges that children are quite sincere in making moral judgments on their own behaviour and so Piaget claims that, for his purpose, words are indicative of actions. This rather dubious assumption leads Piaget to rely almost exclusively on verbal evidence as support for his own ideas on moral development. Later the judgment–behaviour relationship problem will be examined further (Sections 4.5, 7.5, and 7.6). But for the moment, let us skate around the issue by accepting Piaget's results on moral judgment tasks as being equally applicable to moral behaviour.

Piaget's method simply consisted of telling children stories which have moral themes and then probing for responses. Much, though not all, of what was found to be characteristic of an adult-constraint/mutual-respect transition can be placed under the following four rubrics: intentions and consequences; immanent justice and naturalistic explanations; punishment and adult authority; and justice among children.

3.3 *Characteristics of Piaget's Stages*

Intentions and consequences

One indication of adult constraint is the "objective" responsibility orientation of the young child; that is, his moral judgments are based on the consequences of an action regardless of its accompanying intention. To look at this issue, Piaget presented pairs of stories to children aged 5 to 13. For example, in one story a little boy named John accidentally broke 15 cups; in a counterpart story, another little boy, Henry, irresponsibly broke one cup. The children were asked to judge who was naughtier, John or Henry. Those with an objective responsibility orientation (average age 7) chose John, as he was the one associated with the greater damage. Those with a subjective intent orientation (average age 9) disregarded the extent of the damage and chose Henry because he was the one who was deliberately naughty. Piaget (p.126) gives the example of 6-year-old Schma who has an objective notion of responsibility:

Interviewer: Are those children both naughty, or is one not so naughty as the other?
Schma: Both just as naughty.
I: Would you punish them the same?
S: No. The one who broke fifteen plates.
I: And would you punish the other one more, or less?
S: The first broke lots of things, the other one fewer.
I: How would you punish them?
S: The one who broke the fifteen cups: two slaps. The other one, one slap.

There are two other facets of moral judgments related to the intentions–consequences theme. First, young children confuse lies with mistakes. They do not yet understand that lying involves a deliberate attempt to deceive, whereas mistakes are accidental. For example, children were told two stories: one about a boy who deliberately misled a gentleman asking for directions, the other about a boy who faithfully tried to help. In the first story, the man eventually found his way but, in the second, he became lost. The children judged the well-meaning boy to be naughtier than the mischievous one.

Secondly, children under the age of 9 maintain out of unilateral respect that it is worse to lie to an adult than to another child. They claim that "It's naughtier to lie to a grownup because they are older" or "It doesn't matter to a child. You can tell him lies. But you mustn't to a grownup" (Piaget, 1932/1977, p.165). Only later is lying to a friend considered to be just as naughty or even naughtier.

Immanent justice and naturalistic explanations

Here again children are told stories. For example, a boy who has disobeyed his mother later meets with misfortune. In trying to cross a stream, he walks across a rotten plank and falls into the water. Why did this happen? An immanent justice response typical of the 6- and 7-year-olds' adult constraint morality would be that the boy fell in because he disobeyed his mother. A rational, naturalistic response would be that the boy fell in because the plank was rotten. Thus "to young children, things such as planks are the accomplices of grownups in making sure that a punishment is inflicted where the parent's vigilance has been evaded" (Piaget, 1932/1977, p.247). Adult authority is so powerful that it enlists the help of inanimate objects in sustaining its control. In contrast, for the older mutual respect child, disobedience is not related to such misfortune.

Punishment and adult authority

Compared to children who have achieved a morality of mutual respect, those constrained by adult authority are also more apt than mutual respect ones to choose to punish offenders in an arbitrary expiatory manner that is unrelated to the content of guilty acts. Responses to the following short story provide an example:

> A child is looking at a picture book belonging to his father. He carelessly makes spots on the page. What should the father do? 1. The child will not go to the cinema that evening. 2. The father will not lend him the book anymore. 3. The child often lends his stamp book to his father. The father will not take care of it as he had until then. (Piaget, 1932/1977, p.196)

The first punishment is expiatory; it is unrelated to the misdeed. According to Piaget, the child who chooses this punishment accepts the "righteous anger" and authority of the adult, and accepts that an effective punishment must carry the weight of adult constraint. In contrast, the choice of the second punishment is more mature in that it is suited to the misdeed and is aimed at preventing similar incidents in the future. The third punishment is midway between the first two in sophistication. It is related to the misdeed but only creates greater damage instead of preventing a recurrence.

Justice among children: the development of co-operation

For Piaget, there are sharp differences with age in children's ideas on justice. Younger children associate justice with obedience to authority; since age implies authority, they judge that older individuals rightfully deserve more rewards and less punishments than do younger ones. By contrast, older children may equate justice with equality and judge that rewards and punishments should be dispensed equally without regard for subjective factors such as effort and need on the part of the individual recipients. But even more characteristic of the judgments of older children is their belief in the fairness of equity, that rewards and punishments should be distributed according to subjective factors, especially individual needs.

Piaget's (1932/1977, p.299) evidence here comes partly from children's responses to the following story:

> Two boys, a little and a big one, once went for a long walk in the mountains. When lunch-time came they were very hungry and took their food out of their bags. But they found that there was not enough for both of them. What should have been done? Give all the food to the big boy or to the little one, or the same to both?

Examples of the younger children's responses, predominantly those of 7-year-olds, indicated the prevalence of authority-based reasoning: e.g., "The big boy should have had most because he's bigger" and "The big boy should have most because he's the eldest". In comparison, the older children either claimed that it was fair for each to be given the same or for the little one to receive more because of his smaller size. Piaget claims that such answers adequately document the development of co-operation in children towards considering others' interests and intentions.

3.4 *The Antecedents of Moral Development*

In describing these processes of transition, Piaget minimizes the role of the parent. Contrary to any theory (including one of social learning) which emphasizes the strength of adult influence, he maintains (p.190) that children's

> sense of justice, though naturally capable of being reinforced by the precepts and example of the adult, is largely independent of adult influence, and requires nothing more for its development than the mutual respect which holds among children.

Thus the adult may be able in home and school to promote moral development. But the transition primarily involves cognitive factors which are associated with a broadening of the child's former egocentrism. Among these are an increasing solidarity among children, a realization that adults are fallible, and the experience of suffering injustice to oneself through the misinterpretation of one's intentions.

As we have seen, Piaget claims that the effects of adult constraint are most prominent in young children. In contrast, the older child has reached a state of co-operation; he has attained an "equilibrium" of mutual respect. Nevertheless, it may be suspected that this achievement is complicated by factors which Piaget has neglected to consider fully, factors related to the role of adult influence which—far from being independent of child development—forcefully directs the rate and outcome of personal, practical experience gained through participation in peer-group activities. For though Piaget's ideas on the child's cognitive development are excellent, his approach to the relevant experimental evidence is often "cavalier" (Bryant, 1971); and the term "cavalier" might also be used here to characterize

Piaget's approach to experimental evidence pertaining to the child's moral development.

One of these neglected factors which Piaget plays down is that adults may surreptitiously or overtly recognize the immanent nature of children's moral reasoning and use this to maintain obedience. Thus moral development may be obstructed by adult-instilled fears and, for example, despite having been immersed in peer-group experience, children may come to believe that disobedience of adult authority will inevitably be punished by natural calamities.

Another factor which Piaget largely ignores is that adults themselves may not be so inclined to inquire after intentions. Whatever the circumstances, they may punish the child more severely for breaking 15 cups than for breaking one (Costanzo *et al.*, 1973; Cowan *et al.*, 1969). Piaget himself makes this point (p.130), but claims that the injustice of being punished for a well-intentioned act enables the child to make mature intentional moral judgments. Yet it is at least equally plausible that the child learns much about consequences and little about intentions, again despite having been immersed in peer-group experience. To this end, studies have shown that young children aged 6 years are capable of inferring intentionality in making moral judgments, but they may not spontaneously do so unless directed to do so by others (Bearison and Isaacs, 1975).

Even to what extent adults themselves make intentional moral judgments is unclear (Fishbein and Ajzen, 1973). There may even be some cases in which the consequences alone, regardless of intentions, are the prime determinants of moral judgment in adults (Lane and Anderson, 1976). An example comes from automobile accidents. In such situations, adults may judge a driver who causes heavy damage more severely than a driver who causes light damage even though the drivers are equally negligent (Walster, 1966).

Despite all this, Piaget does little to dispel the notion that moral development is complete before adulthood at the age of 12 or 13. Though in later work he says that personality development continues after the age of 13 (1967, pp.64–70), Piaget does not attempt to provide empirical evidence bearing on the development of moral reasoning in adolescents and adults. Instead, he merely asserts that once mutual respect has come into existence in one aspect of behaviour, it has the "right to be applied to everything" (p.91). But though logically sound, Piaget's claim is psychologically misleading. In making a moral judgment within certain isolated circumstances, a person may imagine the interests and intentions of others. Yet in exactly or relevantly similar circumstances, he may ignore these interests. Thus the ideals of equilibrium, co-operation and mutual respect may be more closely tied to hypothetical experimental situations than Piaget has stressed. Even

4-, 5-, and 6-year-olds at times give mature, mutual-respect-oriented responses; yet at other times even older children give constraint-oriented responses.

It should be noted that Piaget himself (1932/1977, p.32) does not deny that young children demonstrate some semblance of a mutual respect morality:

> through imitation and language, as also through the whole content of adult thought which exercises pressure on the child's mind as soon as verbal intercourse has become possible, the child begins, in a sense, to be socialized from the end of his first year. But the very nature of the relations which the child sustains with the adults around him prevents this socialization for the moment from reaching that state of equilibrium, in which the individuals, regarding each other as equals, can exercise a mutual control . . . .

By this account, the stages are far from clear-cut; and, if the adult does exert any effect at all, this inevitably is at the expense of moral development.

Piaget's de-emphasis of normative influences is in keeping with a commitment toward formulating a cognitive theory of moral development. But why Piaget particularly derogated the effects of adult influence is something of a mystery—especially when we recall that in his autobiography Piaget describes himself as strongly influenced by his parents and that from a very early age he substituted work for play with other children. This would imply that in Piaget's case the effects of peer-group interaction were minimal, which is of course anomalous to his own theory. It is tempting to speculate that Piaget's ideas on moral development are flavoured by those of Rousseau. If children are born good and are then corrupted by adult society and its institutions, does it not follow that adult authority should be an obstacle to the child's moral development?

Such speculation aside, following the publication of his 1932 book, Piaget from time to time returned to touch on the subject of moral development. But he never again conducted an in-depth study on the subject, preferring instead to devote his efforts to work on infancy and cognitive development as well as to philosophical subjects. According to one account (Elkind, 1970), Piaget used to disappear alone each summer to a farmhouse in the Swiss Alps, his whereabouts a closely guarded secret. By the start of classes, Piaget habitually emerged having written several books and articles during his sojourn. This enormous productivity fuelled the Piaget legend. Though Piaget's work has been critically scrutinized in recent years (Bryant, 1974; Donaldson, 1978), a strong, enduring interest remains in his research findings, notably including those on children's moral judgments.

Perhaps nowhere in the world has this interest been greater than in the United States where the advent of the Cold War set the stage for an enthusiastic acceptance of Piaget. With the launching of the first Sputnik by the USSR in 1957, concern mounted that the Soviet Union was outstripping the United States in technological achievement. A culprit was soon found and the finger was pointed at the American education system. The Soviets are outperforming the Americans, went the argument, because Soviet children are outperforming American children. Up came a gigantic push toward research in education and child psychology and in the process American psychologists "rediscovered" Piaget. For Piaget was involved in the study of imagination, thinking, and reasoning—skills which are obviously necessary for technological innovation. American psychology had been aware of Piaget's work for decades (Piaget was given an honorary degree at Harvard in 1936) yet the indigenous behaviourism movement was so dominant that it had cast Piaget out from the mainstream of study for his allegedly unscientific concern with cognitive processes. It was hardly surprising that when the need for information on these processes arose, American psychology could not meet the demand and turned to Piaget for inspiration.

Thus after 1960, Piaget's ideas on many aspects of child development spearheaded a voluminous amount of research, particularly in the United States. For example, they have become both the cornerstone and foundation for the influential work of Lawrence Kohlberg (1963, 1976, 1978) which aims to describe moral development in childhood and throughout adolescence and adulthood. In this approach, responses to a set of hypothetical moral dilemmas are scored; individuals are then classified as having either a preconventional, conventional, or postconventional (i.e., principled) moral orientation. However, as might be expected, hypothetical responses do not fall into easily scorable categories, nor do they give a clear picture of actual moral behaviour. For such reasons, the scoring system has undergone continuing revisions and amendments, particularly with regard to the categorization of responses as principled.

What follows is a discussion of the extensive research on Piaget's theory; later (Chapter 7) the Kohlberg theory will be examined in detail. The evidence suggests that heterogeneity in Piaget's stages of moral judgment is to a large degree dependent on an adult influence which can both stimulate and obstruct. This influence is exerted partly along ways proposed by social learning theory such as reinforcement and imitation. It is related to (1) the extent and (2) the type of damage caused by children and, as might be suspected, (3) it also reflects social class differences in childrearing methods, and (4) cultural differences in the existence of co-operation. The implications of the research outlined below serve to question the viability of the egocentrism concept and point to a possible convergence in the Piagetian and social learning approaches.

3.5 *Research on Piaget's Theory*

The extent of damage

Suppose then that adults punish according to the severity of the damage regardless of the child's intentions. The greater the damage, the heavier the punishment; and the heavier the punishment, the more likely are children's moral judgments to be consequence-based. Conversely, intentional moral judgments should reflect light damage and mild punishment.

There is strong support for this view. In one study (Armsby, 1971), children aged 6 to 10 were given a set of four story-pair situations. Each pair had four levels of accidental consequences. For example, children were asked to compare a boy who deliberately broke one cup while setting the table with: (1) a boy who broke one cup accidentally; (2) a boy who broke 15 cups accidentally; (3) a boy who broke all his mother's cups accidentally; or (4) a boy who broke a brand new television accidentally. In both the 6- and 8-year-old groups, the hypothesis that moral judgments are related to the extent of damage was supported. As predicted, when both deliberate and accidental damage resulted in relatively minor damage, even the 6-year-olds tended to respond intentionally. Others have reported similar findings despite differences in method of story presentation and differences in story content (Berg-Cross, 1975; Gutkin, 1972; Hebble, 1971; McKeachie, 1971; Rule and Duker, 1973).

Given that children are more likely to give intentional responses when consequences are light, consequence-based answers may be purely a function of unusually severe damage. In fact, contrary to Piaget, young children may have a preference for consequences over intentions only in very special situations involving a great deal of damage such as the smashing of 15 cups.

There are other types of frequently occurring situations which Piaget does not consider. For example, Piaget confines his discussion on intentions and consequences to situations with negative consequences. But if a well-intentioned and an ill-intentioned act both met with positive consequences, children could not then judge according to an "objective" criterion of naughtiness. Might they be more apt to give intentional moral judgments in these situations?

To answer this question, Costanzo, Coie, Grumet and Farnill (1973) compared the effects of good and bad consequences on intentional responses. Their subjects were boys aged 5 to 11 years. They were presented with stories one by one, and were instructed to rate story characters on a 9-point scale from most good to most bad. Findings indicated that the use of intentions increased with age for judgments of story characters accidentally producing negative consequences. However, all age groups tended to use intentions in judging characters associated with positive consequences.

The explanation advanced by Costanzo *et al.* (1973, p.160) is consistent with the imitation and reinforcement interpretation of social learning theory:

> The child himself is evaluated by quite different criteria when he produces positive consequences than when he produces negative consequences. That is, most children may receive negative feedback, either directly or indirectly when they produce negative outcomes, regardless of their intentions. Such is less likely the case with positive events, since the parent's arousal is less extreme and he is better able to discriminate his child's intentions.

The type of damage

There is other work which stresses the importance of adult influence. In one study (Imamoglu, 1975), children aged 5 to 11 were given 8 stories representing all combinations of three variables: namely, two levels of intentionality (intentional–accidental), two levels of consequence (good–bad), and two of "affected agent" (human being–physical object). For example:

> This little boy and a group of children were playing with a ball in the garden. As the little boy kicked the ball to his friend, it went a little too high and broke a window (accidental; bad outcome; physical object). This boy was riding on the bus to school. When he saw an old lady who did not have a seat, he gave his seat to the old lady; the lady was very pleased (intentional; good outcome; human being).

The stories were again presented separately and were supplemented with pictures as an aid for comprehension. Subjects then rated the story characters on a 4-point scale of "very good", "good", "bad", and "very bad". Again, the results indicated that children were better able to distinguish between deliberate and accidental acts in the good-outcome than in the bad-outcome stories. Moreover, as early as 7 years, this distinction was clearer in stories involving human beings than those involving physical objects, a finding which has since been replicated (Elkind and Dabek, 1977).

Once more, these results are attributed to the effects of imitation and reinforcement. According to Imamoglu, when children and adults are engaged in a two-way relationship, both parties are expected to be able to understand the implicit intentions behind acts. But when acts involve only material damage, adults cannot be expected to understand intentions since often these are not readily apparent. Thus adult reinforcement is often related to the type as well as to the extent of child-caused damage.

Social-class differences in the acceptance of adult authority

Piaget claims that young children of about 5 to 9 years have a unilateral respect for adult authority; they are very willing to accept that an effective punishment must be severe enough to carry this authority's weight. Yet Piaget's observations are based on children from the poorer parts of Swiss cities, and it has been commonly observed that there are social class differences in childrearing methods. For example, working-class parents are more likely to use physical punishment as a disciplinary technique than are middle-class parents (Hoffman, 1970). Might then middle-class children, for example, be less accepting of adult authority?

Harrower (1934) was one of the first to examine this question. Two groups of 5- to 10-year-old English schoolchildren, one group from poor homes and one from well-to-do homes, were given the following story and questions:

> One day, Tommy and Peter were playing together, and Peter had a lovely new engine . . . one that you could wind up and then it runs along the floor. Now Tommy was a naughty little boy and suddenly he kicked Peter's engine, and smashed it up so that it could not go anymore. Now what should we do to the naughty Tommy? Shall we smack him (expiatory punishment), or shall we break up his boat (reciprocity proper), or shall we make him save up his pocket money until he can buy Peter a new engine (restitutive punishment)?

The responses of the children from poor homes were consistent with Piaget in that within this group there was a significant developmental shift in response category. The majority of the 5- to 7-year-olds chose the expiatory punishment, while the majority of the 8-to 10-year-olds gave mature restitutive responses. In contrast, there was no developmental shift in the children from well-to-do homes. At all ages, they tended to give restitutive responses. Harrower's conclusion was that the well-to-do home imparts an intellectual atmosphere which the poorer home does not. Therefore, the moral judgment development of the poor children lags behind their well-to-do counterparts.

Similar social class differences on these types of stories have been found in Switzerland (Lerner, 1937a) and the United States (MacRae, 1954). However, the differences found in an American study by Boehm and Nass (1962) were largely insignificant though in the same direction. But in this case, the questions differed from subject to subject. Moreover, the subjects themselves were chosen from the same demographic areas and were not divided into two clearly distinct and homogeneous groups.

A study by Lerner (1937b) was designed to examine the influence of "sociocultural" factors on the moral judgments of working-class children.

A series of stories and questions were presented to Genevan boys aged 6 to 12. For example, "A boy here in your school told me that the boys in *X* school [another local school known to the subject] tell more lies than the boys here; while a boy there [the other school] told me just the opposite . . . who is right? Why?" As one might expect, even the responses of the older group centred on the omnipotence of familiar, respected persons and institutions; 44% of the subjects aged 10 to 13 based their judgments on the infallibility of schoolmates, while 65% gave similar responses regarding family members and 26% regarded the community. In Lerner's interpretation (1937b, p.264), "We have here the genetic psychology of so-called race prejudice, religious, occupations, or class bias".

In contrast, Lee (1971) did find a significant decrease with age in authority-based responses. But while Lerner's subjects were the sons of manual labourers, Lee's were boys of "average intelligence or above", living in an upper-middle-class community. Thus the disappearance of authority-based responses may be accelerated in, if not restricted to, children from well-to-do or middle-class homes. All of this implies that, contrary to Piaget, moral judgment development is highly dependent on adult influence.

It may be argued, of course, that such social class differences are an artefact of differences in IQ scores or formal education (cf. Higgins, 1976). Nevertheless, this seems implausible since the Piaget and Lerner studies were based on a sample of children with similar demographic characteristics. Yet Lerner's results appear to conflict with Piaget's. They suggest that a respect for authority does continue to dominate the moral judgments of working-class children aged 10 to 13, and that development is stimulated in children from middle-class homes. To this end, other evidence to be reviewed in Section 5.4 with regard to the issue of a sensitive period in moral development lends little support to Piaget's claim that, with increasing peer-group interaction, the authority of the adult becomes less legitimate and influential to the child.

Crosscultural differences in co-operation

Piaget's theory proposes that children with age develop a morality of genuine respect and co-operation in which the needs of others are acknowledged. But though children's co-operation has not been intensively investigated by contemporary psychologists (see the review by Cook and Stingle, 1974), recent research suggests that preschool children do demonstrate a considerable amount of co-operation (Strayer, Wareing and Rushton, 1979). In certain contexts, children may actually become less co-operative, and, at the same time, more competitive with age. Moreover, children from industrial Western societies tend to be less co-operative in general than are children from traditional cultures on all continents worldwide (Werner, 1979, pp.316–324).

Co-operation has been studied by examining children's performance in same-type situations. One of these involves the use of a "circle matrix board". For example, in one study (Kagan and Madsen, 1972) Anglo-American and Mexican children aged 7 to 9 years were shown a board with seven rows of circles connected by lines along which they could move a marker from one circle to another (Fig. 6). In each experimental session, two children were seated on opposite sides of the board. The marker was placed in D4, the centre circle. One of the children was given a toy to keep (e.g., a pen, magnifying glass, magnet, or ring) and asked to place it by

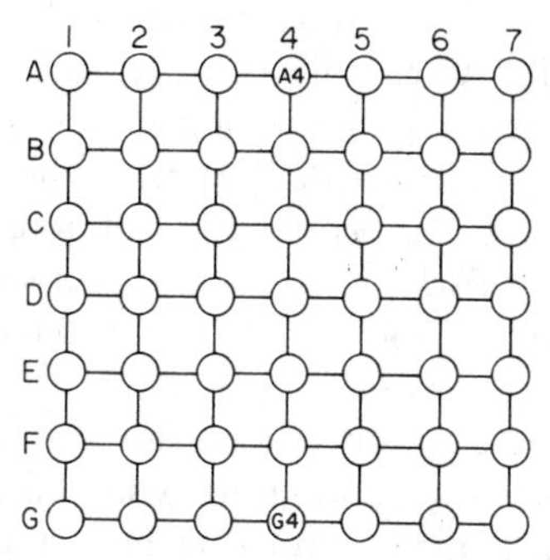

Fig. 6. ***The circle matrix board used in studies on co-operation.***

the middle circle of the row nearest him. The second child was then told that he could take the first child's toy by moving the marker to G4 or could let the child keep the toy by moving the marker in the opposite direction to A4.

The results indicated that the Anglo-American children were significantly more competitive than the Mexican children in taking the toy from the other child. The less-competitive behaviour of the Mexican children was attributed to their traditional non-industrial culture. Subsequent studies (e.g., Knight and Kagan, 1977a, b) have compared the co-operation of Anglo-American and Mexican-American children. Findings have been that Anglo children become significantly more competitive with age in contrast to Mexican children who tend to become slightly more prosocial. As Mexican-American children become progressively more immersed over generations in the broad Anglo-American culture, they become less altruistic and more competitive. Therefore, at least in some circumstances, children may become less co-operative with age in moving away from a belief in equality and equity to one based on competition. In their judgments of rewards and punishments, more emphasis may be placed on the competitive outcome of the situation rather than on individual needs. Such findings clash with Piaget's generalizations made on observations of children's marble game play.

3.6 Theories of Egocentrism and Imitation: A Contrast and Convergence in Viewpoints

By now it should be apparent that Piaget's theory might be seen to clash with social learning theory. Piaget claims that peer-group interaction disturbs the child's egocentrism and undermines his unilateral respect for adult authority. This development toward understanding others' interests and intentions is irreversible. When children reach the point where they make mature moral judgments, they cannot be conditioned to ignore intentions.

For Bandura, moral judgment development should be reversible given the appropriate "observational learning", and additional support for this notion might be inferred from research on Piaget's theory. The extent and type of damage as well as social class background are related to moral judgment development; this would seem to involve imitation and reinforcement effects. Thus a child who is trained through imitation and reinforcement to give consequence-based judgments should readily do so even if he has previously attained Piaget's mutual respect stage and has developed a mature moral judgment orientation.

The proposition that moral judgments are acquired through social learning is a difficult one to substantiate. The issue of the ecological validity of the experimental situation arises once more. Even so, the social learning of moral judgment was examined in an experiment by Bandura and McDonald (1963). The results were as predicted, and are consistent with evidence suggesting that adult reinforcement and modelling contribute to children's moral judgments.

The participants in the study were children aged 5 to 11 years. They were given a pretest which consisted of 12 story-pairs. In each pair, a story involving good intentions and heavy consequences was contrasted with one involving bad intentions and light consequences such as in Piaget's story-pair about the broken cups. On the basis of their pretest responses, the subjects were assigned to one of two groups: a group with clearly intentional responses and a group with clearly consequence-based responses. The aim of the experiment was to expose the members of each group to a level of moral reasoning opposite to their own.

In the experimental conditions, all the subjects were presented with an additional 24 story-pairs. The intentional group was trained "downwards" to make consequence-based responses to the story-pairs. By contrast, the consequence-based group was trained "upwards" to make intentional responses.

Each group was sub-divided further into three others. For one sub-group trained upwards and one sub-group trained downwards, the children observed an adult model giving a "correct response". Then they themselves were asked to respond. Both the model and the children were reinforced for responding correctly with verbal approval from the experimenter. For a second sub-group trained upwards and a second sub-group trained downwards, only the model was reinforced and not the children; and for the

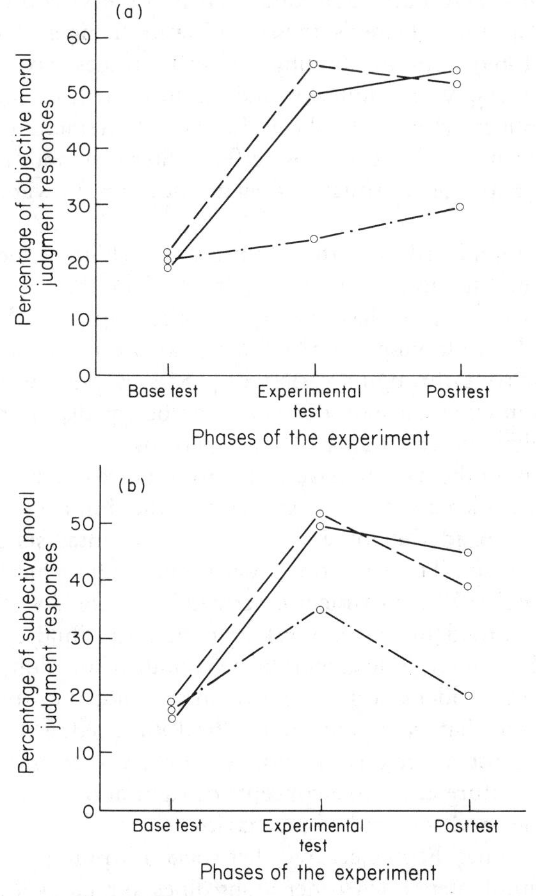

Fig. 7. *The effect of reinforcement on children's moral judgments. (○——○) Model and child reinforced; (○— —○) model reinforced, child not reinforced; (○— · —○) no model present, child not reinforced. (From Bandura and McDonald, 1963.)*

other two sub-groups, only the children were reinforced, without a model present. During the posttest phase, a second experimenter, one who did not conduct the pretest, presented all the children with 12 different story-pairs.

Findings (Fig. 7) were that by observing an adult model, children could be trained upwards or downwards with equal effectiveness to give about 50% of their responses in the conditioned direction. Reinforcement of the child without a model present was ineffective. It was therefore concluded that "subjects' responses are readily modifiable, particularly through the utilization of adult modelling cues" (Bandura and McDonald, 1963, p.280).

These results have been replicated even by others who have sought to provide evidence for Piaget's theory (Cowan, Langer, Heavenrich and Nathanson, 1969). But the findings of such studies have not dissuaded Piaget's followers. While imitation and reinforcement can stifle the effects of peer-group interaction, it has been shown that interaction over a number of months can in turn reverse these effects (Sternlieb and Youniss, 1975). Children in naturalistic situations again develop upwards to respond intentionally.

It is in fact abundantly clear that neither approach has earned a monopoly on research in this area. It is also quite evident that the confrontation between the two theories has been overworked. Just as a hiker can reach a destination by following a variety of paths so can a child attain a sense of right and wrong through a variety of processes. To this end, modelling and peer-group experience on occasion may be equally effective in broadening the child's understanding of other persons.

Social learning theory emphasizes the importance of adult reinforcement and imitation. Piaget's theory emphasizes the importance of practical experience in considering others' intentions and interests as acquired in peer-group contact. There are times when one might cancel out the other (as in the White, 1972, experiment described in Section 2.4). But very often both of these broad processes work together, for children may initially share when they observe the generous behaviour of an adult. But imitation is not the same as identification and often it is not until others refuse to share with them that they gain the practical knowledge that sharing is in the interests of other persons, including themselves. In this way, children may develop mature adult-like concepts of right and wrong in identifying with adult rules and standards for behaviour.

Therefore, it may be conjectured that social learning and Piagetian processes can complement each other along lines similar to those originally proposed by Baldwin and Vygotsky. This would allow for a synthesis of the two theories in a framework for the study of fairness and moral development.

Much of the anomalous evidence which has come from research or Piaget's theory casts doubt over the appropriateness of the egocentrism concept in theories of moral development. Granted, the child may not give a verbal indication of an ability to co-ordinate different points of view simultaneously when questioned by an adult experimenter—implying that such an ability is associated with unconscious affective-conative strivings. But contrary to Piaget, the young child—though *cognitively* unsophisticated—is surely not shut in according to his or her own point of view.

Historically, when Piaget's position on egocentrism was first elucidated in the 1920s, it was roundly condemned by many psychologists (for a review, see Houssiades and Brown, 1980). An alternative proposition widely shared among these critics was that in real life children may show at most a slight degree of egocentrism in the company of other children and very little with adults. The egocentric responses found by Piaget were often attributed to the allegedly idiosyncratic nature of the tasks used. In other words, much of what Piaget formed as egocentrism was assumed to be an artefact of the experimental situation and ecologically invalid.

It can be said of modern attempts at establishing the construct of egocentrism (and its converse, the development of "role-taking" abilities) that their outcome has been consistent with this historical prognosis. Egocentrism as a unitary concept has been measured using a great variety of tasks which have tapped a great variety (and perhaps a plethora) of abilities (Damon, 1977, 1979; Shantz, 1975). But to date, as emphasized by several thorough reviews of the literature, no meaningful constellation of abilities has been found which can be given the global label of "egocentrism" (Ford, 1979; Kurdek, 1978; Rubin, 1978). There are often negligible correlations even among those test items which attempt to measure a specific aspect of egocentrism (e.g., to assess children's ability to infer what different child protagonists are thinking from information contained in short stories). By and large, the results of such tests have also yielded only equivocal relationships with overt measures of moral behaviour such as sharing and helping (Kurdek, 1978; Strayer, 1980). Refinements have been made to increase the predictive value of the tests, only to suggest that children's responses are more indicative of a desire to answer in a socially desirable way rather than of a genuine egocentrism (Eisenberg-Berg and Hand, 1979).

Though these tests may be more useful in assessing, for example, the effects of training in role-taking skills (cf. Silvern, Waterman, Sobesky and Ryan, 1979), the obstacles to devising a meaningful test of egocentrism as it relates to moral development do not appear to be easily surmountable ones. Consequently, the answer to the question "Are children egocentric?" remains elusive. But this much can be stated in opposition to Piaget's notion of an early morality of unilateral respect:

(1) Young children have at least a tacit knowledge of others' viewpoints. Though this knowledge may not be expressed verbally in certain experimental situations, young children *can* communicate, co-operate, and play effectively.

(2) However, children may not actually *spontaneously use* this knowledge appropriately in considering the interests and intentions of disadvantaged others. They may maintain, without a self-awareness of what they share in common with others, that their own interests and intentions are more important. Three elements can be noted in the development of this self-awareness:

(a) Children *learn* a conscious self-awareness of what they have in common with others through experience and stimulation, by wanting to be like others, especially adults. Overt imitative behaviour may be indicative of identification with others, but not necessarily so.

(b) In the same way, they *learn* what they do not have in common with others. They realize that others, especially adults, with whom they identify, are in fact fallible and cannot provide a complete picture of the ideal self. This awareness of the similarities and differences in viewpoints between self and others, this "consciousness of cognitions" is perplexing and worrying. It propels individuals into a dialectical reasoning process out of which principles of behaviour can be independently generated.

(c) At the same time, children *practise* their identifications especially through peer-group experience and stimulation. In this way, children come to give mutual consideration to the other's point of view in codifying and generating moral rules and principles. Often, through practice in the peer group, children come to develop a sense of control and self-direction in their moral behaviour. They are also able to make more accurate judgments of how well they can handle stressful conflict situations.

While this position borrows from Piaget in stressing the role of peer-group influence, it is also akin to that taken by Baldwin. Because Baldwin in his *Social and Ethical Interpretations in Mental Development* (1899/1973) maintained that imitation held the key to moral development, Piaget (1932/1977, p.380) asserted that Baldwin's theory was one which wrongly "gave priority to the relation of constraint over and against that of the relation of co-operation". For Piaget, imitation only had the function of allowing us to perceive similarities between ourselves and others. He believed that the distinctive consciousness of self, which is so essential a part of moral development, can only come about through opposition and discussion. But Baldwin's imitation may be reconsidered specifically in terms of an identification which eventually leads to the child's unnerving discovery that this other self, which was the ideal to be revered and adopted, is flawed. In such circumstances, Piaget's objection would seem to lose its force and indeed Piaget himself (1932/1977, p.132) does mention the child's realization of the adult's fallibility as an antecedent of moral development.

In addition, Baldwin (1899/1973, p.17) believed that adults and peers played fundamentally different roles in moral development. Children generally learn from adults and practise with peers. Far from weakening the adult's authority, practice in the peer group serves to complement the adult's instructions which, according to Baldwin, are at first blindly followed and understood only in the abstract by the child.

Consequently, the point to the adult's efforts becomes apparent to the child through practical experience with peers, though somewhat paradoxically it is the adult who can exert a stabilizing force here in promoting this experience as children grow older. What follows is a discussion of evidence for the notion of learning through adult identification.

Chapter Four

COGNITION, IDENTIFICATION, AND FAIRNESS IN CHILDREN

4.1 *Identification and Psychoanalytic Theory*

PIAGET'S THEORY aimed to provide a cognitive foundation for children's moral development. Yet evidence suggests that moral psychology is by no means explainable merely in "cool" cognitive terms. There is a recurring quality to moral development which cannot be characterized in terms of operational stages; and children may be scarcely conscious of what it is which motivates them to act fairly or unfairly. Despite a child's high intellectual capacities, he or she may not attain anything resembling Piaget's morality of mutual respect. The tendency to backslide is all too tempting and appears to be closely related to the nature of adult–child relations. In harmony with what has been suggested previously, the missing affective-conative ingredient in moral development may be found in the process of *identification* with adult rules and standards of behaviour. For it is a strong identification which may give meaning to children's knowledge of the right and good as evidenced in their fairness toward others.

Historically, identification as a non-cognitive process has long held a pivotal place in theories of social and personality development. It was first discussed thoroughly by Sigmund Freud (1856–1939) in his psychoanalytic theory. Identification was a key concept which emerged from Freud's observations of the pathological side to individual development in what he regarded as a fundamentally irrational society. For Freud, development and its frequent pathology was affective rather than cognitive in nature. His was a theory coloured by a pessimistic outlook on human relationship and industrial civilization. It departed sharply from Piaget's assumption of the eventual emergence during adolescence of a rational mutual respect morality.

As Phillip Rieff (1968, p.110) has shown, it is impossible to write about psychoanalytic theory without some reference to Freud's own intellectual history. The young Freud was obsessed with the desire to be famous. Like Piaget, he first studied in the natural sciences. But while Freud eventually qualified as a physician, he is also reported as having been overwhelmed by a tremendous intellectual need; he once wrote to his friend Wilhelm Fliess (1954, p.119): "A man like me cannot live without a hobby-horse, a consuming passion . . . . I have found my tyrant and in his service I know no limits. My tyrant is psychology." Freud became interested in abnormal psychology and in his Vienna studio pursued the study of hypnosis as a method for treating mental illness. In hypnotherapy, patients can be made to recall forgotten incidents while, for example, the therapist makes suggestions to change their behaviour. But Freud came to believe that hypnosis is a band-aid treatment for symptoms which still remain under the surface personality. He found that not every patient was susceptible to hypnosis, that there was often symptom substitution, and that he could stir up emotional episodes in which the memories of old would appear. After these bursts of emotion which showed semi-sexual overtones, the patient would get better. For Freud, patients have "knots" in their psyches which produce emotional discharge if lanced by the therapist during analysis.

Freud became intrigued by his patients' rationalizations and defence mechanisms which served to protect the ego, the part of the personality which is conscious and in closest contact with reality. He became concerned with what he claimed was a buried unconscious malignancy. He attempted to delve into this problem by examining the patient's non-hypnotic free associations to the therapist's suggestions. There were two "persons" inside the head, the conscious and the unconscious which provided the data for free association and psychoanalysis.

The crossroads in the formulation of Freud's theory came in his collaboration with the neurologist Josef Breuer (together in 1895 they published a book entitled *Studies on Hysteria*, reissued in 1956.). Breuer found that something seems to develop between the analyst and the patient. Once hypnotized, one of his female patients was encouraged to talk about anything which came to mind and then, having recalled painful early experiences, made sexual advances. Breuer was disturbed by this and gave up his research into the psychoanalytic method. But Freud was undeterred. This sexual phase interested him. He labelled it a "transferrence relationship", one thrown by the patient on to the analyst. The patient surfaces unconscious needs and transfers these upon him in a dynamically significant way.

When Freud decided that sex drives are an important part of the problem, he started to sit behind his patients out of their sight. He became a "disembodied voice" which disallows transference. By listening to his patients, Freud was led to the following line of reasoning. The psyche contains instincts and emotions which are repressed by society in early childhood. Phenomena such as dreams and slips of the tongue are manifestations of a conflict between unconscious wishes and exterior sensibilities. As "proof", the scientific status of which will be examined shortly, Freud also analysed legends, jokes, wit, and works of art. These statements of prototypical conflict situations appear in his many writings.

Freud's theory became primarily one of an undifferentiated reservoir of sexual energy or "libido" which serves to "cathect" objects of gratification, through which process the individual acquires reality and personality. The child will have a series of emotional attachments and these will lay down the strategy for adult personality. The libido flows out to the world in stages, and gratification is a wandering target. A critical stage in development is reached after the child has achieved bowel and bladder control when interest is focused on the genital area. During this phallic stage, the child's libidinal pleasure can be gratified by possessing the opposite-sex parent. Boys, with whom Freud's theory was mostly concerned, have mothers for their objects of attachment. To attain sexual pleasure, the boy has to displace his father as his mother's sexual partner. But his father is a powerful figure and can retaliate in punishing the child for his desires. The boy comes to believe that the most drastic kind of punishment is possible: castration. This belief is reinforced by his glimpses of girls' genitals, that they once had penises like boys but were punished by castration.

Freud claimed an evolutionary basis for the boy's castration anxiety. During prehistoric times, he speculated, the father within the primal horde chased the sons away in order to keep all of the women for himself. Disobedience was punished by castration. At last, the father was killed by the sons acting together. To avoid further competition and to ensure the survival of human society, they relinquished the conquered women as objects of gratification and enacted incest taboos. This set of taboos was handed down from generation to generation; and in order to reduce castration anxiety, the defence mechanism of *identification* evolved in which the energy addressed toward possessing objects of gratification and displacing barriers to these objects was redirected. The boy unconsciously identifies with both his mother as a source of love which can be lost (anaclitic identification) and more importantly with his father's powerful authority (aggressive identification). Both forms of identification are narcissistic insofar as the child internalizes the representations of nurturance and power in his superego. This Oedipus complex of the male child gives rise to a sense of guilt and conscience against causing injury to his parents. A strong potentially very punishing superego is achieved primarily through aggressive identification and gives rise to the boy's adoption of lofty moral positions (Freud, 1923/1961).

Freud was less clear about the psychology of women. The anxiety of girls during the phallic stage, he surmised, results primarily in anaclitic identification. The girl notices that boys have a penis, an organ which she lacks. Out of penis envy, she then turns to her father for gratification but fears that she will then be punished by her mother, not by castration since she has "already been castrated", but by loss of love. Freud further speculated that the girl's "Elektra complex" is resolved by relinquishing the father and incorporating the personality characteristics of her parents (particularly the mother) into her own personality. Once again this sex role development is linked to the internalization of her parents' moral positions. Yet because of her mainly anaclitic identification and an aggressive identification which is largely absent, the girl allegedly fails to achieve the same degree of conscience development as does the boy.

Freud (1930/1961) believed that there was tension between biological instincts and the society which demanded the renunciation of instincts. Thus implicit in human civilization was a considerable degree of unhappiness:

> Civilised man has exchanged a portion of his possibilities of happiness for a portion of security (p.62) . . . . A threatened external happiness—loss of love and punishment on the part of the external authority—has been exchanged for a permanent internal happiness, for the tension of the sense of guilt. (p.75).

4.2 Empirical Evidence for the Psychoanalytic View on Identification

Freud regarded identification as a defence mechanism buried deeply within the "hot-core" of the psyche. Such theoretical assumptions are not easily tested. But it would be wild and reckless to dismiss Freud's writings out of hand. He himself saw much of what he was doing in terms of a vision rather than as the product of a man of science. The untestable propositions of his theory arise from the assumption that personality is rooted in the unconscious and that unconscious phenomena can only be indirectly inferred from overt and often pathlogical behaviour. Evidence for psychoanalytic concepts and complexes frequently comes not from systematic experimentation and observation but from case studies and anecdotes. Perhaps the best support can be taken from Bettleheim's (1943) account of aggressive identification among prisoners in a Nazi concentration camp. He reports that prisoners who had been deprived of their liberty for some years came to adopt the Gestapo's values as their own. In identifying with the aggressors, believing in a childish way that powerful father images should be kind, these prisoners sought to mimic the toughness of the Gestapo. Some would even scrupulously obey the ridiculous edicts of the guards long after these had ceased to be enforced. For example, one day on a whim the allegedly dirty prisoners were ordered to wash the insides of their shoes with soap and water. Though the Gestapo soon forgot about implementing this rule, some prisoners (the number unspecified) continued to wash the insides of their shoes every day and cursed their fellows who did not follow suit.

But Bettleheim's report is admittedly an impressionistic one as he himself was an inmate of the camps and could hardly be expected to play the role of a detached observer. To test the existence of the Oedipus and Elektra complexes under controlled experimental conditions is a very difficult task and may be impossible at present. In view of this quandary, how scientific is Freud's theory? By one definition of the word "scientific" it is not, for scientific theories have a degree of precision and determinateness which allow them to be verified or falsified. In this connection Freud's own theoretical vacillation certainly does not help. For example, within one paragraph he asserts that a child's very strict conscience may be independent of his childrearing, may be "determined by the amount of punitive aggression he receives from his father", and at the same time can be acquired through a lenient upbringing (Freud, 1930/1961, p.77).

Yet again it would be a mistake to dismiss psychoanalytic theory as a doctrine of a faith or as merely interesting mythology. As Farrell (1963) has written, Freud's theory may represent an "empirical speculative synthesis" which is years in advance of the availability of supporting or disconfirming proof. It was certainly a brand-new window on social and personality development, one which captured the imagination of intellectuals everywhere and found popular expression in many books, plays and films. Like Piaget, Freud provided a stage theory of development involving subject–object relations. Like Piaget, he also opposed the stone wall of American behaviourism, "a theory which is naive enough to boast that it has put the whole problem of psychology completely out of court" (Freud, 1935, pp.95–96). He certainly disliked intensively what he regarded as the crassness and commercialism of American society, a view which was reinforced when he received (and not surprisingly refused) offers of huge amounts of money from American newspaper proprietors and movie producers to psychoanalyse celebrities.

But Freud differed from Piaget in several ways. By his own account (1935, p.14), he believed that his Jewish origins permitted him to act freely without the prejudice that restricted others and so to remain in opposition without seeking the agreement of the majority. He believed that sexual instincts and personality directed cognition: in his aloof intellectual posture,

Freud was a maverick in a Victorian moral era. He did not mind that his ideas did not acquire a respected academic stature, although certainly he was disturbed by defections of his closest disciples from the psychoanalytic movement.

What has academic psychology done with Freud's theory, particularly his concept of identification? Because of its alleged vagueness and untestable properties, negative reactions abound. Piaget himself has been quoted as regarding psychoanalysis as mythology to be disproven eventually through advances in the field of neurology (see Hess, 1972, p.49). As noted earlier (Section 3.5), social learning theorists such as Bandura have equated identification with imitation for pragmatic experimental reasons. Nevertheless, an important consideration remains unresolved by this manoeuvre regarding the motivations behind imitative behaviour. Branding the concept of identification as imprecise and untestable carries with it an enormously high price. In restricting attention to the acquired similarity between parent and child as evidenced in imitation behaviour:

> . . . We would risk losing sight of an important psychological phenomenon, as well as an intriguing theoretical issue. In concerning himself with identification, Freud was not asking why and how a child might learn an isolated piece of behaviour from his parent. He was interested in what he felt to be a more sweeping and powerful phenomenon—the tendency of the child to take on not merely discrete elements of the parental model but a total pattern. Moreover, as Freud saw it, this acquisition was accomplished with a considerable emotional intensity which reflected the operation of motivational forces of considerable power . . . . If the core of identification is a *motive* to become like another person, then the presence of similarity is, at best, only a by-product rather than an essential feature of the phenomenon.
>
> (Bronfenbrenner, 1960, pp.27 and 29)

Furthermore, the parental model emulated by the child is not the one whose behaviour is observed by researchers or reported by the parents themselves. It is an ideal and hence a child's identificatory strivings may grossly depart from a parent's actual behaviour. For this reason, children's own *perceptions* of their parents should be more predictive of their behaviour than actual childrearing practices whether directly observed or reported. This is a position which has been given the name of "symbolic interactionism" (Acock and Bengtson, 1980; Scheck and Emerick, 1976).

4.3 The Testability of Aspects of Identification

The symbolic interactionist position clashes with that of behaviourism and positivism. It is consistent with the notion that identification may still be the key to understanding more of children's moral development. In this

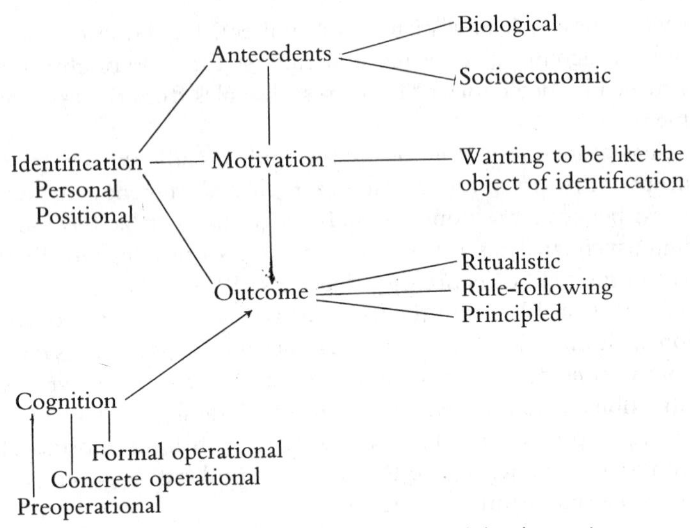

Fig. 8. *Aspects of identification in moral development*

connection, there remains a school of contemporary psychologists who continue to believe that the concept may be of considerable worth to the extent that identification-related behaviours are regarded as more than mere by-products. For example, it has been maintained that distinctive aspects of identification can be usefully studied provided these are separated and clarified (Staub, 1979, p.25): (a) the antecedents of identification; (b) the motivated disposition to identity; and (c) the consequences or outcome of the identification process. These are depicted in Fig. 8 in hypothetical relationship to cognitive development and moral behaviour.

The antecedents

Freud dwelled at length on the biological antecedents of identification. Put simply, his approach was one in which anatomy determined destiny. But is it in fact necessary to reduce the nature of human relationships to explanations centring on the libido and objects of sexual gratification?

Freud's writings overlapped with the sexually repressive Victorian era. During this period, fathers participated much less than mothers in the caretaking of young children. Thus it was not surprising that the mother was assumed to be the first object of gratification for both boys and girls. Today much has changed, in no small way owing to the switch from breast- to bottle-feeding infants. There are now many families in which the father is an equal participant in childrearing or has become even the primary caretaker (Parke, 1979).

Would this historical development entail massive changes in the process of identification in sex-role and moral development? Such a complex question is of course not easy to answer, but it would seem at least as plausible to attribute these changes to changes in socioeconomic conditions as to changes in biological development. If girls were to adopt more masculine roles in society owing to economic pressures to contribute to the family income, this phenomenon may be explained without recourse to biology. As regards girls' identification, it is worth noting that studies of empathy have found that girls are more empathic than boys, as Freud's notion of anaclitic identification would suggest (Hoffman, 1977b). However, most of the observed sex differences are statistically insignificant and barely noticeable. Even these may disappear as girls are increasingly exposed to working mothers and attain greater occupational roles and responsibilities in Western society (L. W. Hoffman, 1979). Certainly then, identification with a parent can be examined in terms of prevailing socioeconomic conditions (Section 8.1).

The motivated disposition and its outcome

But while identification's antecedents may be plagued by an irresolvable biology v. socioeconomic system controversy, the motivated disposition to identify is an entirely separate issue. According to Freudian theory, a child may be motivated to identify with a parent in an aggressive or anaclitic fashion. But in any case, the child *wants to be like* the parent. Since this desire is often unconscious as are many processes researched by experimental psychologists (Shevrin and Dickman, 1980), again it might be assumed that any measure of actual identification would have to be inferred indirectly from overt behaviour. However, as noted previously (Section 2.4), there are some problems with this less than optimal approach. On the one hand, a child's behaviour may appear similar to that of his or her parents not out of identification but out of coincidentally overlapping interests which may be motivated toward different goals. On the other hand, a child may be motivated to be like a parent but not have the necessary intellectual or physical capabilities to manifest evidence of identification in overt behaviour. He or she may then display identification in situations where these requirements are met or are unimportant. For example, a child may attempt to adhere to the rules of parliamentary procedure in chairing a student council meeting, thus emulating a parent's behaviour witnessed in a similar situation. But the child's desire to be like the parent does not ensure that these rules have been understood well enough to be followed.

Suppose it could be assumed that children are able to convey accurately their desires to be like their parents. In that event, the strength of identification might be measured by simply asking children questions such as

"Who do you want to be like when you grow up?" Children who maintain strongly that they would like to be similar to their parents could then be presumed to have a high degree of identification. This method may be promising. While the extent to which motivations and behaviour can be consciously and accurately verbalized by adults, let alone children, is once more a matter of continuing controversy (Nisbett and Wilson, 1977), evidence has recently been reported that individuals do indeed demonstrate a considerable measure of consciousness about their own behavioural states. Such awareness does not appear to require a sophisticated level of cognition (White, 1980).

By comparison, children's abilities to verbalize their motivations and behaviour accurately are largely unknown. But it might be assumed that those who want to be like their parents may be more conscious of their wanting to identify than those who do not. Consequently, children's answers to questions seeking to establish the extent of their identifications may be one reasonable measure of identification. Yet the problem then arises as to what kinds of behaviour such a measure could predict. Though a child may want to be like a parent it is clear that he or she will not be able to emulate the parent in situations which demand sophisticated cognitive skills beyond those available to the child.

Most middle-class children, for example, have parents who maintain that they should follow school rules. Children who identify with their parents should tend to internalize such rules, assuming that these are comprehensible and match their level of cognitive development. Some rudimentary support for this assumption comes from the work of Martin Hoffman (1971). Because this study is so important it merits a detailed discussion. The participants were primary school children (Grade 7) from middle- and lower-class homes in the Detroit metropolitan area. As an "identification index", the children were asked three questions: (a) "Which person do you admire or look up to the most?" (b) "Which person do you want to be like when you grow up?" and (c) "Which person do you take after mostly?" Separate identification scores for mothers and fathers were obtained by adding the number of responses mentioning the mother and father respectively. Measures of rule conformity came from teacher's ratings of the extent to which the child usually follows or breaks the rules. Other related measures included ones designed to assess guilt, confessions and acceptance of blame. Data on guilt were collected by presenting children with the beginning of a story in which a child character has trangressed under circumstances which are not detectable by a superior authority (e.g., a child cheats in a swimming race and wins). Subjects were asked to complete the stories. Their reactions would be labelled as demonstrating guilt if there were indications of self-criticism rather than of a concern with external detection. Data on confession were gathered from mothers' responses to the interview question, "When (name of child) has done something that he knows you would not approve of, and you haven't found out about it yet, how often does he come and tell you about it without your asking?" Teachers' reports of how the child reacts when "caught doing something wrong" formed the basis for the index of blame acceptance.

Findings were that mother identification was associated with rule conformity in middle-class boys and that father identification was associated with rule conformity in both middle-class boys and girls. There were no such significant associations in lower-class children, and no relationship between identification and guilt or blame acceptance in either social class group. These results are not easy to interpret but Hoffman's tentative conclusion was that identification is not an "all-pervasive process"; it contributes to children's rule-following behaviour though not that behaviour which occurs in the absence of authority. According to Hoffman, this identification process may proceed most effectively between middle-class boys and their fathers since it is the middle-class father who, by acting empathically toward the same-sex child, facilitates his identification.

But alternative sociological and economic explanations for the antecedents of identification are logically possible. It may well be, for example, that the middle-class child envies the economic resources and power of the middle-class parent—a situation which does not exist so sharply in the comparatively materially impoverished relationship between working-class parent and child. Indeed this may be an equally plausible explanation. Even if it could be established that working-class parents act less empathically toward their children than do middle-class parents, the difference itself might be attributable to the economic pressures faced by the working-class family. Consistent with this explanation are the results of a subsequent study by Scheck and Emerick (1976). Grade 9 boys (mean age 14.6 years) from two medium-sized midwestern American cities were given a questionnaire designed to ascertain perceptions of childrearing practices used by their parents. Low amounts of perceived parental support, control and consistency were found to be associated with low parental socioeconomic status, suggesting that working-class parents provide a weaker model for identification than do their middle-class counterparts.

Aside from the issue of interpretation, there are several other points to be noted about the Hoffman study. First, the measures of guilt, confession, and acceptance of blame are of questionable ecological validity. There is no established association between actual behaviour and story-completion measures of guilt (cf. Schaffer, 1968). The story content itself varies enormously from a story for which the child may have a real-life acquaintance (winning a race by cheating) to one in which this acquaintance is usually lacking (contributing to the death of a younger child through negligence). Moreover, Hoffman himself qualifies the usefulness of the confession and blame-acceptance measures. The former, based on teacher's reports of how children react to an authority figure following the discovery of a transgression, is hardly a measure of spontaneous, freely volunteered confession. The latter, based on parental reports, may be particularly unreliable. Since parents want to convey a good impression to our interviewer, they tend to give socially desirable answers which are not necessarily accurate (Danziger, 1971).

A second point is that children's actual behaviour may not be accurately reflected in the ratings of teachers. While many teacher ratings can discriminate behaviour, there are clear individual differences among teachers (Bolstad and Johnson, 1977). In fact, some teachers may rate as best behaved those children who are observed as misbehaving the most; others appear to tolerate disruptions as long as students perform well academically, an orientation which may contaminate teacher ratings of children's behaviour.

Third, with regard to teachers' reports of rule-following behaviour, it is important to know *what* rules the teachers mentioned. Different teachers rated different children on rules which may have varied from teacher to teacher in content, extent of application, and enforcement.

Fourth, as Hoffman mentions, these techniques may have been inadequate in investigating the cognitive prerequisites of much which would presumably be the outcome of identification. For example, it is possible that there are children who want to adopt the adult's behavioural rules and standards but do not actually do so because they are not yet able to comprehend the rules.

Finally, it may be that identification may be a more pervasive process in individuals at ages other than at the onset of adolescence. By Grade 7, many children may have become disillusioned with their parents, even if only temporarily (Section 6.1), and this factor might partly account for the pattern of results in the Hoffman study.

4.4 *A Social-cognitive Approach*

Identification and children's rule-following behaviour

A recent study was designed with regard to these issues (Siegal and Francis, in press). Rather than using teacher's ratings, children's actual behaviour was observed both under and without teacher surveillance. The rule which the children were to follow was explicity presented, easily comprehensible, and evenly enforced.

The participants were 18 children aged 5 to 7 years. They attended first grade in a primary school located in an upper-middle-class suburban district. The children were given concrete operational measures of cognitive development (from Form C of the Piagetian-based Concept Assessment Kit, Goldschmidt and Bentler, 1968) as well as the parental identification index items devised by Hoffman (1971). All the children were asked to say whom they admire, whom they would want to be like as a grownup and whom they take after mostly. Finally, as a measure of peer-group contact and experience, each child was asked to say which of his classmates he would prefer to play with during freetime.

The situation itself was envisioned to be a clash between a ritual (an idiosyncratic regularity of individual behaviour) and a collective rule comprehensible to those who had entered a concrete operational level of cognitive development. The ritual v. rule conflict situation involved "napping" or relaxation periods which were customarily scheduled immediately after lunch each day. A wall was installed in one corner at the front of the classroom. Built into the wall was a three-foot-high trap door above which was a one-way mirror. The top of the wall was about eight feet high and was graced by six floral illustrations. At the centre of each flower was concealed a camera lens, only one of which was operative and connected to videotape equipment hidden in a space behind the wall.

Thus the wall was unobtrusively present in the classroom and did not attract the children's attention. The children's behaviour was observed and recorded during nine relaxation periods over a space of three weeks. The observations began when the teacher told the children that it was time for relaxation, that there was a school rule to be quiet, and that it was not fair to bother others during relaxation. After two minutes the teacher told the children that she had to go out for a while and that they should remember the rule about remaining quiet and not disturbing others. When two further minutes elapsed, she reappeared in the room and told the children to keep napping. The period ended six minutes after it began.

The children's rule-violating behaviour was scored by two independent judges for restlessness and acts which succeeded in distracting others during the six-minute periods. This situation allowed for high agreement among observers in which a stationary position was the modal category. As in other such studies (Epstein, 1979), there was a high degree of ritualistic consistency in this behaviour over the three weeks of taping, as well as a high level of agreement between the judges on the nature of the rule-violating behaviour. The children's rule violations were correlated with the cognitive, identification, and peer-group popularity measures. It was predicted that identification would account for children's rule-following behaviour both in the presence and absence of the teacher-experimenter.

The children's rule violations were scored in two main categories: initiated rule violations directed toward disturbing others and rule violations as reactions elicited from others' provocations. Behaviour in both categories significantly increased when the teacher left the room and decreased when she returned. The mean numbers of initiated rule violations in each of the two-minute periods were 4.8, 15.4, and 5.4 respectively; comparable numbers for reactions were 3.7, 7.7, and 3.1. Only negligible non-significant relationships existed between initiated and reactive rule violations indicating that the reactions were not a function of the initiated provocations.

The major finding of the study was that there were significant negative correlations between children's reactions and their self-reports of mother identification in all three periods. Moreover, the strength of these correlations was greatest by far during the period when the teacher was absent (−0.64 v. −0.44 during the teacher's presence and −0.46 during the teacher's return). When mother identification in the absent phase was statistically partialled out and its effects held constant, the relationship between mother identification and reactions in the return phase disappeared almost completely (−0.04), suggesting that identification can importantly account for the level of reactive rule violations. One interpretation of this result is that the mother is a source of children's "ego-strength" which is associated with children's ability to resist others' provocation directed toward breaking rules, particularly in the absence of adult authority (Section 7.6).

By contrast, initiated rule violations did not correlate significantly at all with identification. But initiations did correlate significantly with concrete operational measures of cognitive development in the teacher-present phase only (−0.40), indicating that reactions are unlike initiations in that their origin resides in the behaviour of others rather than in the head of the subject. Thus the suppression of rule-violations as reactions is more highly related to perceptions of important others than to a "cool" cognitive development. It may embody a push or pull of affective strength toward a compliance with adult rules.

There were generally no significant relationships between reactions and self-reports of father identification, sex of child, cognitive development, and play popularity as rated by peers. Such results can be compared with those of an earlier study by Hoffman and Saltzstein (1967) aside from the fact that it used seventh-graders as subjects. Children and their parents were asked to describe disciplinary techniques used in the family. This procedure demonstrates the value of using self-reports as a measure of identification. There was a significant relationship between both middle-class boys' and girls' mother-identification scores and *the child's own* perceptions of the mother as a warm, affectionate individual who uses reasoning as a disciplinary technique. By contrast, mother-identification scores were insignificantly related to the mother's report and once again there were no significant relationships involving father identification.

In the child's eyes, the mother with whom he or she identifies attempts to communicate the consequences of her child's actions for others by use of reasoning to develop empathy and perceptions of others' needs. That perceived induction can be associated with fair behaviour has been shown by Dlugokinski and Firestone (1974). Using fifth- and eighth-graders in a midwestern American parochial school as subjects, perceived induction was found to be positively correlated with peer ratings of kindness and consideration.

In sum, mother identification appears to be related to perceived inductive "maternal socialization behaviour". Much other research is indirectly related to identification and attempts to relate systematically observations or parent reports of childrearing methods to actual behaviour. This work will be examined later together with other studies which focus on the role of the father. Amongst a number of possibilities, the evidence suggests that the father still has an important role in moral development, if only an indirect one, in influencing the quality of the mother–child relationship (Section 8.3).

Identification and principled acts directed toward upholding human rights

This evidence from studies of elementary school children suggests that identification may play a pervasive role in fairness and moral development. But of course development does not end in childhood. It continues through adolescence and adulthood. While mother identification is highly associated with children's rule-following behaviour, the antecedents and correlates of principled acts which may clash with rules appear to be different and complicated. In general, two hypotheses have been advanced about families of children who protest against rules: one is a generational continuity hypothesis, the other is a hypothesis of discontinuity and rebellion of youth against parental authority.

The continuity hypothesis proposes that parents' moral-political ideology and values are transmitted continuously from one generation to another; liberal parents have liberal children and conservative parents have conservative children. Values are shared across generations (Braungart, 1975; Horn and Knott, 1971). By contrast, the discontinuity hypothesis draws upon psychoanalytic theory (e.g. Feuer, 1969). It proposes, for example, that much of what can be described as left-wing political activity can be understood as a type of Oedipus complex, as a protest against the father's conservative lifestyle. Children revolt against what they regard as the undeserved authority of the father and seek out substitute persons and causes to which they may become closely identified. In this regard, children may—though not necessarily—seek a nurturant relationship with their mothers in forming an alignment against the father. The mother's empathic qualities and altruistic behaviour are imparted to her children who develop a sensitivity for those disadvantaged by laws and rules. In violating such rules by performing acts directed at upholding human rights, children are emulating their mothers, hoping that their mothers will be pleased even secretly, for their children have done what they themselves would not dare to do (Fishman and Soloman, 1963).

Because of this special mother–child relationship, it could be said that the two hypotheses are not completely contradictory. According to the continuity version, children adopt their parents' moral-political ideology without rebellion. While discontinuity assumes conflict between generations it still allows for an intense identification with the idealized image of the mother in that children will strive to adopt her moral-political ideology.

As might be suspected, the testing of the two hypotheses in the context of moral development has been marred by numerous methodological problems. Perhaps the hardest hurdle to clear has been to find situations in which there is an unambiguous scope for clash between a rule and a principle, then to determine that the rule-breakers were actually acting on principled grounds. A tremendous amount of research has been conducted on this subject, much of which has studied the student protest movement against the Vietnam war and related issues (see Keniston, 1973, for an annotated bibliography of 303 studies in the area). Students have had many reasons for protesting. These have ranged from an optimistic concern for the future of society to a gloomy dissatisfaction with Western civilization and a personal aversion to joining the military (Block, Haan and Smith, 1969; Keniston, 1967). To illustrate the difficulty in categorizing the motivations underlying individuals' actions, it is possible that those who claim a principled, other-oriented rationale for protest may in fact privately hold views of self-gain (cf. Cowdry, Keniston and Cabin, 1970).

Another methodological problem emerges in this context. Because law-breaking may be unpopular with society at large, activists may be unwilling to be questioned by outsiders (e.g., non-protester psychologists). For this reason, studies of civil disobedience have been continually plagued by small participation rates and subject samples which may be unrepresentative of activists as a group. Generally, claims for a representative have come from studies of moral-political ideology, not actual behaviour.

Table 1 summarizes the results of ten major studies mostly on incidents of civil disobedience in the United States. Perhaps the most important investigation was made by Haan, Smith and Block (1968). This came at the time of the 1964–1965 Free Speech Movement at the University of California, Berkeley, when activists sought to overturn a university endorsement of a rule construed as an infringement on civil rights which prohibited the distribution of political leaflets on campus (for a history of the FSM, see Lipset and Wolon, 1968, and Heirich, 1971). The subjects, with a wide spectrum of political views, were sent a questionnaire through the mail. It asked for information on their relationships with their parents as well as on their parents' political preferences. Also included were a number of hypothetical moral dilemmas for which a principled course of action was possible. The subjects were asked to respond by justifying their behavioural choices to each dilemma. Responses were scored using Kohlberg's method (detailed in Section 7.1). This assumes that responses can be "stage-typed" according to whether or not, for example, they fit the criteria of a principled morality (e.g., taking the role of the other in judging moral behaviour and universalizing this decision in all other relevantly similar situations).

The findings were complex and not easy to interpret. But in comparison with those who gave non-principled justifications, principled subjects indicated that there was a lot of conflict between themselves and their parents and rated their parents' political preferences as liberal on a conservatism–radicalism scale. Parental conflict and ideology were not directly examined in terms of actual behaviour. Yet both were related to principled moral reasoning which in turn correlated with reported civil rights activism such as being arrested during the FSM.

These results would appear to lend some support to both the continuity and conflict hypotheses. While the principled subjects reported more conflict with their parents than did the non-principled, their parents were indeed further to the left politically (although not as far left as many of the activists themselves). But the Haan *et al*. study, though very important, has serious drawbacks. As is pointed out in the original article, the sample was not representative. How unrepresentative is indicated by figures calculable from those provided both in the original and in a subsequent article (Smith, Haan and Block, 1970). Of a total University of California sample of 696 only 342 returned their questionnaires for reasons which are largely unknown. Consequently the possibility cannot be discounted that the non-returnees would have given much different answers than did those who actually participated in the study. Of these 342 students (111 former undergraduate arrestees and 231 non-arrestees), only 214 could be classified as "pure" moral-stage types according to the Kohlberg scoring system in use at the time. Of these 214, 53 were arrestees and 161 were non-arrestees. Thus only 53 (or 47.7%) of the total of 111 arrestees who answered the questionnaire could be classified as pure as contrasted with 161 (or 69.7%) of

Table 1. *Studies of Parent–Child Relations and Actions in Support of Civil Rights*

Study	Subjects	Location	Procedure	Results
Watts and Whittaker (1966)	FSM students	University of California, Berkeley	Asked to give biographical details	Parents more academically elite
Westby and Braungart (1966)	College students	Public university in eastern United States	Asked to give views on Vietnam war, parents' social class and political affiliation	Parents more academically elite, ideological positions consistent with parents' political orientations
Flacks (1967)	Undergraduates	University of Chicago	Responded on political attitude scales	Political activists more "radical" than parents. Parents more liberal than parents of non-activists.
Haan, Smith and Block (1968) Block, Haan and Smith (1970)	FSM students	University of California, Berkeley	Responded on parent–child relations questionnaire	Indicated both political conflict and closeness with parents

Keniston (1968)	Full time anti-Vietnam war activists (aged 19–29 years, mean = 23)	Cambridge, Massachusetts	Gave semi-structured interview on family background and politics	Living out expressed but unimplemented parental values (Keniston's interpretation)
London (1970)	Christian rescuers of Jews from Nazis	Israel and the United States	Asked to give biographical details	No data but impression of intense parental identification
Rosenhan (1970)	Civil rights activists	North-eastern United States	Interviewed on parent–child relations	Fully committed higher on identification than partly committed
Kraut and Lewis (1975)	White male freshman students	Yale University	Responded to scales of parental and political ideology and parent–child conflict	Both leftist ideology and conflict were related to leftist student ideology
Zalkind, Gaugler and Schwartz (1975)	Non-students median age in 26- to 30-year-old category	New York City	Responded on civil rights questionnaire	Higher economic status correlated positively with support for civil rights

the 231 non-arrestees. The significant difference in the classifiability of the two groups attests to the difficulty of using the Kohlberg method in scoring the responses of anti-authoritarian groups. For this reason, it is hardly surprising that the "principled" responses predominant in the arrestee group were scored by a technique which has since been abandoned as unreliable (see Chapter 7 on Kohlberg's theory).

Still another problem is the extent to which any of those espousing principles in hypothetical situations were genuinely committed to activism directed toward the upholding of civil rights of others (cf. Haan, 1978). In the absence of decisive sanctions on the part of law-enforcement authorities, the scenario for many of the protesters became one permeated by drama, entertainment and excitement. Instead of a serious and bloody confrontation which would have involved only the truly committed and their opponents, many hippies and dissenters without a cause participated in the movement (Whittaker and Watts, 1969).

Overall, this study was not without its share of problems. A non-representative sample was given an unreliable measure of principled reasoning. Subjects' motivations in their protest behaviour were not easy to determine, and the FSM situation was not a clear instance of a clash between a rule and a principle in which rule-violation behaviour could have grave consequences. To be sure, on the positive side of the ledger, these results have been somewhat substantiated in subsequent work. In a study of white male Yale University undergraduates, Kraut and Lewis (1975) found that leftist political ideology was related both to leftist ideology of parents and high family conflict. But in neither the Haan *et al.* nor the Kraut and Lewis studies can ideology be easily assumed to translate into principled actions, and certainly it cannot be simply assumed that attaining a principled morality is equivalent to possessing a leftist political ideology (cf. Fishkin, Keniston and McKinnon, 1973).

Consequently, it is imperative to look elsewhere for clear-cut clashes between rules and principles in which it is doubtful that a rule violation could have been performed by anyone but persons concerned with others' interests and intentions.

In this respect, what little information is available on principled behaviour in wartime is invaluable. Though much of this is anecdotal, it fits in well with the generational continuity hypothesis that principled actions are associated with a strong parental identification. In an attempt to find stable character traits among Christians who risked their lives to save Jews in Nazi-occupied Germany, Perry London (1970) interviewed 27 rescuers. He found that nearly all his subjects tended to identify very strongly with at least one parent though not necessarily with the same-sex parent. This parent held quite firm opinions on moral questions. One of the rescuers in describing his religious views responded: "Lutheran Protestant . . . . Protest is Protestant. I protest. Maybe I inherit it from way back . . . my mother . . . always in life she gave me so much philosophy. She didn't go to high school, only elementary school, but so smart a woman, wisdom, you know. It is born in you . . ." (London, 1970, p.247).

London notes that his data were "broad and complex" and that "they were never formally analyzed". Yet they are consistent with many anecdotes in the diaries of those who witnessed wartime heroism. For example, Jessica Mitford's (1960) account of the roles of those who volunteered to fight fascism in the Spanish Civil War bears a close resemblance to London's description of the rescuers.

Ideally, then, a study of principled actions must focus on an example from which motivations can be clearly inferred, such as in wartime. It should have a representative sample of co-operative subjects contacted by a researcher in whom trust can be placed. Additionally, although, in the study of Kraut and Lewis the subjects' perceptions of mothers and fathers are combined, a test of the conflict hypothesis would demand that these be separated. In this regard, it would be important to control for the effects of cognitive development and social class variables which tend to correlate together but which could each independently contribute to activism.

The participants in a study designed to meet this requirement (Siegal, 1982) were university students during the late 1970s when the Queensland (Australia) State Government proclaimed an Act of Parliament prohibiting street marches. Since then the act has been rescinded in practice. But at the time it had the effect of banning demonstrations against the conservative government policies of the ruling coalition of National and Liberal Parties. When the Premier of Queensland announced the street-marching ban, his words were given massive publicity across Australia:

> Protest marches are a thing of the past. Nobody, including the Communist Party or anyone else is going to turn the streets of Brisbane into a forum. Protest groups need not bother applying for permits to stage marches because they won't be granted [4 September, 1977] . . . . The day of the political street march is over. Anybody who holds a street march, spontaneous or otherwise, will know they're acting illegally. . . . Don't bother applying for a permit. You won't get one. That's government policy now. [5 September, 1977]

Thus the situation was similar to that of the Berkeley Free Speech Movement of the 1960s except that none of the protesters were hippies or yippies: the whole situation was very serious. The law was rigidly enforced by physical intervention on the part of the police which resulted in considerable violence. (For a detailed history of the Queensland civil liberties movement and the street-marching issue, see Plunkett and Summy, 1980; the legal ramifications are discussed in Brennan, 1979.)

During 1978 and 1979, there were a series of marches held in Brisbane to protest the withdrawn right of free speech and assembly. Numerous arrests were made. In the eyes of the activists this well-publicized issue was clearly a clash between a rule and a principle of civil rights. To examine both the continuity and discontinuity hypotheses, 33 university students (14 males and 19 females) arrested in several marches were given a questionnaire in which they were asked to justify their actions, to indicate their own and their parents' political preferences as well as to rate the extent of conflict between themselves and their parents. Their responses were compared with those of a non-marcher group consisting of undergraduate psychology students (19 males and 22 females).

This study departed from many previous ones in three major ways. First, unlike in some other studies, the two groups were equated for age, social class and intelligence. Scores on psychometric and Piagetian tests indicated that both groups were of higher than average intelligence and were at formal operational level as measured by their performance on Inhelder and Piaget's (1958) pendulum problem.

Second, it could be assumed that this sample of arrestees was a representative one. Of the 90 students arrested, approximately half had left the city and could not be contacted. It is unlikely that this mobility would systematically bias the results in that the protesters who did not leave would give significantly different answers than those who had left. The remainder were approached individually by a research worker openly sympathetic to their actions. Of these, 41 agreed to participate in the study though six had to be excluded because divorce and death prevented their reporting on relationships involving both parents and parental political preferences. Two others were excluded because of incomplete responses.

Third, the study looked at a situation in which a principled moral orientation could be unambiguously inferred from behaviour. This is further shown by the subjects' reasons for marching in contravention to the law. The following are prototypical justifications offered by three of the arrestees. Their responses are directed toward upholding the rights of disadvantaged in stark opposition to the law:

> *Arrestee No. 1 (male, age 25).* Streetmarching on a political level raises civil rights (individual rights) to democratic rights (the rights of groups, parties, etc.). As such it represents a form of opposition that is effective for a movement (social or political). If a group is dependent upon it for political expression and organization it is an absolute necessity to defend it. I am firmly of the conviction that repression is effective in limiting all political expression and organization . . .. If the opposition to legal streetmarch restrictions raises the character of organizations and expression of the class or group dependent on

it (those without political power) and weakens repression, then it is the most effective form of opposition to such measures.

Arrestee No. 2 (female, age 33). I have participated in almost all streetmarches, legal and illegal over the past 2–3 years in Brisbane because of my strong convictions that the attack on our civil liberties must be resisted at all costs. I have always supported moves not to apply for permits to take part in illegal streetmarches. The rationale, as I see it, is that the government has to be shown that there are enough people who are normally law-abiding citizens who are willing to break a law which they consider unjust or immoral. There is a point, I believe, in a demonstration where you can make the decision whether or not you will be arrested on a point of principle . . . I do not regret my arrest at all.

Arrestee No. 3 (female, age 23). My justification for participation is that I really don't believe laws that repress freedom are real laws for people to follow . . . . There is something wrong with a system that doesn't give its people even the freedom to say what they believe in. In marching in an illegal streetmarch, I expressed my dislike for the law prohibiting marches and also expressed my dissatisfaction with the present government in Queensland.

These three responses were typical of the arrestee group. Very similar ones were given by the others who participated in the study. By contrast, many of the non-marchers—though virtually all sympathetic to the goals of the arrestees—expressed personal fear of the consequences of marching. Some felt they could be injured while others did not want to risk jeopardizing their future careers by the possibility of arrest and the stigma of a criminal record.

The results were clear-cut. Not surprisingly, the arrestees supported the opposition Labor Party in significantly greater numbers than did the non-marchers. But at the same time, the arrestees reported significantly less conflict with their mothers than did the non-marchers (mean of 3.26 v. 4.04 on a 7-point scale). Moreover, they agreed with their mothers' political preferences significantly more often than did the non-arrestees. Taking only those subjects who expressed political preferences for themselves and their mothers, 23 out of 29 arrestees agreed with their mothers in contrast to only 16 out of 34 non-marchers (see Table 2). There were no significant differences between the two groups in perceived level of father conflict or in their agreement with their father's political preferences. Amongst those who expressed political preferences for both themselves and their fathers, father agreement was indicated by 20 out of 29 of the arrestees and 22 out of 35 of the non-marchers. While the arrestees did perceive father conflict to be greater than mother conflict (mean of 3.96 v. 3.26), there were no such significant differences in the non-marcher group (mean of 3.76 v. 4.04). No sex differences were revealed in the responses of either group.

Consequently, once again, mother–child relations, as perceived by the child, are an effective predictor of moral action. These findings are supportive of the continuity hypothesis that children adopt their parents' moral-political ideology without rebellion. This process appears to be characterized by a particularly close mother–child relationship, rather than a revolt or poignant opposition toward the father. The affective-conative strivings associated with an intense, ideal mother image may be translated into actions aimed toward correcting what are recognized as unfair situations.

It is also noteworthy that these findings on actual adult behaviour are wholly in line with a recent study on ideology. Acock and Bengtson (1980) studied 446 young adults randomly drawn to be a representative middle-class sample of a large population (849 000) belonging to a Los Angeles area medical care plan. The youths, mothers, and fathers were asked to state their opinions on several political questions such as "The United States should be ready to answer any challenge to its power, anywhere in the world". Again, children's perceptions of their parents' orientations had

Table 2. *Relationship of Marchers' and Non-marchers' Political Preferences to Those of Their Parents*[a]

Parent's political preferences	Marchers' political preferences (n = 33)				
	National-Liberal coalition	Labor	Democrat	Communist	Don't know
Coalition		5/6			
Labor		*23/20*		1/1	3/3
Democrat		0/2			
Communist					
Don't know		1/1			

Parent's political preferences	Non-marchers' political preferences (n = 41)				
	National-Liberal coalition	Labor	Democrat	Communist	Don't know
Coalition	*6/10*	4/3	3/2		4/4
Labor	6/4	*10/12*	3/4		1/1
Democrat	1/0	1/0			
Don't know	2/1				

[a] Mothers' preferences are cited first, fathers' second; agreements between subjects and their parents are shown in italics

much more effect on their own opinions than did the actual stated opinions of their parents which were frequently distorted. Moreover, as in the Queensland study, perceptions of the mother's orientations had a greater impact on those of the child than did the father's orientations which were largely non-significant as predictors. Finally, again there were no sex differences. Mother perceptions were equally important for males and females. Additional and similar findings have been reported by Langston (1969).

4.5 *Is Moral Development a Unitary Process?*

Altogether, these studies supply evidence for the notion that mother identification has a pervasive impact on moral development in both children and young adults. Such identification embodies the hot cognition which may reveal the affect and motivation underlying moral behaviour. In this way, identification may importantly predict children's fairness.

But the extent to which such results are generalizable across situations outside those studied has been a longstanding issue of controversy (Bem and Allen, 1974; Bowers, 1973; Burton, 1963; Epstein, 1979; Mischel and Mischel, 1976). It is certainly not easy to predict instances of behaviour from behaviour demonstrated in one test session. Often given as evidence against the stability of moral character are the classic studies of Hartshorne and May (1928, 1929; Hartshorne, May and Shuttleworth, 1930). Over eight thousand children in the Chicago school system were given tests of honesty and deceit. These included circumstances as varied as cheating in a classroom, stealing money, and falsifying athletic records. Many commentators (e.g., Kohlberg and Mayer, 1972, p.478) have claimed that Hartshorne and May were dismayed to find the non-existence of stable personality traits of honesty. Cheating allegedly was highly determined by the nature of the situation.

However, that is but one disproportionately publicized feature of the results. What Hartshorne and May actually did find was that, although honesty in any single situation has a disappointingly low predictive value for honesty in another single situation, it is possible to predict behaviour averaged over a sample of situations.

> Just as one test is an insufficient and unreliable measure in the case of intelligence, so one test of deception is quite incapable of measuring a subject's tendency to deceive. That is, we cannot predict from what a pupil does on one test what he will do on another. If we use ten tests of classroom deception, however, we can safely predict what a subject will do on the average whenever ten similar situations are presented.
>
> (Hartshorne and May, 1928, p.135; and cited by Epstein, 1979, p.1101)

In the aforementioned rule-ritual conflict, for example, there was, on the average, a good deal of stability in behaviour. Some children were consistently fair in not disturbing their classmates while others were considerably less so. From this knowledge and that from the related measures of cognitive development, identification strength, and peer-group popularity, it should be possible to predict usefully future behavioural incidents. However, the napping situation is only one of many possible rule–ritual conflicts. How correct is it to generalize from one situation to another?

Generalizability would appear to be at least partly a function of the similarity of the situation. The more similar the situation, the more accurate the generalization (Mischel, 1968). Since the napping situation is similar to many others in which children are expected to act fairly in a school environment without direct supervision, it should also be possible to predict behaviour in these circumstances, but as the situations diverge in similarity, predictions become less accurate. To take an example offered by Epstein (1979), it would be ludicrous to observe swimming behaviour in a library as well as in a swimming pool and expect consistency in persons' behaviour across the two situations. Thus behaviour outside the school should be more difficult to predict because the situations are liable to be dissimilar to those at school. Likewise the results of the street-marching study are more generalizable to similar principle–rule conflicts than to dissimilar ones. An area in need of further study concerns the relationship between two or more rule–ritual or rule–principle conflicts across a variety of ages, together with an examination of other types of conflicts such as those between two rituals, two rules, and two principles (see Chandler, Siegal and Boyes, 1980, for a discussion of this question).

To this end, it should be noted that behaviour does not always have to be laboriously observed over a number of occasions to ensure stable and reliable measurements. As Epstein (1980) has shown, some events are so potent and "ego-involving" that the influence of incidental variables becomes unimportant. The experience of arrest in defiance of the law may fall into this category, taking account of the subject's cognition of the situation and his or her identification strength. Self-ratings and ratings of others may also be stable and reliable measures. Ratings themselves are made on a single occasion. But they may be based on an average impression made over behaviour in numerous past events such as children's perceptions of child-rearing techniques and their relationships with parents.

In summary, Freud may indeed have been on the right track when formulating his loosely defined but theoretically intriguing concept of identification. It may be that his identification concept is akin to Lavoisier's concept of oxygen which had to be modified before combustion theory could be incorporated into the body of established scientific knowledge. So too might Freud's identification have to undergo changes (i.e., become more verbal, conscious, and hence more testable) before a pale form of psychoanalytic theory can come in from languishing alongside the periphery of experimental psychology and enter its mainstream (cf. Farrell, 1981, p.193).

It may be that an avalanche of evidence is about to fall in this direction. But only a start has been made and a cautionary note is warranted as most of the evidence is correlational in nature and the direction of effect is unclear. While the correlation between children's behaviour and perceptions of their parents reflects the parent's influence on the child, it is still conceivable that the correlation may instead at least partly reflect the child's influence on the parent. Perhaps because children follow adult rules, they perceive themselves to be similar to their parents. Such similarity could attract parental rewards and approbation.

However, a reasonably convincing case can be made for the parental effects model (Hoffman, 1975b). As a means for exerting control, the parent has greater physical and psychological resources at hand than does the child. For this reason, the parent may constrain the child more than the child constrains the parent. Moreover, children develop into adults and not vice versa. Consequently, a justifiable working assumption is that children's behaviour and their perceptions of their parents can be attributed to parental socialization techniques.

Though only the tip of the iceberg has been located at best, and resolution of the correlational problem awaits further research, the broader implications of identification can be examined. These will be closely tied to peer-group influence and to the issue of critical periods in children's development.

Chapter Five

CRITICAL PERIODS IN CHILDREN'S DEVELOPMENT

THE CONCLUSION that identification is a pervasive process in moral development operates on the assumption that children are as susceptible to adult influence in later childhood and adolescence as they are in the preschool years. But this is inconsistent with a possibility which is difficult to rule out completely: namely that adult influence is in fact most effective during one particular *critical period* in children's development. If such influence is to have irreversible effects on the child's later years, it might have to take root during this critical period when the "doors" of understanding are open. Once the doors are closed, the time for understanding may be passed.

Until recently, many psychologists expressed a firm belief in the critical periods hypothesis. In these circles, it was commonly said that a critical period for development takes place during the first three or four years of life. The tender years were surmised to be the formative years. Yet a large body of evidence (Clarke and Clarke, 1976) has now challenged this idea. The critical periods hypothesis will be examined in this chapter: first as it relates to children's development in general and then to moral development in particular. In either case, there appears to be little supporting data; children's development is astonishingly resilient despite the effects of early deprivation. Moreover, children's moral judgments seem to be as susceptible to adult influence in later childhood as in the early years. These findings have important ramifications for any social-cognitive approach to the study of moral development.

5.1 *Attachment and Deprivation*

During much of the history of modern psychology, many of the same issues have remained controversial. The comparative contribution of environment and heredity to intelligence is one example; the existence or non-existence of critical periods is another. It was firmly believed by Sigmund Freud and others in the psychoanalytic tradition that events during the first few years of life are critical for later personality development. A child who can successfully resolve the early conflicts between his biological and social needs will grow up healthy, one who cannot will suffer. Freud (1930) in fact believed that each of us is obligated to sacrifice a portion of the happiness derived from the satisfaction of biological needs in order to establish security within adult society. The adult personality is produced from childhood experience: the boy, then, is father to the man.

In recent years, the most prominent psychoanalytic advocate of the critical periods hypothesis has been John Bowlby (1951, 1969). He believes that there is first a period during which the child's social and personality development is highly dependent on a mother-figure. Children under the age of 3 who are separated from their mothers and experience "maternal deprivation" are susceptible to adverse effects in later life:

> Direct observations of the ill-effects on young children of complete deprivation of maternal care have been made by a large number of child specialists and have shown that the child's development may be affected physically, intellectually, emotionally, and socially. . . . Wisely handled, these troubles may gradually fade away, though once again the real possibility of unseen psychic scars must not be forgotten which may become active and give rise to emotional illness in later life.
>
> At what age, it may be asked, does a child cease being liable to damage by a lack of maternal care? All who have studied the matter would agree that between three and five the risk is still serious, though much less so than earlier . . . . After the age of five the risk diminishes still further . . .
>
> (Bowlby, 1965, pp.22, 32 and 33).

5.2 *The Skeels Longitudinal Study*

But in contrast to the critical periods hypothesis, there have been several reports which indicate that children who have been deprived of maternal care have later been able to lead normal lives. Among the most prominent of these studies is that of Skeels (1966). This is a thirty-year longitudinal study originating in the early 1930s of 25 white children who had been transferred to an orphanage because no next of kin were available to give support or guardianship. Twenty of the children were illegitimate and five had been separated from their parents because of severe neglect and/or abuse.

The children's orphanage was a bleak place. Infants up to the age of 2 years had good physical and medical care but little more. They had little contact with adults and what they did have was largely restricted to dressing, feeding, and toilet supervision. There was little opportunity to play with toys.

After the age of 2, the children were transferred to "cottages" in which there lived 30 to 35 other children of the same sex under the age of 5. The children's homes were regimented by a matron who was in charge of their cleaning and clothing. Virtually nothing was owned by the children themselves.

Skeels at that time became involved in the placement of these children through the Iowa Board of Control of State Institutions. He was entrusted with the delivery of psychological services to several institutions including the orphanage. Almost at the outset, he noticed the rapid progress of two girls aged 40 and 43 months. As they had suffered from malnutrition and been ignored by their mothers, they had been committed to the orphanage. Their psychological tests indicated that the girls when aged 13 and 16 months respectively had developmental levels of 6 and 7 months. For this reason, the children were regarded as non-placeable and were put into a special institution for the mentally retarded. There, the two girls were placed in one of the wards of women whose chronological ages ranged from 18 to 50 years but whose mental ages ranged from 5 to 9 years. The children were "adopted" by the staff and inmates, and were lavished with attention and affection. Two years later, psychological testing revealed scores well within the normal range of intelligence.

These observations led Skeels to make a radical proposal to the appropriate authorities. He requested that a group of developmentally backward orphanage children be transferred to the institution for the mentally retarded. An agreement was reached that 11 more children would be transferred to this type of institution. At the time of transfer, the mean age of the group was about 1½ years and IQ scores were in the sub-normal range with a mean of 64.3. By the time the children reached the age of 3–4 years, their average IQ score increased to 91.8. Following the time spent in the second institution, 11 out of the 13 children were placed in an adoptive home; the remaining 2 were returned to the orphanage. In the adult follow-up study, all 13 were self-supporting, 11 were married, 9 out of these 11 had children with a total of 28 children in all. These second generation children had mean IQs of 104 (range = 86–125).

It was important for Skeels to compare these results with those of a second group who remained in the orphanage at approximately 4 years of age and were *not* transferred to the institution for the mentally retarded. Skeels located a contrast group of 12 such children whose mean IQ at the approximate age of 1½ years was 86.7. At the age of 3–4 their IQ scores had declined to a mean of 60.5 points. Whereas the contrast group then recorded an average loss of 26.2 IQ points, the experimental group recorded an average gain of 28.5 points. The comparative years of schooling are startling: the contrast group completed an average of 3 years as opposed to the experimental group which completed 11 years. Further comparisons

Table 3. *Experimental and Contrast Groups: Occupations of Subjects and Spouses (from Skeels, 1966)*

Case no.	Subject's occupation	Spouse's occupation	Female subject's occupation previous to marriage
Experimental group:			
1[a]	Staff sergeant	Dental technician	
2	Housewife	Labourer	Nurses' aide
3	Housewife	Mechanic	Elementary school teacher
4	Nursing instructor	Unemployed	Registered nurse
5	Housewife	Semi-skilled labourer	No work history
6	Waitress	Mechanic, semi-skilled	Beauty operator
7	Housewife	Flight engineer	Dining-room hostess
8	Housewife	Foreman, construction	No work history
9	Domestic service	(Unmarried)	—
10[a]	Real-estate sales	Housewife	—
11[a]	Vocational counsellor	Advertising copy-writer[b]	—
12	Gift-shop sales[c]	(Unmarried)	—
13	Housewife	Pressman-printer	Office-clerical
Contrast group:			
14	Institutional inmate	(Unmarried)	—
15	Dishwasher	(Unmarried)	—
16	Deceased	—	—
17[a]	Dishwasher	(Unmarried)	—
18[a]	Institutional inmate	(Unmarried)	—
19[a]	Compositor and typesetter	Housewife	—
20[a]	Institutional inmate	(Unmarried)	—
21[a]	Dishwasher	(Unmarried)	—
22[a]	Floater	Divorced	—
23	Cafeteria (part-time)	(Unmarried)	—
24[a]	Institutional gardener's assistant	(Unmarried)	—
25[a]	Institutional inmate	(Unmarried)	—

[a]Male [b]B.A. degree [c]Had previously worked as a licenced practical nurse

between the two groups provide quite striking differences (Table 3). In the contrast group, 5 out of the 12 children remained in institutions as adults, and were supported by the state. Only 2 of the 12 had married. One male subject had a family of four children of average intelligence; the other had one retarded child and was then divorced. This pattern is very unlike the successful marriage and employment histories of the experimental group.

The Skeels study is not without its problems. For example, one glaring drawback is that the contrast group members were chosen after some of the early data from the experimental group were analysed. Had the contrast group been randomly selected as part of a larger group at the same time as the experimental group was selected, it may have had a different composition. Only those few children could be included who had been given intelligence tests when they were under the age of 2. Because of this problem only 3 of the 13 experimental group children were males while there were 8 boys out of the 12 contrast-group children. Thus the experimental group might have been more advanced because it was predominantly female, and particularly amenable to the care of the inmates of the institution for the mentally retarded and to success in school and marriage. Had the contrast-group children also been predominantly female, they might have developed their potentialities more fully despite deprivation. For these and other reasons, it is impossible to assign an unambiguous interpretation to Skeels' results; and one recent critic has gone so far as to claim that this often-cited study is scientifically worthless (Longstreth, 1981, p.624).

5.3 *Additional Studies Bearing on the Critical Periods Hypothesis*

The Freud and Dann study: an example from the Holocaust

Nevertheless, there are other studies which complement the Skeels report. These also indicate that deprivation during the tender years neither has an irreversible effect nor does it exert a disproportionate influence on later development. Two such studies are especially noteworthy. First, Anna Freud and Sophie Dann (1951) report an observational study of 6 Jewish children orphaned during the Second World War. Before the age of 1, they had all lost their parents. Between the ages of 1 and 4, they lived together in several concentration camps and institutions. Then they were brought to Bulldog Banks, a home in the English countryside which had been converted to a nursery for war orphans.

At the start of their stay at Bulldog Banks, the children were very hostile toward adults but they showed altruism toward each other which was astonishing for such an early age. The children, who very quickly damaged much furniture and toys and ignored or spat on adults, would protect each other. A sick child was carefully watched by the others; a frightened child was comforted by the others; a child who was deprived of a second helping of dessert was spontaneously given some of the others' portions. The children did not want to leave each other for a moment despite the attractiveness of incentives such as pony rides offered by adults.

A follow-up project conducted one year after the children's transfer to Bulldog Banks indicated that the children had made substantial progress in their ability to form relationships with grownups, though their attachments to their peers were still stronger than their adult attachments. Despite severe deprivation during a hypothetical critical period of 0–4 years, there was no evidence to suggest that the children were lastingly delinquent in their social and personality development.

The Kadushin study: an example from adoptions of older children

The second study which supports the Skeels' interpretation is that of Kadushin (1970). Ever since the work of Goldfarb (1945), there has been concern that children who spend their early years in orphanages and are later adopted are likely to suffer lasting damage from this experience when compared with children who are adopted shortly after birth. Kadushin's study was designed to test this notion. His subjects were 49 boys and 42 girls of average intelligence. All had been removed from their own homes for reasons of neglect and abuse. They had come from poor homes in which one or both of the parents often suffered from personality disorders; very frequently there was considerable disharmony between the parents.

Prior to adoption by foster parents which occurred at the average of 7.2 years, the children had changed care on the average about 2.3 times. The criteria for calculating the success of the placement were mainly the foster parents' satisfaction with the new circumstances as expressed in questionnaires and interviews. Successful cases of adoption were found in about 85% of all cases, a figure no different than that obtained in studies of infant adoptions. Although the children were deprived of an enduring attachment with a mother-figure during a "critical period" extending at minimum from birth to 4 years, these traumatic effects proved reversible.

The results of a recent study by Tizard and Hodges (1978) also indicate that many late-adopted children do not suffer lasting effects from institutionalization. In addition, Tizard and Hodges point out several methodological difficulties in conducting research on the effects of adoption and institutionalization. Three of these are particularly notable. First, it is virtually impossible for an investigator to be unaware of the individual circumstances of his subjects. This knowledge may bias the observations of the children under study. Second, for the collection of some important data, a reliance on interviews with parents and children is often unavoidable. The subjects may deliberately or unconsciously either not tell the truth or act differently than usual in order to create a favourable impression with the interviewer. Third, even if it can be ensured that a difference between the deprived and normal groups is not an artefact of the method of investigation, this difference still might be attributed to factors other than a lack of stimulation during a critical period. It is possible, for example, that children fostered from birth have been placed in homes superior to those given to the late-adopted children. For this reason, any difference between the two groups might be attributable to social class differences; for instance, the early adopted may be more likely to be placed with middle-class parents than the late adopted. Therefore, in any event, it may be difficult to establish the presence of a critical period which gives rise to lasting effects on late-adopted children.

The Kagan and Klein study: a crosscultural example

The studies discussed so far have been conducted in either England or the United States. The case might be made that any environment in the modern industrialized world is enriched as compared to that of the environment of developing or Third World countries where the deepest poverty is widespread. Yet even here there have been studies which are inconsistent with the critical periods hypothesis and which indicate that severe deprivation during early experience is not irreversible.

To investigate the effects of early experience on children in Third World countries, Kagan and Klein (1973) went to the isolated village of San Marcos la Laguna (pop. 850) located in the mountainous north-west of Guatemala. According to Kagan and Klein's account, San Marcos infants are rarely spoken to or played with by adults during the first year of life. They spend most of their time inside a small dark hut, and are not usually allowed to crawl on the hut's dirty floor. Compared to Western babies, those in San Marcos are extraordinarily passive and much less alert. They are guarded by their mothers like a cashmere sweater, as a precious item to be safely stored away and left unattended. At the age of about 15 months, the San Marcos infant becomes mobile and starts to leave the dark hut to play with other children.

Kagan and Klein tested the effects of this early deprivation on children's cognitive development by administering tests of memory recall and

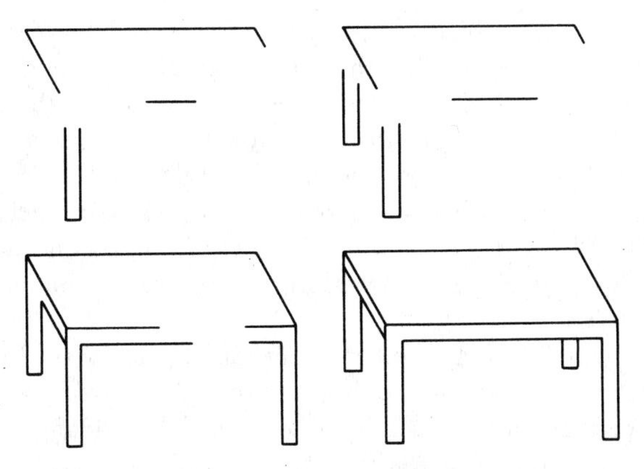

Fig. 9. *Sample item from the Perceptual Inference Test*

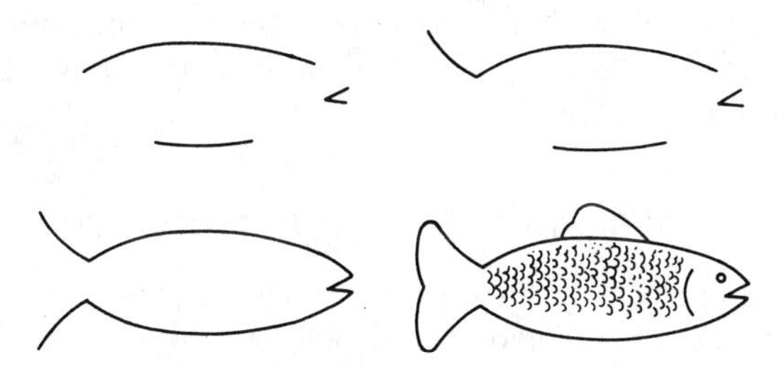

Fig. 10. *Sample item from the Perceptual Inference Test*

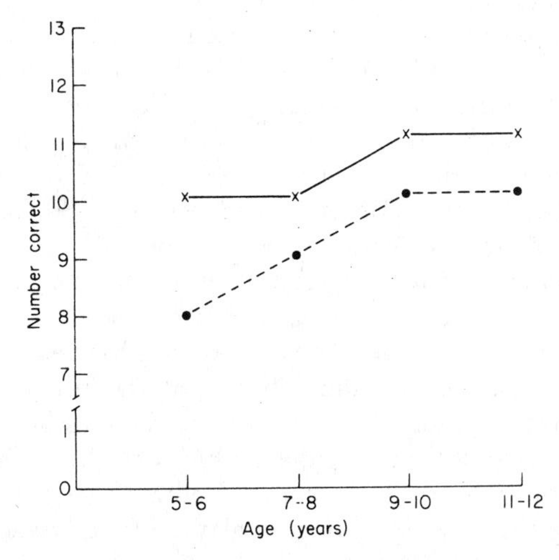

Fig. 11. *Number correct on the Perceptual Inference Test.* (●– – –●) *San Marcos;* (×——×) *Cambridge.*

recognition for familiar objects at the ages of 5, 8, and 11 years. At 5 and 8 the Guatemalans were outperformed by a sample of American children living in Cambridge, Massachusetts. But at 11 years, there were no differences between the two groups. The same pattern of results was found on a Perceptual Inference Test on which the child's task was to make an inference from minimal information given in the rough outlines of a design (Figs 9 and 10). While at 5–6 years American children again outperformed the Guatemalans, there were no significant differences in the 7- to 12-year-old group (Fig. 11).

These results should be regarded with caution, especially as a later research report has suggested that the findings are closely related to the specific nature of the task given to the children (Kagan, Klein, Finley, Rogoff and Nolan, 1979). Moreover, this study says nothing about children's social and personality development. But it can be assumed that most San Marcos children whose early experience consists of lying on the floor of a dark hut grow to be at least as "socially adjusted" in their culture as those who grow up in Western countries.

Longitudinal studies of North American children

In still another approach to the critical periods question, several efforts have been made to examine the extent to which later cognitive and social development can be predicted from measures taken during early experience. These have proceeded in two directions: (1) attempts to predict development from the nature of early mother–child interaction, and (2) attempts to predict development on the basis of intelligence and language-test scores during the first year of life. With regard to the former, the accuracy of early mother–infant interaction in predicting cognitive development at age 2 and 3 years is a matter of some controversy for which both supporting evidence (Cohen and Beckwith, 1979; Ramey, Farran and Campbell, 1979) and non-supporting evidence (Bakeman and Brown, 1980) exists. With regard to the latter, there does seem to be a modest degree of continuity, for example, between infant test scores during the first year and language development at 3 years, suggesting that infant tests have usefulness in detecting delays in language at 30 and 36 months (Siegel, 1979).

However, to establish the durability of effects during a critical period it is necessary to look at development beyond the preschool years. This was done in a study by Kagan, Lapidus and Moore (1978). Infants aged 4, 8, 13 and 27 months were brought to a laboratory at Harvard University. They were given a variety of free play and experimentally structured measures designed to assess attentiveness and vocalization. At 10 years of age, the children's scores were correlated with intelligence and reading ability. Infant attentiveness was significantly related to IQ and reading. However, both infant and childhood variables were significantly correlated with parental social class, again demonstrating the importance of examining children's development within a socioeconomic context. Once the variance attributable to social class was statistically removed, no signficant infant–childhood relationships remained.

To date, no similar study on social development has been reported, but the closest is that of Bakeman and Brown (1980). The subjects were a group of Atlanta mothers and their babies. Among numerous measures of infant development, the verbal responsiveness of the baby at 20 months was scored during a home visit by a social worker. This variable significantly correlated with IQ and social ability at age 3 (e.g., rated co-operativeness with peers at a day camp). However, as in the Kagan, Lapidus and Moore study, the infant and childhood variables were all associated with the mother's level of formal education, an indication of social class.

Thus in both longitudinal studies the continuity in development was significantly explained by social class measures. These results suggest that social class may be more predictive of children's development than is a critical period of early experience.

Enrichment and critical periods

Just as it was once often believed that deprivation during the early years would necessarily result in lasting harmful effects, it was also often believed that early enrichment would necessarily result in lasting beneficial effects. But the effects of enrichment have also proved to be reversible in later years.

Intervention through innovative nursery school programmes designed to aid disadvantaged children has been largely unsuccessful in producing long-term intellectual and academic gains. Some of the programs stressed problem-solving, others language skills, and still others stressed "discovery through play". With a spirit of wishful optimism characteristic of the 1960s, programs were funded to give the disadvantaged a "head start" in their early years. The guiding assumption in these bygone days was that children's early progress would be enduring.

There is no need to go into the details of the programs for they generally shared the same outcome. The results of 12 program evaluation studies involving children aged 1 to 6 years are neatly summarized by Bronfenbrenner (1974):

1. Almost without exception, children showed substantial gains in IQ and other cognitive measures during the first year of the program, attaining or even exceeding the average for their age.

2. Cognitively structured curricula produced greater gains than play-oriented nursery programs.

3. Neither earlier entry into the program (from age one) nor a longer period of enrolment (up to five years) resulted in greater or more enduring cognitive gains.

4. By the first or second year after completion of the program, sometimes while it was still in operation, the children began to show a progressive decline, and by the third or fourth year of follow-up had fallen back into the problem range of the lower 90s and below. Apparent exceptions to this general trend turned out to be faulted by methodological artefacts (e.g., self-selection of families in the experimental group).

5. The period of sharpest decline occurred after the child's entry into regular school. Preliminary data from the follow-through program suggest that this decline may be offset by the continuation of intervention programs, including strong parent involvement, into the early grades.

In fairness to the advocates of these programmes, it should be pointed out that if lasting effects were not clearly orchestrated by the age of 9 or 10, funding which would have permitted the examination of possible "sleeper effects" in later years was cut off (Palmer and Semlear, 1977). It is also uncertain whether or not an adequate measure of the effectiveness of preschool programs exists. Intelligence tests are commonly used to assess progress but perhaps a more comprehensive index is needed which includes measures of physical health, school attendance and achievement motivation, and acts of delinquency (Zigler and Trickett, 1978). This type of improvement has not yet been developed and implemented.

The issue is certainly not yet closed. On a different tack, a claim has recently been presented for the successfulness of preschool programmes. Darlington, Royce, Snipper, Murray and Lazar (1980) argue that IQ is only an indirect measure of programme effectiveness. A more valid indicator is actual school success. In 1976, the school records of 1599 children who had attended preschool programmes in the 1960s were examined. The numbers of these children who were held back and placed in special education classes during their school careers were significantly lower than those of a comparable control group who did not attend the preschools. These results are interpreted to indicate that early intervention was a success after all.

But there are still other explanations which cannot as yet be ruled out. Most notably, attendance at the programmes was voluntary. It could well have been that the children who participated would have done better than the non-participants in any event had they not attended before the programmes began. Their parents may have been more favourably disposed toward school in general (including preschool) and this attitude might have been reflected in school success.

The Snow and Hoefnagel-Hohle study: an example from second-language learning

All in all, the evidence to date which has accumulated from studies of enrichment as well as deprivation, lends little support to the critical periods hypothesis. To be sure, it still has been said (Lenneberg, 1967) that there is a critical period for language acquisition—if in no other area—and that it is much easier to learn a language as a young child than as an adolescent or adult. The issue may be of particular relevance to moral development as the learning of moral rules and principles has often been likened closely to language learning. Brown (1965, p.407), for one, has made the analogy that "To speak a language one must have a system of general rules by which infinitely many sentences can be constructed. To distinguish right from wrong, one must have another such system." Consequently, should a critical period be established in the course of language development, the same might be suspected with regard to moral development.

However, even this idea does not meet with unequivocal support. In a well-conceived study, Snow and Hoefnagel-Hohle (1978) studied English speakers' attempts to acquire the Dutch language during the first year of their residence in Holland. There were, in fact, two groups of English speakers who participated in their project. In addition to the group of beginners who were just starting to learn Dutch, the study included an advanced group who had been living in Holland and learning Dutch for at least 18 months. Both the beginners and the advanced group were divided into the following age groups: 6–7 years, 8–10 years, 12–15 years, and adults. The beginners, who also counted among their ranks a number of 3- to 5-year-olds, were tested three times during the year at 4- to 5-month intervals, while the advanced subjects were tested only once. The test battery itself was designed to assess a wide range of abilities in the second language: pronunciation, auditory discrimination, morphology, sentence repetition, sentence translation, sentence judgment, story comprehension, story telling, and finally vocabulary comprehension as measured on the Peabody Picture Vocabulary Test.

The results, including those on the translation test (reproduced in Fig. 12), showed that older groups outperformed the 3- to 5-year-olds on all the measures and that the 12- to 15-year-olds indicated the most rapid learning of the Dutch language. On this basis, Snow and Hoefnagel-Hohle find grounds to reject early childhood as a critical period for language acquisition.

This conclusion appears to stand even in the face of rather obvious objections. It might be argued that the youngest children did not receive as much exposure to the language as did the adolescents and adults. However, as Snow and Hoefnagel-Hohle point out, the children were immersed in a Dutch language environment for at least 30 hours a week at school, whereas the adults did not use Dutch regularly at work and their class time devoted to learning Dutch did not exceed a total of 26 hours in any one case. Despite this comparatively shorter exposure to the language, the adults learned Dutch more quickly than did the children.

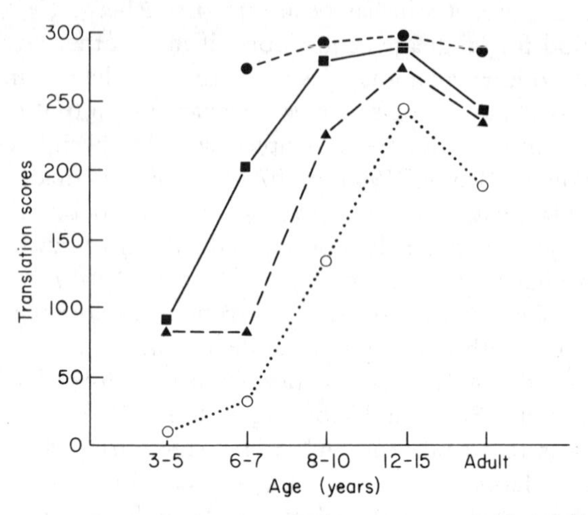

Fig. 12. *Median number of grammatical structures correctly translated in the Translation Test. (●---●) Advanced; (■——■) Time 3; (▲--▲) Time 2; (○···○) Time 1.*

It might also be argued that the inferior performance of the younger children can be attributed to the sophisticated nature of the testing material. To counteract this objection, Snow and Hoefnagel-Hohle claim that there the content of the tests was specifically designed to ensure that this problem would not arise. The test material was thus rather elementary and childish; and in this respect attention is drawn to a comparison of the test performance of the second language learnings with that of a group of native Dutch speakers. Within age groups, the 12- to 15-year-old language-learners approached native abilities more quickly than did the 3- to 5-year-old learners when compared to a group of 3- to 5-year-old native Dutch speakers.

It is also pointed out that these results are consistent with other language-related findings bearing on the critical periods hypothesis. Thus once again, there is a lack of evidence for the notion that the early years exert a disproportionate influence on later development. Even the existing evidence that children outperform adults in learning a language without an accent is shown to be equivocal and open to question. So those adults who believe that the time to become bilingual has past should take note.

5.4 Is There a Sensitive Period during Moral Development?

The studies discussed so far do not specifically bear on moral development. Nor do they establish whether or not there is a *sensitive* period in development—a period in which children are particularly sensitive to socialization influences though not necessarily critically affected. What follows is an examination of these issues.

The research on identification and the delineation of sensitive periods in the development of moral behaviour is very meagre. For this reason the best evidence here comes from the long years of exhaustive research on Piaget's theory of moral judgment development. As seen earlier (Section 3.4), Piaget maintains that with the advent of peer-group influence, the child is "liberated" from adult constraint and the authority of the adult loses much of its legitimacy. This claim implies that a sensitive, if not a critical, period exists in early childhood during which adult influence is most effective. However, the findings of subsequent studies suggest that, while there are some areas in which authority might wane with an increase in peer-group interaction, it may actually if anything become more influential in the area of moral judgments.

Judgments of acts committed by adult and peer transgressors

If, as Piaget claims, children have a unilateral respect for adult authority, they should judge adult transgressors less severely than peer transgressors. Yet several recent studies have indicated that young children's moral judgments are not affected in this way by the age of the transgressor. In one study (Rybash, Sewell, Roodin and Sullivan, 1975), kindergarteners (mean age = 6 years) were presented with a single moral problem in which either an adult or a peer accidentally broke a number of Easter eggs. The adult and peer were judged as equally naughty, regardless of their ages. Similar findings have been reported elsewhere (Suls and Kalle, 1978). Children aged 5 to 10 were given four moral problems involving, for example, an adult or a peer who broke all the dishes. Again adults were not judged less harshly than children causing identical damage, even by subjects as young as 5 years.

Judgments of acts involving adult and peer victims

Piaget's notion of adult constraint also implies that younger children, having a unilateral respect for adult authority, should be more likely than older children to believe that to harm an adult is naughtier than to harm a child.

On this score, Piaget himself offers some data which he interprets as convincing and critical support for his position. Children aged 6–13 were asked, "Is it just as bad to lie to one's companions as to grownups or is it different?" The results appeared to support Piaget's expectations. These were that the constraint-oriented younger children would answer that it is worse to lie to grownups while the older mutual respect-oriented children would answer that it is equally bad or even worse to lie to one's companions. It was found that

> 81 percent of the subjects between 6 and 9 think it worse to lie to adults, while 51 percent of those between 10 and 12 that it is equally bad to lie to children, and of these, 17 percent are even of opinion that it is worse to lie to a companion than to an adult. (Piaget, 1932/1977, p.297)

However, there are at least four serious faults to this study. First, the question itself implies that it might be worse to lie to grownups but does not imply that it might be worse to lie to one's companions. Had the question been, "Is it just as bad to lie to grownups as to one's companions or is it different?" the results might have been much different. Second, mention of the grownups occurred later in the question than mention of the companions. Thus the younger children might have chosen the grownup simply because it was more recent in their memories. Third, Piaget gives no breakdown of the percentages at 6, 7, 8, or 9 years: it might well have been that 95% of the 9-year-olds as opposed to 50% of the 6-year-olds answered that it is worse to lie to a grownup. Fourth, even according to the percentages which Piaget does supply, only 17% of the older children thought it worse to lie to a child as opposed to presumably 32% who thought it was worse to lie to an adult and 51% who thought it equally naughty. This hardly proves that mutual respect is prevalent over a respect for adult-imposed constraints. So while there is an increase with age in the percentage of children choosing "equality", this development might have been accompanied by a deeper respect for the adult than before, perhaps within a process of identification. Of course an interpretation of Piaget's results is also made difficult by the fact that the size of the population sample is missing.

Thus Piaget's evidence is inconclusive. Moreover, there is a plausible alternative to Piaget's argument. Adults try to instruct the child's moral behaviour. But the child will not follow what he is being taught unless he has a respect for adults. Perhaps then this respect should actually increase rather than decrease with age during the course of a process of identification (Section 4.4). Thus older children should be more respectful of adult instruction than younger ones: e.g., they should actually be more likely to think it worse to lie to a grownup than to a friend.

So once more Piaget's work is cleverly conceived but rather loosely presented, and it is inconsistent with a study designed to control for these difficulties (Siegal, 1979). Children aged 5, 7, 9, and 11 years were asked to compare identical moral acts (lying, stealing, sharing, and helping) committed by a child culprit against either an adult or peer victim. The results are shown in Table 4. Only the 9-year-olds judged that it is naughtier to harm (and better to help and share with) an adult than a child. The 5- and 7-year olds displayed no clear preference for either type of act while the 11-year-old group maintained that both acts are equally naughty (or good) regardless of the age of the victim involved.

It is interesting to note that not one child spontaneously gave a "mature" mutual respect explanation similar to that of 12-year old Cal (cited by Piaget, 1932, p.170): "Sometimes you almost have to tell lies to a grownup,

Table 4. *Numbers of Children (out of 20) Choosing "Friend", "Grownup", or "Both the Same" in the Experiment on Judgments of Acts Affecting Adults and Peers (Siegal, 1979).*

Range and mean of age group	Moral acts			
	Giving	Helping	Pinching	Lying
5:0–5:11 ($\bar{x} = 5:5$)				
Friend	9	6	9	11
Grownup	7	10	6	5
Both the same	4	4	5	4
7:0–7:11 ($\bar{x} = 7:6$)				
Friend	5	3	6	6
Grownup	5	11	3	10
Both the same	10	6	11	4
9:0–9:7 ($\bar{x} = 9:4$)				
Friend	5	2	5	1
Grownup	7	10	8	12
Both the same	8	8	7	7
11:0–11:8 ($\bar{x} = 11:8$)				
Friend	4	1	2	2
Grownup	0	3	4	6
Both the same	16	16	14	12

but it's rotten to do it to another fellow." However, in choosing the grownup, some children spontaneously gave explanations which invariably took the form, "the grownup is bigger" and "the grownup is the right one because he's older".

Contrary to the position advocated by Piaget, adult-oriented responses were increasingly evident with age and preceded the mature "both the same" responses of the 11-year-old group. One interpretation of this result is that the choices of the 11-year-olds may be less the product of the increasing solidarity among friends advocated by Piaget and more the product of a deeper respect for adult authority.

This explanation is further supported by the results of a recent study of children's perceptions of maternal socialization behaviour (Appel, 1977). Kindergarteners (aged 5 and 6) and third-graders (aged 8–10) were given stories in which a highly permissive mother allows a child to misbehave. For example, in one story, a child is permitted to splash others at the beach. The overwhelming majority of third-graders evaluated the permissive mother negatively while the kindergarteners overwhelmingly evaluated the mother positively. These results could be attributed to a response bias on the part of the younger children which would evaluate a mother as "good" regardless of her behaviour. However, the possibility remains that, with age, children appear to develop or "internalize" a deeper respect for the intentions underlying the adult's childrearing efforts. An increasing cognitive awareness of the intentions strengthens and legitimizes adult authority.

According to Piaget, young children's respect for adult authority is especially manifested in their moral judgments. These disregard the transgressor's intentions and focus more on the consequences of the deed which are "objectively" defined by adult rules and punishments. Children with age come to give more weight to intentions, a process which according to Piaget is associated with a freedom from adult constraint. But there is an alternative interpretation which is quite plausible: that is, an increase in children's understanding of intentionality may produce not a decrease but an increase in the authority of the adult.

Attribution of causes to adult authority

In contrast to the evidence on children's judgments of acts involving adult and peer transgressors and victims, research in the area of children's perceptions of causal attributions has been interpreted to support Piaget's claim that adult authority weakens with age. Karniol and Ross (1976) gave kindergarteners, first-graders, second-graders, and college students four story-pairs. In one member of a pair, for example, a boy played with a toy freely without adult constraint. In the other member, another boy played with an identical toy because his mother told him to do so or promised him a reward. The following story-pair was one used in the study:

> Mike was home and there were two of his toys there, a ball and a puzzle. Mike's mother said that Mike could have some cake if he played with the ball. Remember, Mike's mother said that Mike could have some cake if he played with the ball. And Mike played with the ball.
>
> Tony was home and there were two of his toys there, a ball and a puzzle. And Tony played with the ball.

The subjects were then asked, "Who really wants to play with the toy?" The second-graders and college students correctly chose the boy who freely played with the toy but the kindergarteners and first-graders generally chose the constrained story figure. These results are comparable with those reported in a similar study by Costanzo, Grumet and Brehm (1974), and are interpreted to be consistent with Piaget's idea that young children have a unilateral respect for adult authority; an obedient act is better than one which is freely initiated.

However, an opposite explanation is equally plausible. Five-year-olds might judge that the constrained figure is the one who really wants to play with an approved toy only because adult approval implicitly makes a good act better. This does not mean that they respect the adult to the extent that the goodness and badness of acts are dependent on the rewards and punishments dispensed by adults. In fact, Jensen and Hughston (1973) found that 4- and 5-year-olds judge bad acts to be bad independently of whether these acts are rewarded or punished. It might even be the older children who display the greater adult respect here for they are the ones who explicitly recognize that the adult has the power to regulate children's play regardless of their wants and likes.

Before turning to research in other related areas, a word is in order concerning the methodological problem of ensuring children's story recall and comprehension. This problem is serious enough to cast doubt over the findings of many of the studies in this area. For example, in the Karniol and Ross study the stories were audiotaped and presented without visual displays as a memory aid. It is not surprising that, in order for the younger children to remember the second story in a pair, it had to be repeated up to three times. By then they may have forgotten the first story. In addition, the younger children might have chosen the "constrained" figure because his name was more salient than that of the "free" figure. Within a story-pair, the name of the constrained figure was mentioned six times but the name of the free figure was mentioned only twice.

Having children repeat the stories, even with the benefit of illustrations, is probably not enough of a safeguard to ensure their comprehension. Several studies have indicated that a failure to recall story information can affect children's responses to moral judgment problems (Austin, Ruble and Trabasso, 1977; Feldman, Klosson, Parsons, Rholes and Ruble, 1976; Parsons, Ruble, Klosson, Feldman and Rholes, 1976). For this reason, comprehension probes were used in the Suls and Kalle (1978) study mentioned above to assess children's understanding of the stories. Over 20% of kindergarten and first-grade subjects had to be excluded because of recall errors. Indeed, by going to special lengths to guarantee recall and comprehension, it has been shown that young children can correctly identify a figure who freely chooses a toy as the one who really wants to play in contrast to a constrained figure (Berndt, 1977; Shultz and Butkowsky, 1977).

Effects of adult and peer models on moral judgment development

Thus neither the evidence on children's evaluations of adult and peer transgressors and victims nor that on children's perceptions of causal attributions supports Piaget's adult-constraint notion. Much of this work is equivocal or suggests the possibility that adult influence on moral judgment increases with age. The same conclusion can be reached through an examination of studies on the comparative effects of adult and peer models on children's moral judgments.

Piaget appears to make no clear prediction on children's susceptibility to external influence over age. While young children are rigid in their advocacy of adult-imposed rules, older children can be meticulous in their adherence to group norms (Allen and Newtson, 1972). What Piaget's theory does imply is that older children should be less susceptible to the influence of adult models than are younger children, and that adult models should be less effective than peer models in training children to consider a story-character's intentions in judging his moral behaviour.

Yet contrary to Piaget, recent studies have demonstrated that the adult is a generally more effective model than the peer in the case of moral judgment development. Using a design similar to that originally employed by Bandura and McDonald (1963), and described earlier (Section 3.6), Dorr and Fey (1974) gave children aged 5 to 11 a pretest consisting of story-pairs which contrasted the behaviour of a child who accidentally caused heavy damage with the light damage caused by a well-intentioned child. On this basis, the subjects were divided into two groups: those who correctly considered the story-character's intentions, and those who immaturely disregarded his intentions by focusing on the objective consequences of the character's behaviour. The groups were then given additional story-pairs and exposed to the judgments of either adult or peer models; the models gave objective judgments to the subjective (or intentional) group and intentional judgments to the objective group. In both conditions, the adult model was more influential than the peer model although the latter was more influential than no model.

Similar results were obtained by Brody and Henderson (1977). First-graders were simultaneously exposed to two models, a peer and an adult, who in some conditions gave conflicting judgments. An adult who gave mature intentional judgments accompanied by rationales was effective in eliciting intentional moral judgments when he was paired with a peer who

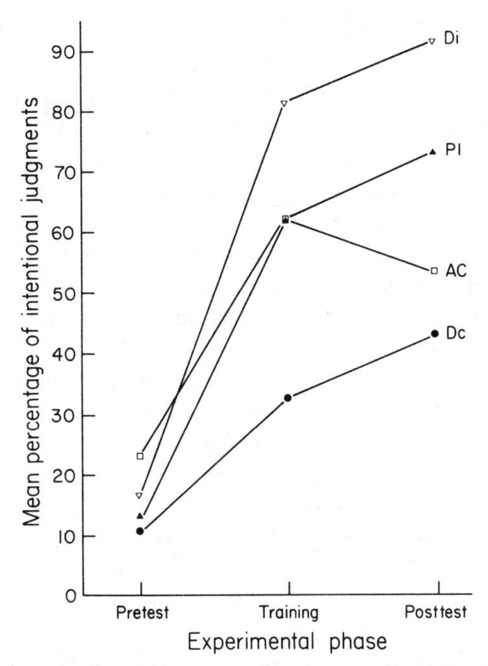

Fig. 13. *Methods of promoting intentional moral judgments in children.* (Di) *Didactic;* (PI) *peer interaction;* (AC) *adult conflict;* (Dc) *decentring.* (*From Lickona, 1973.*)

gave immature objective judgments. An intentional peer model paired with an objective adult was comparatively ineffective.

That adult influence is more powerful than peer influence in stimulating children's moral judgment development is also shown in a study by Lickona (1973, 1976). The judgments of first- and second-graders were trained under a number of conditions. These included a peer-interaction condition involving a face-to-face debate between an objective subject and an already subjective peer and a didactic training condition in which an adult told a subject directly why an intentional judgment was correct. Piaget's theory would imply that the peer-interaction condition should be more successful than didactic training. Yet the opposite occurred; didactic training was the more effective of the two (Fig. 13). As Lickona points out, this finding is difficult to interpret from a Piagetian standpoint.

5.5 *Summary and Implications*

The evidence is indirect in the sense that it has been derived almost wholly from experimental studies. Observational studies of moral behaviour are needed for additional support. Nevertheless, findings from divergent research areas converge in pointing to the same conclusion. Little support exists for Piaget's claim that children's respect for adult authority is liberated with increasing peer-group interaction. Children of all ages judge adult and peer transgressors as equally naughty. With age, children in fact appear to develop a deeper respect for the adult victim and the intentions underlying the adult's efforts at childcare. In the realm of social perception, children also may come to recognize explicitly that the adult has the power and authority to control children's behaviour regardless of their wants and likes. Moreover, the adult is more effective than the peer as a model for stimulating moral judgment development.

There is indeed not much question that the daily proportion of adult–child contact decreases and peer–child contact increases as children enter school (Wright, 1967). Moreover, children's susceptibility to adult influence may well decline for perceptual judgments of unambiguous stimuli and on matters of opinion (Allen and Newtson, 1972; Utech and Hoving, 1969). But as children grow older they become more adept at recognizing that adult rules are deliberately designed to prevent naughty behaviour. The child can identify more strongly with these rules because he or she recognizes their rational quality.

This is a possibility which Piaget (1932/1977, p.99) considers but then dismisses as characteristic of primitive non-Western societies:

> In our societies the child of thirteen escapes from the family circle and comes in contact with an ever-increasing number of social circles which widen his mental outlook. Whereas in so-called primitive communities adolescence is the age of initiation, therefore, of the strongest moral constraint, and the individual as he grows older, becomes more and more dependent. But keeping in mind only our societies of children we see that cooperation constitutes the most deep-lying social phenomenon, and that which has the surest psychological foundations. As soon as the individual escapes from the dominion of age, he tends towards cooperation as the formal form of social equilibrium.

There is little doubt that the increasingly complex moral dilemmas of modern society render Piaget's claim problematic and questionable. An age of initiation exists not only in economically underdeveloped societies but also in the industrialized West. In order to solve these moral problems, a learner, whether child or adolescent, has to be "initiated" into skills of reasoning (Peters, 1967). At this juncture, it is still premature to probe in any considerable way the vast field of education and childrearing (Section 8.3). But one point should be made here: education is a process of initiation and is facilitated by an increasing respect on the part of the child learner for the adult teacher. A lack of respect can impair this process, and evidence suggests that children's readiness to misbehave is associated with disrespectful attitudes toward adults and is comparatively unassociated with attitudes toward peers. For example, using a questionnaire technique developed by Bronfenbrenner (described in Section 6.3), Bixenstine, DeCorte and Bixenstine (1976) found that elementary schoolchildren's readiness to engage in peer-sponsored misbehaviour was significantly correlated with a loss in favourableness toward adults; in contrast, this readiness was unassociated with attitudes toward peers.

To be sure, Piaget (1932/1977, p.190) does allow that children's moral development is "naturally capable of being reinforced by the precepts and the practical example of the adult" though it is "largely independent of these influences". But he claims that traditional educational practice which directly attempts to inculcate adult values is dangerous in that it discourages co-operation and encourages an unreflecting conformity to adult rules. A "new", more original method of education should centre on developing co-operation within the peer group (Piaget, 1971, pp.178-180).

Yet if adult authority does not crumble beneath the onslaught of peer influence, it is especially incumbent upon adults themselves to develop children's sense of right and wrong. To this end, peer-group debates in the classroom have often been used to stimulate children's moral judgment development (Blatt and Kohlberg, 1975; Jensen and Murray, 1978; Power and Reimer, 1978). But perhaps less emphasis should be placed on peer-group-centred programmes and more stress put on the effectiveness of direct adult intervention. This of course is not to deny that peer-group influence can be profitably channelled toward increasing, for example, children's communication skills and their abilities to imagine others' interests and intentions (Section 6.3; 6.4). But at least in the area of moral judgment development, the adult himself may actively and systematically encourage children to consider the interests and intentions of others through modelling, reinforcement, and reasoning.

In sum, evidence from crosscultural and longitudinal studies and from studies of orphans and adopted children have shown that the effects of early deprivation and enrichment are reversible in later years. The same conclusions have come from animal studies; for example, monkeys who have been subjected to severe deprivation under experimental conditions eventually appear to recover (Novak and Harlow, 1975). Moreover, there is no evidence to suggest that children's early moral development as defined by Piaget is particularly sensitive to adult influence. And at times even Bowlby (Bowlby, Ainsworth, Boston and Rosenbluth, 1956, p.240) has allowed that the case for a critical period is not a strong one:

> statements implying that children who are brought up in institutions or who suffer other forms of serious privation and deprivation in early life commonly develop psychopathic or affectionless characters are seen to be

> mistaken . . . . Outcome is immensely varied, and of those who are damaged only a small minority develop those very serious disabilities of personality which first draw attention to the pathogenic nature of the experience.

All of the findings to date must be regarded as tentative. But in the absence of firmer evidence, there is little which contradicts the presumption that in general adult influence can be as effective in later childhood and adolescence as in the preschool years. During the ages 6 to 12 much can be done to develop intellectual abilities as well as a sense of fairness in children. On the one hand, these efforts will not necessarily be wasted owing to the effects of deprivation in the "critical" early years. It is abundantly clear that many children are not lastingly damaged by deprivation and that "experiences at all ages have an impact" (Rutter, 1979, p.298).

In this regard, as Bronfenbrenner points out, to sustain the gains arising from preschool "enrichment" programmes, adults must actively encourage and support their children's development during the primary and secondary school years. Without a follow-through in later years, the effects of early enrichment may be no more lasting than the effects of deprivation. In order to sustain children's identifications with rules and standards for behaviour, peer-group interaction may be structured by adults.

Chapter Six

ADULT INFLUENCES ON PEER-GROUP PRACTICE

6.1 *Recognition and Status in the Peer Group*

CHILDREN, according to Baldwin, practise in the peer group what they learn from adults (Section 3.6). Though much has been written on how peer-group crosspressures can cancel out the force of adult explanations, this phenomenon has not been linked to the attractiveness of peer culture. Rather it has been attributed to a growing lack of adult involvement in the time-consuming childrearing process, accompanied by a loss in favourable attitudes toward adults on the part of children (Bixenstine, DeCorte and Bixenstine, 1976; Bronfenbrenner, 1967, 1970a, b; Devereux, 1970). That is, children become disenchanted with learning from adults rather than their becoming enchanted with the misbehaviour endorsed by peers.

But there exist several important ways in which the peer group might be influenced by adults so as actually to comply with rules of fairness, especially those against cheating (leaving aside momentarily the case of principles of fairness, cf. Section 8.4). Some of these ways involve situations in which young children experience privilege and deprivation relative to their peers; others involve situations in which children who have been assigned responsibility become experienced in acting fairly toward peers without the continuing guidance of an adult authority.

The work in this area is fragmented in that a variety of topics have been studied in isolation from each other without a grand design or even an underlying thread. But though an airtight case cannot be made for many of the conclusions which have been drawn from the research, a number of these studies have generated some extremely interesting suggestions.

Deprivation in peer-group interaction

A concept of a status hierarchy is necessary in order to understand how others may be relatively deprived or privileged and to judge whether or not these circumstances are fair. Children have to be able to locate their position on a totem pole of characteristics such as intelligence and toughness, and to compare their abilities and achievements with those of peers.

Evidence suggests that the capacity to recognize hierarchies increases dramatically as children enter into more frequent and varied peer-group contact at school (Section 1.2). In one study (Omark and Edelman, 1975), children attending kindergarten and the first three grades of a private middle-class school in the United States were shown snapshots of themselves and a classmate. The children were asked to identify the "tougher" child. The results (Fig. 14) indicated that the kindergarteners tended to overestimate their own toughness and that there was only about 40% agreement among the children on the structure of a "toughness" hierarchy within the class. In contrast, children in Grades 1 to 3 displayed over 60% agreement and were able to identify fairly accurately the leaders and followers in the class.

That many preschoolers do not have a clear understanding of status has been reported by others (Edelman and Omark, 1973; Sluckin and Smith, 1977) and this finding has been replicated crossculturally in a Swiss school (Omark, Omark and Edelman, 1973). With increasing age, children increasingly seek information about how well they perform on a task relative to others (Ruble, Feldman and Boggiano, 1976).

In the case of both schoolchildren and adults, the effects of status deprivation on moral behaviour have been intensively studied and are rather complicated. Generally, it may be said that peer-group acceptance is associated with the development of sense of fairness; and that an individual can acquire much recognition and status through participating in peer-group activities. To deprive an individual of this recognition and status may lead to dishonest behaviour in children (cf. Sampson, 1969; Walster and Walster, 1975) as well as contributing to strained family relationships (Section 8.1).

In one study (Kanfer and Duerfeldt, 1968), for example, children in Grades 2 and 5 participated in a guessing game. The children were allowed to reward themselves for correct responses; but since the probability of guessing correctly was near zero, there was a temptation to cheat. Findings were that those who were rated by their teachers as having a low class-standing cheated significantly more than those rated as having a high class-standing. Thus it can be argued that low-class-standing children cheat because they are deprived of status relative to their high-class-standing peers. By the same token, adults also appear likely to cheat when they have

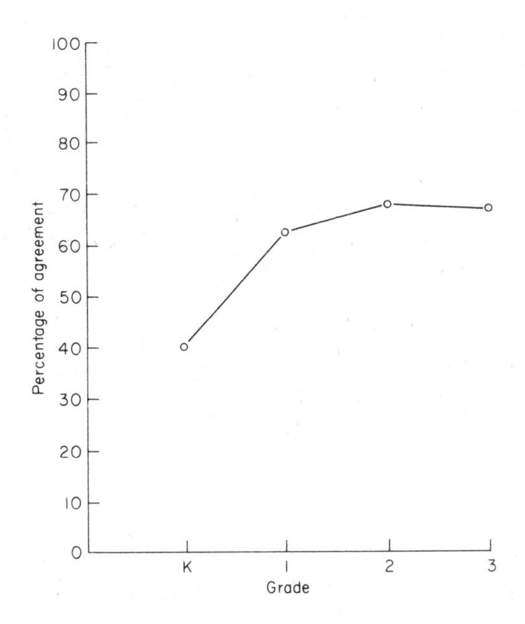

Fig. 14. *Estimated percentage of agreement on the comparative toughness of classmates. (After Omark and Edelman, 1975.)*

been led to infer that they are lower than average achievers and would be embarrassed by this lowly status (Millham, 1974).

However, it is possible that such results may be due to other factors besides status deprivation. For example, cheaters have been shown to be less able to wait for large rewards (Mischel and Gilligan, 1964), to be less attentive (Grim, Kohlberg and White, 1968), and to have lower IQ test scores than non-cheaters (Hartshorne and May, 1928). It might seem that many low achievers would fit better into one of these categories than into that of the status deprived. Moreover, even if the status-deprivation characterization is accurate, it might have nothing to do with adult influence on peer-group contact. For example, though it appears that high-status boys tend to have fathers who give favourable evaluations of their sons' abilities (Winder and Rau, 1962), this type of correlation does not imply that favourable evaluations contribute to this high status. It is equally plausible that parents' evaluations may result from observations of their sons' success in the peer group.

But two cleverly designed experiments by Stephenson and White (1968, 1970) give some support to the adult-influenced deprivation interpretation. The participants in both studies were 10-year-old boys living in Nottingham,

England. In a first experiment, injustice was manipulated in the context of a model racing-car game. Four levels of "injustice" were created: privileged, equity, relatively deprived, and absolutely deprived. The privileged group raced cars all the time and the equity group raced cars half the time and retrieved half the time. The deprived groups retrieved all the time; the relatively deprived group retrieved adult-raced cars while the absolutely deprived retrieved cars raced by the privileged group. All the children then had the chance to win prizes by cheating on a motor-racing quiz. The results indicated that cheating was greater in the absolute than in the relatively deprived group, and greater in the relatively deprived than in the equity or privileged group. One reasonable explanation is that because the deprived groups participated in an unjust adult-endorsed social interaction, status frustration and comparison were aroused. Therefore, these groups cheated significantly more.

The subjects in the second experiment were given a word-making test. Some were told that they did well and were assigned to a privileged group which raced model cars all the time. Others were told that they did poorly and were assigned to a deprived group which retrieved cars raced by the privileged group all the time. Following the car-racing, half of the privileged children and half of the deprived children were told that a mistake had been made; the privileged children were told that they had actually done poorly on the word-making test while the deprived ones were told that they had actually done well. So the car-racing roles should have been reversed. These children formed the "unjustly privileged" and "unjustly deprived" groups as opposed to the "justly privileged" and "justly deprived" groups for whom no mistake had been made. As in the previous experiment, all the children were then given the chance to win prizes by cheating on a quiz. It was found that cheating was significantly greater in the justly privileged and unjustly deprived groups than in the other two. The justly privileged group sought to retain its status; they cheated in order to maintain high outcomes. In contrast, the unjustly deprived cheated in order to right the contradiction that their performance did not equal their rewards. The two other groups did not have as strong a justification for cheating. Being "unskilled" at word-making provided a rationale for foregoing prizes.

It is also quite plausible that the justly privileged and unjustly deprived cheat because the former can get away with it while the latter is expected to. On the one hand, the justly privileged have earned their reward in the eyes of the group. These privileged may include some elected student council officials and sports heroes. They are overprotected from the consequences of dishonest behaviour, and hence have a motivation for cheating. Perhaps this misbehaviour is reminiscent of "white-collar" crime in the adult world. On the other hand, the unjustly deprived live up to the expectations of the peer group. They are expected to cheat especially because their situation is undeserved; and perhaps such misbehaviour is reminiscent of "blue-collar" crime.

A later study (Stephenson and Barker, 1972) replicated the Stephenson and White results, but suggested that they are limited to introverted children. Thus any such speculative explanation must be regarded as highly tentative, and subject to qualification from further research. Certainly not enough is known about how disruptive peer relationships may affect a child's self-perceptions of how well he or she can solve moral conflicts (cf. Bandura, 1981).

In this connection, some initial evidence has come from a certainly ingenious, if rather devious study (Harari and McDavid, 1969). A group of 11- to 13-year-olds were asked to nominate the five students whom they considered as best qualified to represent their classes at a social function for all the local schools. The subjects then witnessed the misbehaviour of a peer who, for example, stole change from the teacher's desk. The culprit was either a higher-status peer (one who had received the most nominations) or a low-status peer (one who had received no nominations). The witnesses were questioned by an adult to discover who was guilty. When questioned alone, every child was willing to reveal the identity of the culprit. But the presence of an innocent classmate during the interrogation deterred potential "finking". Moreover, the incidence of finking was significantly greater when the culprit had low status than when he had high status. In fact, while not one out of seven witnesses were willing to incriminate a guilty high-status peer with an innocent one present, seven out of seven incriminated the low-status peer. Similar results have been found in other related experiments on aggression. Children who are unjustly deprived relative to their peers tend to be aggressive (Perry and Perry, 1976; Santrock, Smith and Baurbeau, 1976).

Presumably the high-status peer is overprotected from the consequences of rule violations while the low-status peer is underprotected. How such phenomena may be associated with children's self-perceptions has been explored in a study by Furman and Masters (1980) using preschoolers as subjects. On a sociometric status measure, each child was asked to nominate three liked and three disliked peers from an array of pictures of their classmates. Then the child was told that a rule against playing with certain toys had been established either by the teacher or by peers. Regardless of who instituted the rule, unliked, low-status children deviated significantly more often than their liked, high-status counterparts.

In the naturalisitic, observational study discussed earlier (Section 4.4), peer-group popularity was unassociated with rule violations. However, this study used older children and a different rule. The data from Furman and

Masters' experimental study suggests that under some circumstances, children's recognition of their unpopularity may determine their rate of rule-violating. Alternatively, children's rule-violating may influence their unpopularity among peers. Consequently, more information is required to establish the direction of effect. A discussion of such possibilities will be included in what follows.

Contact with same-age and younger children

Some children come into contact mainly with children their own age while others interact with children who are older and younger. There is reason to believe that mixed-age peer contact is particularly important for the development of fairness. It fosters a relationship in which the younger child is dependent on the older one and the older one is forced to develop a concern for the younger one's needs. Bizman, Yinon, Mivtazari and Shavit (1978) examined the altruistic behaviour of Israeli children attending kindergartens in which classmates were similar or different in age (about 50% younger and 50% older). The children were given three measures of altruism: two story items in which the children were asked to say whether a central character should give up a pleasurable activity to help a person in need, and a situation in which they could donate prizewinnings in a game to other children who did not have a chance to play. All three measures would appear to be relevant to fairness as well as altruism, for the children had the choice of indicating that some pursuit should be given up for the benefit of others; and on all three, children from classes heterogeneous in age responded more altruistically than those from homogeneous classes.

Further research is needed to ascertain whether these findings would be replicated in nursery or primary school children, and in cases where there is unequal mix of older and younger classmates. In this regard, it has been suggested that mixed-age peer contact can contribute to the development of "sociability" in isolated children. Evidence on this topic has been supplied mainly from one study to date (Furman, Rahe and Hartup, 1979). Twenty-four Minnesota children aged 48 to 68 months were observed over a period of several weeks to be low on measures of peer interaction which would appear to overlap with fairness (e.g., positive reinforcement through help-giving, guidance, praise, affection, giving status and co-operative playing). These isolated children were then assigned randomly to one of three groups: 8 children were given younger partners from the general child population, 8 were given same-age partners, and 8 were assigned to a no-partner control condition.

Each pair of children was placed in a playroom and given the opportunity to play with two attractive toys (e.g., puppets and train sets) for 20 minutes

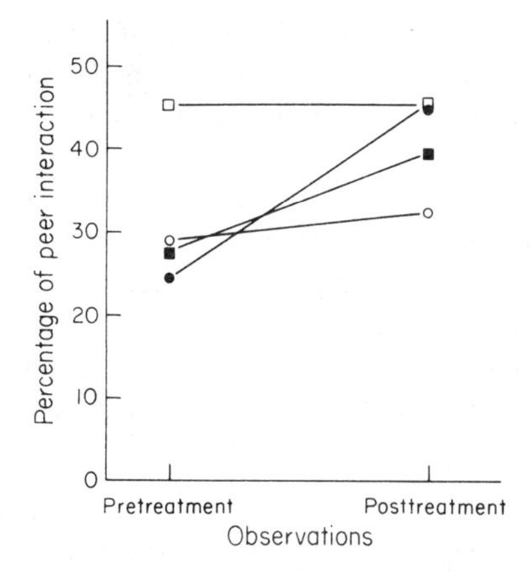

Fig. 15. *Isolates' peer-interaction rates before and after sessions with mixed- and same-age partners. (●——●) Younger partners; (■——■) same-age partners; (○——○) no treatment; (□——□) general population. (From Furmon, Rahe and Hartup, 1979.)*

in each of 10 play sessions over a 4- to 6-week interval. Afterwards, the isolates' behaviour was once again observed in the classroom and compared to that initially observed before the experimental sessions. Results indicated that the children with younger partners now interacted significantly more than the control-group children and with the same frequency as those in the general population (Fig. 15). Much of this effect was due to an increase in positive reinforcement. By contrast, the same-age and free-control groups did not differ in the frequency of interaction.

Furman *et al.* do not say whether this postexperimental increase in interaction occurred specifically between the formerly isolated child and the newly found partner or whether interaction generalized to other children. Yet it is optimistically concluded that (p.921):

> The play sessions must have provided the isolates with experiences that occurred infrequently in the classroom. We believe these experiences included the opportunity to be socially assertive (i.e., to direct social activity). Previous research suggests that social isolates are deficient in leadership skills (Kohn and Rosman, 1972). . . . The play sessions may have fostered increased peer interaction because they provided situations in which assertive behaviours met with a higher probability of success than in the classroom. Experiences with younger children, as contrasted with experiences with age mates, would provide the isolate with the most opportunities to initiate and direct social activity.

According to this interpretation, isolated children lack social behaviour because of a deficit in skills of leadership; and it may be that to encourage leadership responsibilities (and their commensurate status) can lead to an increase in social behaviour, including fairness. Another area in need of further research is to determine the degree to which "sociability", as induced and measured by Furman *et al.*, extends to a wide range of behaviour both inside and outside of the classroom.

A similar study using 9-year-olds as subjects has been reported by Oden and Asher (1977). An adult coach isolated third- and fourth-grade children from middle-class schools in Urbana-Champaign, Illinois, in skills relevant to making friends. The coaching procedure had three components. First, each child was instructed for 5–7 minutes on the meaning of concepts such as, participation, co-operation, and communication. An example is as follows:

> *Coach:* Okay, I have some ideas about what makes a game fun to play with another person. There are a couple of things that are important to do. You should *cooperate* with the other person. Do you know what cooperation is? Can you tell me in your own words?
> *Child:* Ahh . . . sharing.
> *Coach:* Yes, sharing. Okay, let's say you and I are playing the game you played last time. What was it again?
> *Child:* Drawing a picture.
> *Coach:* Okay, tell me then, what would be an example of sharing when playing the picture-drawing game?
> *Child:* I'd let you use some pens too.
> *Coach:* Right. You would share the pens with me. That's an example of cooperation. Now let's say you and I are doing the picture-drawing game, can you also give me an example of what would *not* be cooperating?
> *Child:* Taking all the pens.
> *Coach:* Would taking all the pens make the game fun to play?
> *Child:* No!
> *Coach:* So you wouldn't take all the pens. Instead, you'd *cooperate* by *sharing* them with me. Can you think of some more examples of cooperation? [The coach waited for a response.] Okay, how about taking turns . . . . Let's say you and I . . . [etc.]. Okay, I'd like you to try out some of these ideas when you play [name of new game] with [other child]. Let's go and get [other child], and after you play I'll talk to you again for a minute or so and you can tell me if these things seem to be good ideas for having fun at a game with someone.

The child then practised these social skills by playing games with peers for 12 minutes. Lastly, there was a 3–5 minute "postplay review" in which the coach asked the child, "Did you get a chance to try out some of the ideas we were talking about?" In all, there were six play sessions over a four-week period. Results indicated that the coaching procedure significantly increased the isolated children's peer-group acceptance, an effect which showed some tendency to endure on a one-year follow-up assessment. While no observed changes in behaviour were observed, the subjects were rated more highly by their peers in response to the question "How much do you like to play with this person at school?" While other results have suggested that children's self-perceptions of unpopularity affect their behaviour, this finding illustrates the opposite direction of effect: how children's behaviour can affect their unpopularity.

6.2 Self-direction and Practice

Recognition and status in the peer group, however, is not the only kind of personal experience which contributes to the development of a sense of fairness. There are other experiences which can be initiated by adults to prompt children to "self-direct" their moral behaviour and to practise their ability to imagine others' interests and intentions. The research here seems to relate closely to Bandura's recent explication of the self-efficacy concept, involving how well one can cope in demanding situations (Section 2.4).

For example, in one experiment (Aronfreed, 1963), Grade 5 boys played a soldier–nurse game; they were asked to push a toy nurse into a protective box, though this could only be done by knocking down some toy soldiers. Again at the start of the experiment the subjects were supplied with sweets (cf. Section 2.6). Half the boys were "punished" by an external source for knocking down toy soldiers; the experimenter himself removed some of their sweets. The other half were allowed to direct themselves and decide without external interference how many sweets should be removed. When the doll was made to break on a test trial, the children were given the chance to suggest ways to redress the situation. Those allowed to direct their own punishments offered a greater number of constructive suggestions than those punished by the experimenter. So to give children active control over their behaviour may encourage their helpfulness.

LaVoie (1974) used a different technique to study the effects of self-direction on moral behaviour, in this case, children's ability to "resist temptation". His subjects were children aged 7 to 11 years. All were shown an attractive toy and told that it was not to be played with. Some children were prompted to self-direct their behaviour; they were given an "intention-focus rationale": "It is wrong for you to play with that toy or to think about playing with that toy". Others were given a "consequence-focus rationale": "That toy is not to be played with because it might get broken or worn out from you playing with it". Those given the intention-focus rationale resisted the temptation to play with the toy better than those given the consequence-focus rationale; and, as might be expected, the intention focus was more effective in the older than in the younger children.

In a similar study (Dienstbier, Hillman, Lehnhoff, Hillman and Valkenaar, 1975), children who "felt bad" for their previous transgression owing to their own self-directed behaviour ("guilt") would be less likely to transgress than children in the same situation who believed that they "felt bad" because their previous transgression had been detected ("shame"). Second-graders were asked to watch a slot-car go around a track during an experimenter's absence. Their task was to prevent the car from jumping the track. When the children's attention was attracted by other moving toys, a hidden observer caused the car to fall off and "break". The experimenter then returned and labelled the child's feelings as due to the transgression itself (guilt) or due to being detected (shame). His instructions were as follows (changes from the guilt condition to the shame condition are indicated in parentheses and where a slash occurs within parentheses the shame instructions are followed by the guilt ones):

> I bet you feel a little bad now that (I found out) the car fell off. I've seen other kids feel bad when (someone found out) they weren't able to do exactly what they were supposed to do. When the other kids who tried to watch the car couldn't, they felt bad (when I found out) too.
>
> But it's important that we do stop the car when the light first comes on, and before it flies off the track, so we'll try again with this new car. You won't feel bad if (I find this car still/this car stays) on the track—if (I find) you've done a good job, you'll feel good, won't you?
>
> Have you noticed that when other kids (can show people that they) have done the right thing, that they feel good? And when (people find out) they did things they were not supposed to, they feel bad, don't they? (When someone finds out/even if no one ever finds out) they feel bad for not doing what they were supposed to do, don't they?

The children were then told to watch another car that they were assured would not break if it jumped the track. Those in the guilt condition spent significantly more time in complying with the experimenter's instructions than those in the shame condition.

The effects of self-direction on moral behaviour have been demonstrated in a number of other ways such as in experiments on children's self-perceptions of their honesty (Lepper, 1973). In a first session, two groups of 7-year-olds were forbidden from playing with an attractive toy under either a mild or severe threat. In the mild threat condition, the experimenter said that he would be "a little bit annoyed" if the child played with the toy. In the severe threat condition, he said that he would be "very upset and very angry". Another group of children acted as a control and received no threat. In a second session three weeks later, a second experimenter asked all the children to play a game in which they could obtain attractive prizes only by falsifying their scores. The mild threat group cheated significantly less than the control group, and the control group significantly less than the severe threat group. Thus the child in the mild threat condition infers from the mild threat that he is a good child and can self-direct his behaviour. In contrast, the overjustification of a severe threat causes a child to infer that he is a bad child. Those in the control group received no threats and thus could not infer that they were good or bad. Hence they cheated to moderate degree only.

These types of results have been replicated several times (e.g., Lepper, Greene and Nisbett, 1973; Ebbeson, Bowers, Phillips and Snyder, 1975), though there is some evidence that they are more pronounced in middle-class children (Dembroski and Pennebaker, 1975). Furthermore, though children's imitation of an altruistic model cannot be equated with fairness (Section 2.4), it seems clear that such a model may be imitated more by children who perceive their behaviour as self-directed as opposed to externally directed (Grusec, Kuczynski, Rushton and Simutis, 1978). Children's school performance, perceived competence, and self-efficacy may be encouraged by focusing their attention on relevant aspects of the problems and by assigning responsibility to formulate solutions (Deci and Ryan, 1980).

6.3 *Practice in the Peer-group Collective*

This type of self-direction in rule-following behaviour can certainly be accentuated by adult use of peer-group consensus pressure. The effects of the peer group are present at a very early age. Parke (1974) observed the behaviour of 3- to 5-year-old children when placed in a room with forbidden toys. Those told that their peers had decided that no one should play with the toys were more likely to resist temptation. In this context, the children who are well-integrated into the peer group are the ones who best follow the peer-endorsed rule.

Perhaps nowhere else has peer-group pressure been used so effectively to maintain obedience to adult rules as in the Soviet Union. There, following the writings of Makarenko (1967), who might be considered the Soviet Dr Spock or Dr Jolly, children engage in "socialist competition" or competition between "links" within the class and youth group. According to one account (Bronfenbrenner, 1970a), each school link customarily corresponds to rows of double-seated desks. The link encourages its members' adherence to adult rules in competition with other links. Because rewards and punishments are contingent upon group rather than individual performance, it is in the self-interest of each group member to monitor the behaviour of the others. The status of individuals within the group is evaluated weekly by peers and sanctions take the form of public criticism. The link is the vehicle for encouraging group unity and responsibility, as defined by adherence to adult behavioural rules and standards. For example, each member is expected to share in the collective maintenance of standard of academic achievement and physical grooming as well as in the upbringing of younger children. A link which excels its pursuit of these goals is given official recognition from other links, teachers, and even visitors from other schools. In this way, the peer group becomes an accessory to direct adult instruction in inculcating an adult morality.

In studies designed to illustrate the effectiveness of the Soviet link method (Bronfenbrenner, 1967, 1970b). A comparison was made between American and Soviet children. The mean age of each group was 12 years. All the children were given a Moral Dilemmas Test. This consisted of 30 hypothetical conflict situations involving peer-group pressure to contravene adult norms. For example, one item concerned the accidental finding of the answers for a school quiz; friends suggest that nothing be said to the teacher about it, so that all the students can get better marks. Subjects were asked to respond by indicating whether or not they would go along with their friends in this situation.

These items were given to the two groups of children under one of three conditions. In a base or scientific condition, the children were told that their responses would be scored as a group as research conducted by a national scientific society, and that no one they knew would be aware of either individual or group responses. In an adult condition, they were informed that their responses would be posted on a chart to be shown at a special meeting for parents and teachers. Finally, in the third peer condition, it was said that the responses would be charted and shown only to the students themselves.

The results clearly indicated that Soviet children regard themselves as less likely than Americans to engage in peer-sponsored misbehaviour. While both Soviet and American children inclined to give more adult-oriented responses in the adult condition, there was a tendency for the Americans to give anti-adult responses in the peer condition. By contrast, the Soviets responded much the same way in all three conditions.

These findings should not be taken to mean that Soviet children are more "moral" or "fairer" than are their American counterparts, only that Soviet children are more likely to conform to conventional adult rules. As Shepherd (1977) has pointed out, most of the conflict situations on the MDT are ones which have their basis in fear of punishment, where "good" in adult society is defined by simply resisting the temptations of "naughtiness". It may be expected that Western society may place less emphasis on punishment-defined rules than the strict Soviet society. In its place, there is an influential segment of Western society which is more likely to emphasize the importance of expressing a fair evaluation of the rules themselves with respect to critical moral issues such as abortion, capital punishment, and nuclear power. By contrast, the MDT items tend to be based on comparatively minor mischief and pranks. Perhaps adherence to these rules of convention is enforced more strictly in what has been described as an authority-oriented Soviet society (cf. Garbarino and Bronfenbrenner, 1976).

Nevertheless, elements of the Soviet method may be applicable in Western settings. Efforts have been made to assess the effects of placing students in experimental small-group learning situations where classes have been divided into small groups. In a study reported by Blaney, Stephan, Rosenfield, Aronson and Sikes (1977), the subjects were fifth-grade children in the Austin, Texas, school system. The children were assigned to groups whose size ranged from four to seven. Within each group, sex, academic ability and ethnic background (Anglo, black, and Mexican American) were distributed as equally as possible with the proviso that no close friends or bitter enemies be included. A student was to learn only one part of the curriculum (usually social studies) and to teach this material to the group as a whole. The group's function was to piece together the knowledge of each individual in a jigsaw-puzzle fashion. Since all group members were responsible for learning the entire curriculum for testing purposes, the technique was one which encouraged interdependency and co-operation among group members. The children were asked to rate their liking for each classmate. As compared to controls, those who participated in the jigsaw experiment expressed an increased liking for their groupmates and this liking did not come at the expense of a decreased liking for other classmates. Other evidence suggests that while Anglo children perform equally well in jigsaw and traditional classrooms, their black and Mexican-American classmates do better (Lucker, Rosenfield, Sikes and Aronson, 1976; also Aronson, Bridgeman and Geffner, 1978).

Such pioneering field studies seem promising in that they suggest ways by which tensions between children which arise out of a competitive situation can be reduced. Much more work is required to determine whether this technique can produce lasting and generalizable changes both in academic and moral behaviour.

6.4 *Social-cognitive Intervention Programmes: Learning through Directed Participation in the Peer Group*

Consequently, self-direction may be cultivated in peer-group situations which encourage children to take the role of others in imagining their interests and intentions. It should be stressed that the relationship between role-taking abilities and moral development can be viewed as a logical one rather than one which can only be substantiated by empirical evidence. By definition, role-taking is an important part of moral behaviour, for actions which disregard the interests and intentions of disadvantaged others may be regarded as having been taken by those who have not placed themselves in the roles of the affected victims (Coombs and Meux, 1971; Hare, 1963, 1979).

It is difficult to devise a comprehensive measure of egocentrism and its obverse state, that of possessing the ability to take the role of the other (Section 3.6). But the few training studies which used behavioural outcome measures have demonstrated how role-taking experience in the peer group can encourage children to act fairly without the guidance of a superior authority. The point to note is that the source of this experience lies within the influence of the adult. A good illustration comes from the work of Ervin Staub (1975, 1979) in Massachusetts. Fifth- and sixth-grade children were assigned to one of three groups. One group learned to make a puzzle so that they could make one for hospitalized children (prosocial group). A second learned puzzle-making but were also told to read and rehearse a list of statements that pointed out the benefits of making puzzles for hospitalized children (prosocial-induction group). A third group learned puzzle-making but with the reason that "it might be enjoyable for children to know how to make toys for themselves" (non-prosocial group). Some of the children in each group then continued to work on the puzzle themselves; the remainder taught puzzle-making to a younger child. Subsequently all groups were given the opportunity to donate gift certificates to needy children. Results indicated that, regardless of the reason for having learned puzzle-making, those who taught other children donated significantly more than those who did not teach other children. According to Staub (1975, 1979), the practical experience of teaching seemed to make donating behaviour acceptable.

This result dovetails with one found in a previous study using kindergarten children (Staub, 1971). Having been given practice in enacting helping and sharing situations with peers, boys were more generous and girls more responsive to sounds of distress than those without such practice. Similar results were found by Masters and Pisarowicz (1975). In this study, Grade 2 children who copied word definitions to help others learn to read were significantly more generous than those who copied for no particular reason. Parallel findings come from experiments with adults, which indicates that inducing persons to engage in a particular social or moral behaviour increases the likelihood that they will repeat this behaviour (Freedman and Fraser, 1966; Harris, 1972; Pliner, 1974; Snyder and Cunningham, 1975; Uranowitz, 1975).

So self-direction and practice may influence the ability and willingness to act fairly. Provided a child has met with the rudiments of adult instruction and has attained recognition and status in his peer group, he or she may profit by the personal experience practised in actual peer-group situations. Even this experience of course is not beyond the limits of adult intervention, for the adult may structure the child's peer-group relationships. The following two examples are selected from recent work in preschool education; not because the preschool period is one in which children are particularly sensitive to adult influence, but because a great part of the research has been devoted to this area.

Adults may also intervene in a peer-group setting to develop the communication and imagination skills important for considering others' interests and intentions. To this end, social-cognitive problem-solving programmes have been devised. Their aim is to train children's cognitive processes which mediate their social behaviour, in order to "build in" generalization across problem situations (Urbain and Kendall, 1980).

Perhaps the most notable of these intervention programmes is the ongoing ten-year research project of Shure and Spivack (1980). Elementary school children, rated by their teachers as aggressive, over-emotional and inattentive, were hypothesized to have difficulty in using cognitive skills deemed necessary to solve social problems. On this basis, a preventive programme for 4-year-old nursery-schoolers was devised (Spivack and Shure, 1974). The aim was to enable children by themselves to think of ways to solve their social problems and to increase children's ability to take the roles of their peers.

The training programme itself lasted 12 weeks and consisted of three stages. The participants were children living in inner-city Philadelphia. Under the assumption that a use of negation is important for solving problems, the children were first taught how to use words such as "same", "different", and "not". For example, the children would display body movements which were the same and different, sometimes the teacher would lead and sometimes a child would. During the second stage, the children were taught "preproblem-solving"; they were shown pictures of children in certain unhappy situations such as falling off a bike and asked to identify the consequences of these situations and how these children might feel. They were then encouraged to name lots of different ways to make such children happy.

In the final stage, the children were shown pictures and asked to act out the dialogues of various problem situations. For example, one child might hold a puppet. Another would tell the class in what different ways he might get a turn for himself to play. The child holding the puppet would be asked to suggest what might happen and how might his classmate feel if he is not allowed a turn.

Following the programme's completion, the participating children outperformed a control group in their ability to name solutions and consequences to social problems. They also displayed more prosocial behaviour as rated by adult observers. Overall, the programme appeared to be most effective for those with the greatest difficulty in their social relationships. For example, impulsive preschoolers were better able to take turns and share with others.

Further support for the value of this approach comes from studies using elementary school children in which good communication skills have been associated with generosity and the ability to make friends (Rubin and Schneider, 1973; Gottman, Gonso and Rasmussen, 1975). Reports of the programme's success (e.g., Elardo and Caldwell, 1977) have led to its full or partial adoption over widespread locations. More research is necessary to determine whether these reported changes in behaviour are due to one or more skills taught during the training itself or to some extraneous factor such as increased attention on the part of the participants.

One last study which follows in this vein is that of Iannotti (1978). Two age-groups of boys, 6 and 9 years respectively, were trained in role-taking skills. The subjects were seen in groups of five and assigned to take different roles in stories or skits. Unfortunately, the exact number of stories is unspecified and only one example is given of several boys who were in need of money and who found a wallet with money inside. The experimenter asked questions about the thoughts and feelings of others in order to elicit role-taking and gave suggestions when the children did not respond. The training took about 25 minutes on each of ten days, the children were given measures of empathy, aggression, and altruism. There were significant differences only on the altruism measure, which was the number of candies given by the experimenter to the boys and donated to help a needy child: the 6-year-olds gave significantly more than did controls who did not receive training in role-taking. However, this effect might be attributed to the demand characteristics of the experiment in that the children gave to please (perhaps secretly) the experimenter with whom they had been intensely involved during the training. Again, additional studies are required to examine the effects of training in role-taking on children's willingness to give up something important of their own freely, having considered others' interests and intentions.

In sum, a sense of fairness in children may be developed in many intricate ways which involve the child's peer-group practice in acting fairly. Although more definite verdicts await the outcome of further research, adult intervention may serve to structure peer-group experience, to prevent unjust privilege and deprivation, to encourage children's control and self-direction, and to equip children with the cognitive skills important for solving conflicts in a co-operative manner. Consequently, it seems clear that adult and peer-group influences can complement each other. The force of adult explanations can be enhanced by peer-group influence. In fact, to consider that peers exert influence separate from that of adults may be misleading (Hoffman, 1980, p.328). Children can practice with their peers what they have learned from adults within a context of identification. Disillusionment with adults may be accompanied by participation in peer-sponsored misbehaviour.

Chapter Seven

RELATIONSHIP TO KOHLBERG'S THEORY

7.1 *Kohlberg's Cognitive Developmental Approach*

EARLIER (Section 3.4) it was noted that Piaget was comparatively unconcerned with moral development past the age of 12 or 13. Though in later work he does say in broad terms that personality development continues after the age of 13 (1967, pp.64–70), he did not attempt to provide empirical evidence bearing specifically on the development of moral reasoning in adolescents and adults.

Consequently a vacuum was created waiting and ready to be filled by the work of other psychologists. As Piaget's writings became "rediscovered" in the United States, it was almost inevitable that someone there would attempt to characterize adolescent moral development in borrowing from the Piagetian approach. By far the most illustrious theorist who took up this task was Lawrence Kohlberg who has written extensively in the fields of both psychology and education. In fact it was Kohlberg's writings on education which brought him to the special attention of teachers, principals, and headmasters in North America. There Kohlberg's impact has been so strong that no discussion of moral development can be anywhere near complete without a detailed consideration of his work. The purposes of the present chapter are to evaluate Kohlberg's claim that his theory is superior to Piaget's on many points, and to compare the Kohlberg and social-cognitive approaches to moral development. An examination of educational and childrearing issues will be postponed until afterwards.

Kohlberg's original theory (1963a, b) proposed to describe the underlying structure of the content of moral judgment development throughout adolescence and into adulthood by a somewhat complex sequence of six cognitively based stages. In this connection, it is important to distinguish between Kohlberg's theory of ethics which has been influenced by the writings of philosophers (Hare, 1952, 1963; Rawls, 1971), and his psychological theory which was designed to describe the real-life development of moral reasoning. Because it is entirely reasonable to compare an individual's psychological development against a philosophical or logical standard of ethics (see Section 1.1), this chapter will be exclusively devoted to an examination of the empirical support for Kohlberg's developmental stage theory. As Kohlberg (1976, pp.46–47; 1978, p.2) regards his measure of moral development as distinct from other stage-based tests (e.g., Rest, Davison and Robbins, 1978), these will not be discussed here.

From the outset, notice must be taken that the description of the stages themselves has changed rather frequently over the years (e.g., Kohlberg, 1958, 1969, 1973, 1976, 1978a, b). The most recent published exposition (1976) at the time of this writing is as follows. The first two of the six stages comprise a "preconventional level" of moral reasoning characteristic of most children under 9 and many adolescents. Stage 1 is a punishment–obedience orientation in which rules are followed for avoiding punishment. Stage 2 is an instrumental–hedonistic orientation in which rules are followed only within a specific, immediate reciprocal arrangement. Others' interests are recognized only insofar as this is necessary to fulfil one's own. Stages 3 and 4 comprise the "conventional level", one which characterizes the moral reasoning of most adults. A Stage 3 orientation involves living up to a stereotype of "good" behaviour. Stage 4 is a law-and-order orientation involving the preservation of institutions for the purpose of maintaining a social order. Finally, Stages 5 and 6 can be roughly equated with a rationally defined concept of fairness; they involve the acknowledgement of the rights of individuals over the rules or laws of institutions. These two stages comprise the "postconventional level" of moral reasoning and, as Kohlberg claims, are attained by a small minority of adults in industrialized countries and not necessarily by any adults at all in many economically underdeveloped societies (Figs 16 and 17). According to still more recent revision of the theory (Kohlberg, 1978a, p.30), few if any individuals may reach Stage 6. The content of these stages is detailed in Table 5.

As noted earlier (Sections 3.4; 4.4), the predominant stage orientation of an individual is assessed by analysing his responses to a number of moral dilemmas. This sample dilemma is the one most often cited by Kohlberg (e.g., 1969, p.379):

> In Europe, a woman was near death from cancer. One drug might save her, a form of radium that a druggist in the same town had recently discovered. The druggist was charging $2000, ten times what the drug cost him to make. The sick woman's husband, Heinz, went to everyone he knew to borrow the money, but he could only get together about half of what it cost. He told the druggist that his wife was dying and asked him to sell it cheaper or let him pay later. But the druggist said, "No". The husband got desperate and broke into the man's store to steal the drug for his wife. Should the husband have done that? Why?

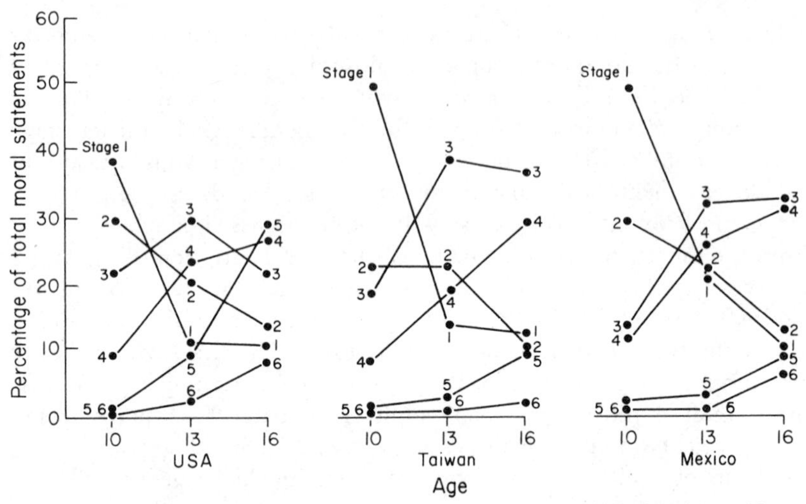

Fig. 16. *Middle-class urban boys in the U.S.A., Taiwan, and Mexico. At age 10 the stages are used according to difficulty. At age 13, stage 3 is most used by all three groups. At age 16, American boys have reversed the order of age 10 stages with the exception of stage 6. (From Kohlberg and Kramer, 1969.)*

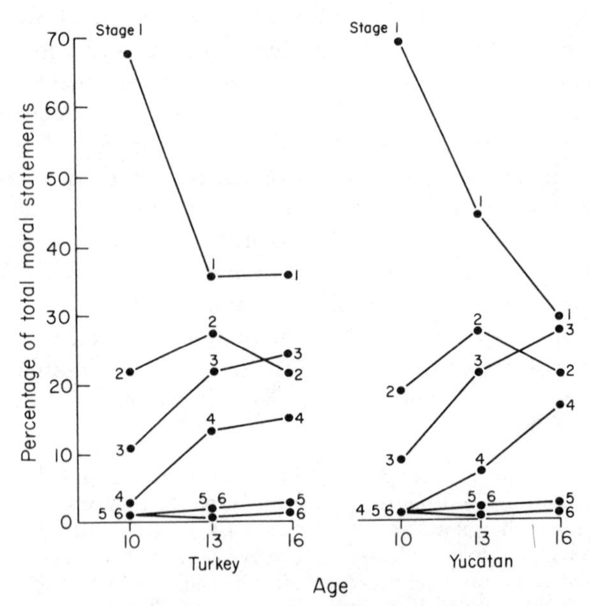

Fig. 17. *Two isolated villages, one in Turkey, the other in Yucatan, show similar patterns in moral thinking. There is no reversal of order, and preconventional stages (1–2) do not gain a clear ascendancy over conventional stages at age 16. (From Kohlberg and Kramer, 1969.)*

Table 5. *Kohlberg's Six Moral Stages (1976)*

	Content of stage		
Level and stage	What is right	Reasons for doing right	Social perspective of stage
LEVEL I—PRECONVENTIONAL Stage 1—Heteronomous morality	To avoid breaking rules backed by punishment, obedience for its own sake, and avoiding physical damage to persons and property.	Avoidance of punishment, and the superior power of authorities.	*Egocentric point of view.* Doesn't consider the interests of others or recognize that they differ from the actor's; doesn't relate two points of view. Actions are considered physically rather in terms of psychological interests of others. Confusion of authority's perspective with one's own.
Stage 2—Individualism, instrumental purpose, and exchange	Following rules only when it is to someone's immediate interest; acting to meet one's own interests and needs and letting others do the same. Right is also what's fair, what's an equal exchange, a deal, an agreement.	To serve one's own needs or interests in a world where you have to recognize that other people have their interests, too.	*Concrete individualistic perspective.* Aware that everybody has his own interest to pursue and these conflict, so that right is relative (in the concrete individualistic sense).

Table 5.—*continued*

Level and stage	Content of stage		Social perspective of stage
	What is right	Reasons for doing right	
LEVEL II—CONVENTIONAL Stage 3—Mutual interpersonal expectations, relationships, and interpersonal conformity	Living up to what is expected by people close to you or what people generally expect of people in your role as son, brother, friend, etc. "Being good" is important and means having good motives, showing concern about others. It also means keeping mutual relationships, such as trust, loyalty, respect and gratitude.	The need to be a good person in your own eyes and those of others. Your caring for others. Belief in the Golden Rule. Desire to maintain rules and authority which support stereotypical good behaviour.	*Perspective of the individual in relationships with other individuals.* Aware of shared feelings, agreements, and expectations which take primacy over individual interests. Relates points of view through the concrete Golden Rule, putting yourself in the other guy's shoes. Does not yet consider generalized system perspective.
Stage 4—Social system and conscience	Fulfilling the actual duties to which you have agreed. Laws are to be upheld except in extreme cases where they conflict with other fixed social duties. Right is also contributing to society, the group, or institution.	To keep the institution going as a whole, to avoid the breakdown in the system "if everyone did it", or the imperative of conscience to meet one's defined obligations. (Easily confused with Stage 3 belief in rules and authority; see text.)	*Differentiates social point of view from interpersonal agreement or motives.* Takes the point of view of the system that defines roles and rules. Considers individual relations in terms of place in the system.

LEVEL II—POST-CONVENTIONAL, or PRINCIPLED Stage 5—Social contract or utility and individual rights	Being aware that people hold a variety of values and opinions, that most values and rules are relative to your group. These relative rules should usually be upheld, however, in the interest of impartiality and because they are the social contract. Some non-relative values and rights like *life* and *liberty*, however, must be upheld in any society and regardless of majority opinion.	A sense of obligation to law because of one's social contract to make and abide by laws for the welfare of all and for the protection of all people's rights. A feeling of contractual commitment, freely entered upon, to family, friendship, trust, and work obligations. Concern that laws and duties be based on rational calculation of overall utility, "the greatest good for the greatest number".	*Prior-to-society perspective.* Perspective of a rational individual aware of values and rights prior to social attachments and contracts. Integrates perspectives by formal mechanisms of agreement, contract, objective impartiality, and due process. Considers moral and legal points of view; recognizes that they sometimes conflict and finds it difficult to integrate them.
Stage 6—Universal ethical principles	Following self-chosen ethical principles. Particular laws or social agreements are usually valid because they rest on such principles. When laws violate these principles, one acts in accordance with the principle. Principles are universal principles of justice: the equality of human rights and respect for the dignity of human beings as individual persons.	The belief as a rational person in the validity of universal moral principles, and a sense of personal commitment to them.	*Perspective of a moral point of view* from which social arrangements derive. Perspective is that of any rational individual recognizing the nature of morality or the fact that persons are ends in themselves and must be treated as such.

Subjects' responses are scored not in terms of "yes" or "no" judgments but with respect to their reasoning which focuses on moral issues such as "life" and "law". Regardless of whether he supports or opposes Heinz's theft, a high-stage subject would consider these issues very carefully in terms of rules or principles while rules and social conventions are external to the reasoning of the Stage 1 or 2 subject. To illustrate the qualitative difference between high and low stages, selected prototypical examples of the range of reasoning exhibited on the life and law issues of the Heinz dilemma are presented in Table 6.

At times, Kohlberg has often illustrated his stages by scoring the moral reasoning of prominent philosophers and politicians. Included among this select group have been Albert Camus, Martin Luther King, Friedrich Nietzsche, Ayn Rand and Jean-Paul Sartre. Perhaps the clearest and most

Table 6. *Samples of Reasoning at Each Moral Stage (after Kohlberg, Colby, Gibbs, Speicher-Dubin and Power, 1977)*

	Reasoning which focuses on the Life issue (Heinz should steal the drug)	Reasoning which focuses on the Law issue (Heinz should not steal the drug)
Stage 1	because if you kill someone you'll be in jail for a long time and for stealing you aren't punished much.	because if he does he will be caught, locked up, etc.
Stage 2	if he thinks his wife would help if he were dying.	because if you commit a crime you have to go to jail long enough to make up for it; because if you steal you only have to pay back the person.
Stage 3	because he tried to be decent but now feels he has no choice; or because he would have the best of intentions.	in order to leave a good impression on the community; or so that others won't get the wrong impression.
Stage 4	because he is obligated by his marital responsibility, wedding vows, covenant of marriage, etc.	because respect for the law will be destroyed if citizens feel they may break the law anytime they disagree with it.
Stage 5	because that is part of the implicit social contract which all human beings have with one another; because responsibility to others is one of the basic principles that life is founded upon, etc.	because if individuals are to live together in society, there must be some common agreement; or because laws represent a necessary structure of social agreement.

convincing of all Kohlberg's examples comes from the reasoning of Adolf Eichmann (Table 7).

But here an important point should be raised; the type and number of aspects or issues or scoring units within the scoring system has changed rather frequently. Kohlberg appears to have once used 30 (1963a, p.14), then 25 (1969, pp.378–379), then 28 (1971, p.36), then 12 (Kohlberg and Gilligan, 1971, p.1068), and most recently 6 (1976, p.45). In general, these revisions have been made with less than a fully documented explanation. Often new evidence requires changes in scoring systems. But each of these changes should be accompanied with a basis for comparing the results obtained through different methods of scoring and data analysis.

7.2 Generality of Stage Responses

Yet despite the fact that a definitive scoring manual is still in preparation (Colby, 1978; Colby, Kohlberg and Gibbs, 1979; Kohlberg, 1978), Kohlberg claims that his own stages are more rigorously formulated than Piaget's. His most direct criticism is that Piaget's moral stages do not meet the criteria which define a stage sequence. One requirement is that each stage, as a qualitatively different mode of thought, forms a "structure d'ensemble" or a "structured whole" (Kohlberg, 1969; Piaget, 1960). For example, responses on logical tasks (e.g., conservation of continuous quantity and seriation of length) considered by Piaget to be indicative of cognitive development should appear empirically as a general cluster of responses. Thus a child who succeeds on one logical task should be able to generalize this logical ability and succeed on other logical tasks if he is at a certain "stage" of development.

According to Kohlberg (1969, 1973), his own stages as well as Piaget's cognitive stages do meet this requirement. Nevertheless, there is evidence which suggests that both may not, though Kohlberg claims that many of an individual's moral judgments "fit" a dominant stage, the remainder clustering about this model category in a normal distribution (Fig. 18). Attempts to find generality across *different* logical Piagetian tasks have not produced high intercorrelations (DeVries, 1974; Flavell, 1971, 1972; Lemerise and Pinard, 1971; McLaughlin, 1963). For example, Tuddenham (1971) correlated the responses of 200 elementary schoolchildren on ten such tasks. The overall picture of results was one of small though significant correlations. These ranged from 0.01 to 0.65 with a mean of 0.21. To be sure, it should be mentioned that there are theoretical problems in equating scores on different tasks, not the least of which is that some scores may be a better reflection of a particular presentation procedure or materials used than of

Table 7. *Scoring of Moral Judgments of Eichmann for Developmental Stages*

Moral judgments	Stage score
In actual fact, I was merely a little cog in the machinery that carried out the directives of the German Reich.	1
I am neither a murderer nor a mass-murderer. I am a man of average character, with good qualities and many faults.	3
Yet what is there to "admit"? I carried out my orders. It would be as pointless to blame me for the whole final solution of the Jewish problem as to blame the official in charge of the railroads over which the Jewish transports travelled.	1
Where would we have been if everyone had thought things out in those days? You can do that today in the "new" German army. But with us an order was an order.	1
If I had sabotaged the order of the one-time Führer of the German Reich, Adolf Hitler, I would have been not only a scoundrel but a despicable pig like those who broke their military oath to join the ranks of the anti-Hitler criminals in the conspiracy of 20 July 1944.	1
I would like to stress again, however, that my department never gave a single annihilation order. We were responsible only for deportation.	2
My interest was only in the number of transport trains I had to provide. Whether they were bank directors or mental cases, the people who were loaded on these trains meant nothing to me.	2
It was really none of my business.	2
But to sum it all up, I must say that I regret nothing. Adolf Hitler may have been wrong all down the line, but one thing is beyond dispute: the man was able to work his way up from lance-corporal in the Germany army to Führer of a people of almost eighty million.	1
I never met him personally, but his success alone proves to me that I should subordinate myself to this man. He was somehow so supremely capable that the people recognized him. And so with that justification I recognized him joyfully, and I still defend him.	1
I must say truthfully, that if we had killed all the ten million Jews that Himmler's statisticians originally listed in 1933, I would say, "Good, we have destroyed an enemy".	2
But here I do not mean wiping them out entirely. That would not be proper—and we carried on a proper war.	1

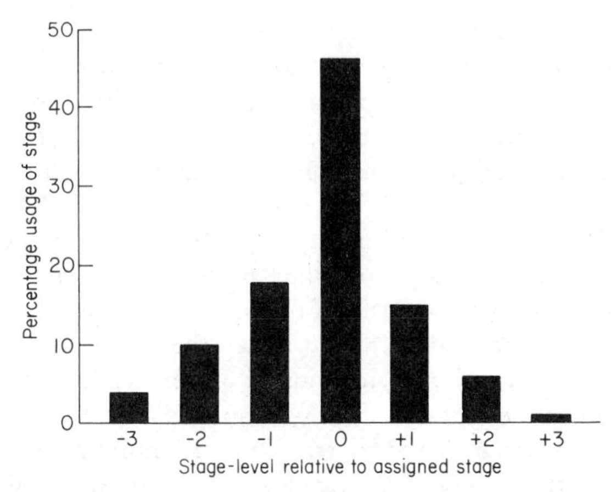

Fig. 18. *Profile of stage usage. (From Kohlberg, 1969, p. 378.)*

the child's attainment of a "logical structure". Even so, the possibility remains that there may be more between-task specificity than generality in performance on Piaget's logical tasks. Moreover, as Piaget (1972) himself pointed out, at least one of his stages of cognitive or logical development, that of "formal operations", is attained by most persons within specific fields only.

Piaget himself also never claimed that responses at each developmental stage form a "structured whole"; and as might be anticipated, scores on different moral dimensions as defined by Piaget do not correlate very highly either. For example, MacRae (1954) found only a 0.26 correlation between objective responsibility and immanent justice. In this regard, Kohlberg fares little better. Santrock (1975) correlated stage scores of pre-adolescents on different Kohlberg dilemmas. These ranged from 0.19 to 0.48 with a mean of 0.33 compared with a range of 0.31 to 0.75 with a mean of 0.51 in Kohlberg's original (1958) study. Quite justifiably, Santrock concluded (p.211) that

> particularly when the strains toward cognitive consistency which are inherent in the Kohlbergian method of obtaining moral judgment information are taken into account, these modest intercorrelations reflect greater situational variability in moral judgment than Kohlberg has assumed.

Similar results have been obtained using secondary school and university student samples (Fishkin, Keniston and MacKinnon, 1973; Rubin and Trotter, 1977). Beyond the finding that Kohlberg's dilemmas are not of equal difficulty, significant sex differences appear on some dilemmas but not on others (Lieberman, 1971). Efforts are currently being made to develop a test on which sex differences in responses are eliminated (Colby, 1978).

So far there seems to be little support for the claim that a "structured whole" underlies responses at each stage of development. But notwithstanding these unsuccessful attempts at finding generality across responses to *different* logical or moral tasks, there may be generality across responses on tasks which tap a *single* dimension or "separate structure" of moral development (cf. Dodwell, 1962; Flavell and Wohlwell, 1969; Inhelder *et al.*, 1967; Rushton, 1976). For instance, with respect to the Piagetian approach, there may be high correlations among responses to story-pairs designed to tap the single dimension of objective responsibility but lower correlations among responses designed to tap the different dimensions of objective responsibility and immanent justice. With respect to the Kohlberg approach, there may be high correlations among responses concerning one single dimension or issue shared by two or more moral dilemmas such as "life". But again there may be lower correlations between responses on dilemmas which do not share any common issues.

Perhaps because the number of issues have undergone continual revisions, this "intra-dimensional" hypothesis appears not to have been tested in the Kohlberg case. However, it does have some equivocal support in the Piaget case. For example, Johnson (1962) found that responses to immanent justice stories intercorrelated with a mean of 0.47 for fifth- and seventh-graders, and a mean of 0.61 for ninth- and eleventh-graders. While the mean intercorrelations on objective responsibility items fell to about 0.35 for all grades, those between the immanent justice and objective responsibility scores fell even further to about 0.16. But though this correlation is miniscule, it is significantly higher than if it were to occur by chance alone.

That less "inter-dimensional" than "intra-dimensional" generality exists on these types of tests has been pointed out by both Burton (1963, 1976) and Mischel (1968). As noted earlier (Section 4.5), when the similarities between the dimensions or story situations are decreased, the intercorrelations are also decreased. So it is hardly surprising that one theory does not surpass the other on the generality issue. Neither in the Piaget nor the Kohlberg case is there convincing evidence for "inter-dimensional" generality. In both cases, the degree of "intra-dimensional" generality is probably modest.

7.3 Development and Regression in Stage Sequences

There is another criterion which a sequence of stages must meet: that the stages be attained in an invariant, irreversible order and that there be no regression from a higher to a lower stage. Kohlberg claims that his own moral stages meet this requirement while Piaget's do not. But on this score, the evidence again suggests that Kohlberg's theory is at best a modest improvement on Piaget's. The two broad stages of adult constraint and unilateral respect appear to occur in an invariant sequence which has been empirically replicated many times. But any more complex six-stage sequence should be harder to establish than a simple two-stage sequence; and not unexpectedly, there are studies which indicate regression in the Kohlberg case.

In a review of moral development research in Western countries, Hoffman (1970) found that in none of the 21 cross-sectional studies derived from Piaget's theory was there a regression with age and in only one (Medinnus, 1958) was there no relationship between age and verbal development (i.e. immanent justice). In non-Western societies, the age of transition to a mutual respect morality may be delayed until late adolescence but the transition eventually does seem to appear at least partially (Dennis, 1943; Jahoda, 1958; Najarian-Svajian, 1966) with the one possible exception of immanent justice in certain American Indian groups (Havighurst and Neugarten, 1955).

Such powerful support from cross-sectional research would seem to lessen the need for stronger longitudinal studies, especially as Piaget's stages appear to describe an almost necessary transition in human development (cf. Deardon, 1968, p.168; Hamlyn, 1967, pp.41–42). Following an objective responsibility child to see whether he later makes intentional moral judgments would be as uninteresting as following a non-conservational child to see whether he later conserves. Nevertheless, as part of a much larger study, Sternlieb and Youniss (1975) did do this and not surprisingly found a significant increase in the intentional moral judgments of 6- to 10-year-olds over a one-year period.

In contrast, the results of two longitudinal studies indicate that regression occurs in Kohlberg's stage sequence. Both of these studies have shown that there is a regression from a higher Stage 4, 5, or 6 to some lower stage. First, Kohlberg and Kramer (1969) found that about 20% of their longitudinal subjects regressed from Stages 4 and 5 to Stage 2 between late high school and the second or third year of college. This Kohlberg (1973) attempts to explain by inserting a "Stage 4B" type of morality between Stages 4 and 5. The "skeptical relativism" which characterizes the college sophomore's "identity crisis" allegedly replaces the conventional law-and-order morality. Rather than a regression to a Stage 2 hedonism, this relativism is to be scored as a Stage 4B, "a transitional state between conventional and principled thinking" (Kohlberg, 1973, p.179), and one which is particularly characteristic of college students. Such an interpretation is consistent with the definition of stage regression advanced by Bearison (1974, p.26). An individual might have attained a structural level of reasoning, but though he still maintains the requisite structures, he may perform below his level of competence because of the debilitating effects of situational factors.

Yet while this interpretation might explain some regression, it might not explain all. Holstein (1976) studied 53 13-year-olds and their parents over a period of three years. Following Kohlberg's suggestion, "skeptical relativism" responses were scored as Stage 4B and not as Stage 2. Nevertheless about 25% of both the adolescents and adults regressed from a higher Stage 4, 5, or 6 to a lower Stage 1, 2, or 3. Given the difficulties in devising a suitable scoring system, this regression may be attributed to measurement error. Or perhaps it is part of short-term oscillations which produce higher-stage movement over a longer term as might be the case in training studies (e.g., Blatt and Kohlberg, 1975).

But in any event, it would still be difficult to establish an invariant, irreversible sequence in Kohlberg's six stages. This is because Stage 5 and 6 reasoning is generally attained in Western societies only; and perhaps even much reasoning which is scored as postconventional reasoning can be attributed to measurement error. Indeed since postconventional reasoning seems to be absent in large sections of Western as well as other less technologically advanced societies, an invariant sequence may be impossible to find (cf. Kurtines and Greif, 1974; p.461). Without a sufficiently large sample of persons who reason at Stage 5 (let alone Stage 6), there can be no useful empirical support upon which to base an invariant five- or six-stage sequence (Peters, 1978, p.149). Once a subject has come to reflect upon rules and laws, it is logically possible that he may adopt reasoning at any stage orientation (Gibbs, 1977; Peters, 1978).

7.4 *Kohlberg's Stage 1 versus Piaget's Notion of Unilateral Respect*

Another important difference exists between the two theories. In opposition to Piaget, Kohlberg (1963b, pp.321-322) claims that 4- and 5-year-olds do not judge acts out of a rigid, unilateral respect for the sacredness of adult rules. Instead, they reason at a Stage 1 level which implies the absence of respect. Whether a specific act is rewarded or punished is critical; whether it contravenes an adult rule is insignificant. Thus a boy who is rewarded for lying is a good boy while one who is punished for helping is a bad boy.

More recently, however, this claim was examined by Jensen and Hughston (1973). Thirty-two children aged 4 and 5 were given 18 stories. In 6 of these, the central character performed a socially approved act, in another 6 the acts were neutral ones, and in the remaining 6 the acts were negative.

In 9 stories, the character was rewarded by an adult; in the other 9 he was punished. The results clearly indicated that the reward outcome had little effect on responses to negative content stories. In other words, a bad act is evaluated as bad independently of whether it is rewarded or punished. These results, which have since been replicated by Ozols and Gilmore (1978), support Piaget in that children appear to respect the sacredness of socially approved, adult rules. But they contradict Kohlberg's claim that 4- and 5-year-olds evaluate an act as bad only if it is punished. In this connection, it is noteworthy that preschoolers' judgments about prosocial behaviour also appear to be generally more rule-governed than oriented toward punishment and obedience (Eisenberg-Berg, 1979; Eisenberg-Berg and Hand, 1979). It may be that children aged 2 and 3 evaluate acts in this way. But it would be very difficult to test this possibility in such young children. Perhaps then Kohlberg's Stage 1 does not necessarily provide a better description of preschoolers' moral judgments than does Piaget's adult constraint notion.

7.5 *Relevance and Comprehensiveness of Cognitive Measures of Moral Development: A Search for a Bridge between Judgment and Behaviour*

There are several other issues relating to Kohlberg's work which merit examination. These concern the relevance and comprehensiveness of moral judgment measures. For example, Kohlberg's claim concerning the superiority of his Stage 1 was derived from his general criticism that Piaget's theory is "not cognitive enough"; it purportedly relies too much on the content of the child's moral judgment and not its underlying structure. Hence, according to Kohlberg, it is necessary to interview subjects to determine this structure. Therefore, "adult constraint children" should be interviewed to ascertain whether their unilateral respect of adult authority is out of genuine reverence or out of a punishment avoidance. Adults who maintain that Heinz should steal the drug should be interviewed to ascertain whether a hedonistic Stage 2 structure or a principled Stage 5 or 6 structure might underlie the content of their reasoning.

Nevertheless, this heavy reliance on subjects' verbal ability to respond in interviews may also be little improvement on Piaget's approach; it probably underestimates subjects' abilities to imagine the interests and intentions of others and inflates the age norms at which these abilities are achieved (cf. Brainerd, 1973). To insist that subjects thoroughly justify their moral judgments in this way might be an overly conservative, sufficient-but-not-necessary basis for scoring responses at a certain stage. It may simply be easier for a subject to say that Heinz's wife would be angry at him if he didn't steal (Stage 1 reasoning) than for a child to talk in terms of "laws" and "social conventions", even though the subject's behaviour may in practice be governed by these conventions. Thus this insistence might result in classifying subjects' responses at stages below those which they actually do reason. The same criticism applies to excessively verbal Piaget-derived tests. Breznitz and Kugelmass (1967) found that requiring subjects to verbalize the principle of intentionality in justifying a transgression delays "the age of intentionality" until late adolescence. It does not of course follow that subjects' verbal justifications are unimportant; only that any interpretation of those justifications must be treated with extreme caution.

In this regard, a study by Moran and Joniak (1979) examined the effects of language sophistication on subjects' preferences for higher- over lower-stage reasoning. A panel of five university teachers was instructed to write a pro and a con response to a Kohlberg dilemma at Stages 2 and 4, using sophisticated terms such as "parental jurisdiction". A group of undergraduates were given these sophisticated arguments and did not indicate a preference for either. By contrast, when asked to choose between an inflated Stage 2 response and a conversational Stage 4 example cited by Kohlberg, the subjects demonstrated a preference for Stage 2 over Stage 4 reasoning. Moran and Joniak (1979, p.338) conclude,

> These findings imply that the evidence offered to support Kohlberg's claim of invariance in the development of moral thought may well have been artifactual—produced by the failure to control for the effect of language.

However this study remains controversial (see the criticism of Rest, 1980). What can be concluded is that more research is needed on the relation of language to moral reasoning.

Familiarity of the dilemma situation

It is also difficult to devise a measure of moral development which is equally relevant to all ages (Von Wright and Niemela, 1966). In this connection, evidence suggests that the themes of some of the Kohlberg dilemmas are beyond the personal experience of many subjects, and particularly schoolchildren (Druck, 1974, pp.35–38; Yussen, 1977). The implications of this problem are serious. Leming (1978) compared the responses of eighth- and twelfth-graders on "classical" Kohlberg dilemmas and practical dilemmas which were generated by the subjects themselves. Subjects' stage scores on the practical dilemmas were significantly lower than those on the Kohlberg ones. Related findings have been reported in other studies (Haan, 1975). To devise a meaningful test of moral development might often force substantial changes in the dilemma content, questions and scoring systems (cf. Lee, 1971). And again, it must be borne in mind that in practice a lack of courage can easily prevent the exercise of heroic, principled ideas which are verbally expounded (cf. Urmson, 1958).

From the standpoint of a social-cognitive approach, a more comprehensive model of moral development can be derived through examining factors such as the types of conflicts which individuals confront, the types of cognitive skills which individuals use in resolving such conflicts, adult influences through modelling, reinforcement and reasoning, and peer-group experiences of status deprivation and responsibility. Kohlberg's theory is a pioneering attempt to examine the interplay of the first two factors. But even though there is some suggestion that cognitive sophistication is a necessary prerequisite for attaining a principled level of resolving moral dilemmas, the dilemmas themselves are not classified in any typology.

Moral reasoning as it relates to moral behaviour

However, the most probable shortcoming of the Kohlberg theory rests in its underevaluation of socialization pressures emanating from adults. Citing a 1969 book which has yet to appear at the time of this writing twelve years later, Kohlberg (1969, p.471) claimed that

> a specific relation to a specific good parent is neither necessary nor sufficient for normal or advanced moral development, since father absence, father's moral level, and the "good" child-rearing techniques, however defined, do not predict to such maturity.

Since then this stance has been reaffirmed in that only a weak relationship appears to exist between children's stages of moral reasoning and those used by their mothers and fathers (Haan, Langer and Kohlberg, 1976). Here Kohlberg has (perhaps unavoidably) slid into the writer's defect underscored so well by Cogswell: "to abandon as platitudinous a good many of the concepts and forms devised by his predecessors which had been a source of wisdom and pleasure to mankind for ages". The ancient Aristotelian concern with the adult's direct effects on children's moral development, so closely warranted by the results of empirical studies, is not shared by Kohlberg.

Before turning to the implications of Kohlberg's theory, one more issue should be discussed. A potential use of moral judgment measures is to predict overt behaviour. But studies have shown relationships which are weak to modest at best between Kohlberg's stages and reasoning about ethnic prejudice (Davison, 1976), political events (Candee, 1976), stealing (Tsujimoto and Nardi, 1978), and capital punishment (Kohlberg and Elfenbein,

1975). Moreover, the relationship between stages and participation in civil rights causes is unclear (see the Haan *et al.* study discussed in Section 4.4). Somewhat stronger relationships have been claimed to exist between stage scores and examples of helping behaviour which would seem to have some affinity with fairness (Krebs and Rosenwald, 1977; McNamee, 1978). However a closer examination of these studies casts doubt over their tentative conclusions owing to the relationship between intelligence and fair behaviour.

A college student experimenter in a study reported by Krebs and Rosenwald (1977) paid adult subjects for filling out personality questionnaires. They were told that if these were not completed and returned in a week and a half, as they had been trusted to do, the experimenter's chances of passing a course would be placed in jeopardy. A significant correlation was reported between moral reasoning and the extent to which the contract was honoured. However, two additional variables correlated with contract-honouring: a possession of an intellectually oriented job and years of formal education. This result would suggest that the well-educated subjects' understanding of the college student's predicament was at least as good a predictor of their moral behaviour as were moral stages.

A similar interpretation can be attached to a study by McNamee (1978) which has been evaluated as giving "the clearest and strongest support for the relation between moral reasoning and independence in moral action" (Blasi, 1980, p.37). Participants in an experiment were confronted with a confederate who claimed he was having a bad time on drugs and needed help. The experimenter refused to help, saying that she was a research psychologist and not a therapist. The moral behaviour recorded was of subjects breaking off participation in the experiment and offering help to the drug user. Again moral reasoning on Kohlberg's dilemmas was related to helping behaviour (although the numbers of subjects classified at each stage of moral development is unclear). Yet an alternative interpretation is at least as plausible: that those who helped were fully aware of what to do and understood drug-user's problems, whereas the non-helpers did not have this knowledge and chose to defer, perhaps sensibly, to the judgment of the more qualified experimenter.

7.6 *Two Theoretical Prognoses*

All in all then, two scenarios may be envisioned. The first is to take a liberal view of the theory's usefulness. Stage 4 and 5 reasoning does exist and should be studied even though the stage responses may be neither homogeneous nor follow in an invariant sequence, nor predictive of moral behaviour independent of intelligence. Here Kohlberg's theory is a modest improvement on Piaget's for it characterizes types of moral reasoning in adolescence and adulthood (Broughton, 1978). To this end, further revisions of the stage definitions might serve to account for some regression and response heterogeneity. These revisions should clarify the scoring process and serve to facilitate the design of studies which use the Kohlberg approach.

It should be emphasized that this is a wholly legitimate approach to theory-building. As Wegner and Vallacher (1977, p.19) write:

> Most scientific theories grow through extension and intention—generalization and refinement; the important point is that this growth is always achieved through an interaction between thought and observation. The way in which reality is logically structured by a theory may change as new observations are made. A theory is not a rigid structure; to be useful, it must adapt to new evidence.

In the Kohlberg case, new evidence demands a restructuring of the scoring system toward an identification of finer distinctions within a process of stage transition. Efforts have been made to identify and define "sub-stages" and, using a newly revised scoring system, preliminary reports claim evidence for the consistency and invariant sequence assumptions (Colby, 1978; Colby, Kohlberg and Gibbs, 1979).

The second scenario is to take a conservative line against the Kohlberg stages as failing to meet the criteria which define an invariant sequence (Nicolayev and Philips, 1979). Suppose that there is no regression or irreversibility in Stages 1, 2, and 3, as indeed there may not be (Kuhn, 1976; White, Bushnell and Regnemer, 1978). If this is so and Stages 4 and 5 are not invariant, Kohlberg's theory can be at least partly reduced to its original Piaget framework. That is, moral development proceeds from an obedience-punishment (adult-constraint) orientation to one based on a (mutual respect) reciprocity. After then, it can be characterized in terms of a conscientious adherence to a "good boy–good girl" orientation. This stage is never fully defined by Piaget (1967) but squares with Kohlberg's difficult-to-score Stage 3. There may be further development to Stage 4 and beyond but this is of a patchwork variety marked by cases of regression. This, of course, is not to deny that a Stage 5 or 6 morality is qualitatively superior to that of a lower stage; only that a Stage 5 or 6 morality in which persons act fairly is difficult to achieve psychologically.

To be sure, arguments have been advanced for a move away from using principles as a logically applicable standard for measuring moral development. For example, Haan (1978) has advocated the adoption of an "interpersonal morality" which strives for balance and agreement among participants. This morality takes into account the ability to use interpersonal and situational detail in moral decisions. Forsyth (1980) goes further in justifying a focus on relativism—a morality based on personal values which are restricted to situations and not generalizable to other circumstances no matter how similar these may be. Both of these efforts have been initiated out of the difficulty of establishing a bridge between moral judgment and behaviour, but to date neither has provided empirical evidence beyond that generated by the Kohlberg approach.

By the present account, it is not so much that Kohlberg's definition of morality is at fault, only that this approach centres on the "cool" cognitive aspects of moral development. Because affective-conative processes such as identification are not seen as directly relevant to moral development, a very important element is neglected which often prevents verbal reasoning about actual moral conflicts from being courageously translated into overt moral action. It is small wonder that, as Kohlberg himself states, the stages may have no necessary bearing on actual behaviour. This pronouncement falls very short of what ought to be an adequate test of moral behaviour: that is, "if we were to ask of a person 'What are his moral principles?' the way in which we could be most sure of a true answer would be by studying what he *did*" (Hare, 1952, p.1). By contrast the present social-cognitive approach deals with actual moral behaviour as well as moral reasoning.

In conclusion, Kohlberg's theory is but a modest improvement on Piaget's. The most recent evidence questions the generality and invariance of Kohlberg's stage sequence (Kurtines and Greif, 1974). It is even doubtful that there is empirical support for Stage 1. Moreover, evidence suggests that Kohlberg's method relies too heavily on verbal explanations to moral dilemmas which are outside subjects' personal experiences. Nevertheless, Kohlberg's Stages 4 and 5 are useful in that they characterize types of moral reasoning in adolescence and adulthood. A revision of stage definitions to account for regression and heterogeneity in responses could add to this usefulness though it may render a complex theory as still more intricate and more difficult to establish.

But any claim that Kohlberg's theory has in some sense eclipsed Piaget's appears quite groundless. At one time it might have been reasonable to treat Kohlberg's theory as potentially more useful than Piaget's because it encompassed many new and provocative but untested ideas (Hoffman, 1970; Wright, 1971). However, this is not the case now, and it is certainly premature to argue as some have (e.g., Lickona, 1976, p.240) that Piaget's theory has been "subsumed" and "supplanted" by a more sophisticated one. It certainly can no longer be said that criticisms of the theory's worth are unjustified because it is still in its infancy. The possibility must be entertained that this incubation period is prolonged precisely because there is a fatal obstacle to its "growing up", namely that the theory (or a significant part of it) is incorrect (see Taylor, 1964, p.272).

Even if it is agreed with Kohlberg that Piaget's theory is not cognitive enough, it is still abundantly clear that Kohlberg's own theory is too cognitive and not social enough. The irony is that a rationalist-empiricist clash has emerged even among those whose approach shares the rubric of "cognitive-developmental" (Section 3.1). Melville in *Moby Dick* (1895) summed up the problem in this way:

> So when on one side you hoist in Locke's head, you go over that way; but now on the other side, hoist in Kant's and you come back again, but in very poor plight. Thus, some minds for ever keep trimming boat. Oh, ye foolish! Throw all these thunderheads overboard, and then you will float light and right.

It is perhaps coincidental to read that Kohlberg himself defines his problem to be one of having to patch a leaky boat (Kohlberg, 1978; Muson, 1979). Yet in the light of evidence his cognitive-developmental approach cannot easily be made watertight: like many theories which have come against a spate of anomalous empirical findings, it must be either discarded completely or overhauled thoroughly and given more precision.

The problems with Kohlberg's approach do not bode well for his ideas on childrearing and education, as he advocates using his shakily supported stages as a basis for moral education programmes. But the dissemination of these ideas to parents and educators is likely to continue until a viable alternative is proposed. Though not an easy task, a desired change would ideally shift attention squarely back to the parent–child relationship and breathe a new vitality into the area of moral education.

Chapter Eight

CHILDREARING IN A SOCIOECONOMIC CONTEXT

THE DISCUSSION so far has been devoted to an examination of how identification processes may contribute to the development of fairness. According to behaviourism and early social learning theory, children's moral behaviour is shaped and learned through imitation and reinforcement. According to Piaget and Kohlberg, moral development occurs considerably apart from social influence; it is an active growth which theoretically culminates in fairness and rationality. The social-cognitive approach accepts this rational theoretical orientation, and follows Baldwin and Vygotsky in assigning importance both to imitation and to cognition. It proposes that both phenomena are related to the nature of parental identification. Through what is at first an unconscious imitation, children become cognizant of their parents' strengths and weaknesses. Together with a "cool" cognitive understanding of the bases underlying rules and principles, children's idealized perceptions of parental characteristics may be linked with their actual behaviour. Wanting to be like their parents may entice children to follow rules and independently generate principles. For their part, parents may use peer-group influence to complement what children have learned in striving to be like adults; and at no particular age does the parent appear to exert a disportionate influence on later development.

It remains, then, to deal with precisely what motivates children to want to be like their parents in the first place. To this end, in terms of what little evidence exists, an investigation must be made of patterns of childrearing and their relation to socioeconomic conditions. In the first part of this chapter, identification will be examined in both Western and non-Western contexts. Then identification will be related to patterns of childrearing and the development of a fair and principled morality.

8.1 Socioeconomic Conditions and the Quality of Parent–Child Relations

Though there exist many different facets to identification, it is difficult to see how the process could come about without considering the often sweeping impact of socioeconomic factors. It is the case that Freud's own ideas on identification were generally not discussed in such terms (Section 4.1). But more recently, Slater (1961) has attempted to free the psychoanalytic concept of identification from its instinctive and dynamic connotations by offering a reclassification: a dichotomy of personal and positional identification. Both kinds can occur together. The personal variety involves identification with a parent out of love and admiration while positional identification involves the child's envy of a parent's power and control over resources.

On either count, it can be expected that identification may proceed most effectively in educated and economically powerful middle-class as opposed to working-class families. Kohn (1963), for example, has described how middle-class parents want their children to love and confide in them, and to share and co-operate. By contrast, working-class parents put more emphasis on obedience and conformity to external authority. Such differences in childrearing values can be attributed to occupational differences. Working-class occupations require obedience while middle-class occupations require relatively more independent judgment and self-direction.

Since the middle-class parent has greater economic power and control than does the working-class parent, identification in general may proceed more effectively in middle-class children. In this respect, it is clear that important aspects of the parent's own individual identity are defined and reinforced by having a role in the economy. Employment gives purpose and structure to behaviour (M. Jahoda, 1979). A parent gains status, authority, and "generativity"—a "concern for establishing and guiding the next generation" (Erikson, 1968, p.138). The breadwinner's self-concept is strongly rooted in an ability to earn a living and provide for the family. Even at the preschool level, the self-concept of middle-class parents is associated with children's behaviour (Tower, 1980).

From the child's perspective, the economic prosperity attached to parents' abilities in employment can facilitate the process of identification. Middle-class boys are more likely than lower-class boys to evaluate their parents as smart, successful, secure and ambitious. They also perceive a greater degree of parental support, acceptance and interest as compared to their lower-class counterparts (Rosen, 1964; Scheck and Emerick, 1976).

In this way, socioeconomic conditions significantly underpin the quality of parent–child relations. They contribute to the maintenance of a system which can be described in terms of a reciprocal model of behaviour (Bandura, 1978). Here the economic environment and the perceptions and behaviour of the parent and child all function as interconnected influences on each other. The economic environment is associated with the parent's self-concept and this self-concept is associated with children's identification. Under prosperous and non-stressful economic conditions, parents may gain a high self-concept and their children develop an intense level of identification. Owing to a sense of generativity, children have worth in their parent's eyes: conversely, children's approving perceptions of their parents give parents worth in their children's eyes. Furthermore, both parents and children have a stake in striving to perpetuate the conditions of purposeful employment in the economy.

But in these times of recession, inflation, unemployment, and general economic hardship, the task of generativity is not an easy one. For a sizeable portion of the workforce, the goal of meeting their children's basic economic needs of food, shelter and medical care—let alone toys—has become more and more difficult. This erosion of economic power threatens the maintenance of parental authority in the home. It is important then to search for answers on what little evidence there presently exists to two questions: (1) "How do children evaluate an underpaid adult who is unable to meet these needs?" (2) "How does a lack of parental economic power affect the quality of parent–child relations?"

Children's perceptions of adult economic needs

In order for children to evaluate economic needs and resources, it is necessary for them to have some understanding of the workings of the economic system. Several incisive studies have recently been carried out to examine this issue. Furth, Baur and Smith (1976; see also Furth, 1978) interviewed children in southern England aged 5 to 11 years about their knowledge of money as used within different roles and occupations filled by adults. The results suggested that 5-year-olds generally do not see a lack of money as a constraint for adults. Adults are perceived as possessing the ability to do what they please and this economic power is characteristic of these in all types of roles. In contrast, 11-year-olds can clearly differentiate among roles. They understand that adults are at times constrained by a lack of money and that occupations carry obligations within a network of social exchange. For example, unlike the 5-year-old who believes that bus drivers alone set the amount of passengers' fares, the 11-year-old correctly understands that the bus driver collects fares on behalf of a company who in turn pays his salary.

In another study by Baldus and Tribe (1978), the participants were children attending elementary school in Toronto, aged 5 to 12 years. They were shown pictures of two men, one well dressed and the other casually dressed. The task was to match the pictures with sets of photographs in which a well-to-do house was paired with an old working-class one, and a luxury automobile with a small old one. Results were that the younger children matched the pictures at a chance level while the 11- and 12-year-olds recognized the social differences in economic power between the two men, correctly placing the well-dressed man with the well-to-do home and luxury automobile and the casually dressed man with the old house and car.

In a similar study (G. Jahoda, 1979), children aged 6 to 12 living in working-class districts of Glasgow were given a role-taking task. Adult experimenters played the roles of customers and suppliers and the child played the role of a shopkeeper. A range of goods was available in a toy "shop" and this was soon exhausted by the customer paying with imitation money. The child was reminded of the selling price and was prompted to contact the supplier for new supplies using a toy phone. The child was then brought the supplies, and if he paid less (with imitation money) than the selling price for the supplies, the child was credited with an understanding of "profit". If he paid the same purchase price or more, it was assumed that the child did not have this concept. The results indicated that a full understanding was not reached until the age of 11 years.

These findings suggest that children's early perceptions of adult economic needs can be generally characterized by an undifferentiated understanding of roles and occupations which gradually gives way by early adolescence to a recognition of occupational differences in the distribution of income. However, comparatively little is known about how children perceive such differences. The information which is available again originates from Piaget's observations on moral development (1932).

According to Piaget, children's ideas on social inequality pass through three stages. In the first stage, justice is equated with obedience to authority; since age implies authority, children judge that older individuals rightfully deserve more rewards than do younger ones. In the second, justice is equated with equality, and children judge that rewards should be dispensed equally without regard for subjective factors such as effort and need on the part of the individual recipients. The third stage is one of equity in which children advocate that rewards should be distributed according to subjective factors, especially individual needs. Therefore older children might judge that adult economic needs ought to be met regardless of what role they play in the community.

But Piaget did not provide a full picture of the issue as he restricted his remarks to certain aspects of justice among children and between children and adults. He did not extend his analysis to children's perceptions of adult justice. Given the prevalent psychology of "more" in adult society (Section 2.1), significant segments of the population certainly condone the existence of social inequality. In the judgment of many adults, resources should be distributed on the basis of effort and ability rather than need. Thus effort and ability also might form the basis for children's evaluations of social inequalities. They may agree with a situation in which a high reward for some entails unmet needs for others under a system of economic constraint where only a finite amount of resources is available for distribution, an assumption commonly held by economists.

These two possibilities of need as opposed to effort and ability were explored in an initial study (Siegal, 1981). The subjects were children aged 6–13 years from working-class districts of Vancouver. They were asked to indicate and evaluate the needs and earnings corresponding to four occupational roles: doctor, shopkeeper, bus driver, and waiter. The children's responses were placed in three categories: (1) those of the many younger children who did not recognize the existence of unmet needs; (2) those of the children recognizing the existence of unmet needs and evaluating this distribution of resources as fair; and (3) those responses evaluating such distributions as unfair. The children in the second category gave justifications for the inequality between doctors and waiters such as "The doctor has more important jobs and abilities" and "It's the waiter's own fault . . . this is what he chose to do." One child even claimed that inequality was fair because "Those who need more than they get paid will be jealous of others and have to work harder. Otherwise they would be lazy." By contrast the children in the third category who claimed that inequality is unfair gave responses such as "It's unfair because everyone is good at their own occupation." At the age of 12–13 years, all the children recognized the existence of inequality but split sharply on the issue of fairness.

Economic deterioration and the worth of parents to children

There are several questions for future research which arise from this preliminary study. For example, what is the relationship of children's perceptions of adult economic needs to occupational sex-typing? How do widespread crosscultural disparities in inequality affect these perceptions? But on the slender evidence which is at hand let us link these categories in children's perceptions of adult economic power with the identification process.

First, there is the young *naive child* who does not recognize the disparity between needs and economic resources. Suppose this child is solely supported by a parent who is inadequately paid or unemployed. In these circumstances, the parent may lose much of the status and identity which accompanied the sense of competence gained through purposeful employment. In some cases, this economic change is accompanied by a propensity toward depression and mental illness (Dooley and Catalano, 1980). Because the parent is less able to meet his or her responsibility for the next generation, and is hard pressed to continue the task of generativity as defined by Erikson, there may be a loss of authority in the family. Here the best information comes from the vast number of observations on economic hardship collected during the Great Depression of the 1930s (Eisenberg and Lazarsfeld, 1938; Elder, 1974). These studies are often based on autobiographies and case histories. But though they lack a certain cohesiveness and precision, they none the less are chilling to read. Children of the underpaid or unemployed may suffer a loss in peer-group status. They may show emotional disturbances from losing the support of authority which deteriorated with the parent's financial situation. Without understanding the complexities of the economic system and its relationship to the parent's resources, children lose both a measure of security and leadership. They have little or no target for ambition and commitment. The child's schoolwork suffers and, according to Eisenberg and Lazarsfeld (1938, p.382), "the younger children suffer more than the older probably because they are more dependent on their parents and have had less opportunity to build up resistance to catastrophic situations." In this connection, more recent systematic studies using data gathered during the depression years have indicated that difficult economic conditions may exacerbate conflict already present in the family, giving rise to problem behaviour in boys (Rockwell and Elder, 1979).

Then there is the *economic child* of about 12 years and above. Though these children can identify unmet economic needs, they maintain that the distribution of resources should be based on the product of effort and ability, perhaps out of society's emphasis on successful achievement (Weiner and Peter, 1973) or its prevalent belief in a just world where persons receive what they deserve (Lerner and Miller, 1978). Suppose again that this child is solely supported by a parent who, despite his efforts and abilities, lacks adequate economic resources. A crumbling parental authority may occur at the very time when it could have come to the aid of adolescent offspring, who are troubled by the necessity to decide on a purposeful occupational identity of their own. To witness the parent's own difficulties in meeting the family's economic needs while still possessing the desire to attain material success could exasperate the child's identity crisis. The adolescent who is about to enter into adulthood without a parental target for commitment and ambition may be plagued by an acute feeling of becoming superfluous and aimless (Zawadski and Lazarsfeld, 1935). Particularly in middle-class families, there may be an increased identification with non-familial adults owing to the father's loss of prestige (Elder, 1974, p.102).

Finally, there is the empathic *psychological child* of about 12 years and above who shares the feelings of the despondent breadwinner. Possibly together with an intense personal identification with the parent, such children may maintain that resources should be distributed on the basis of need rather than strictly on the outcome of effort and ability. They may remain disposed toward the parent's rules and standards for behaviour even though the parent has difficulty in discharging his economic responsibilities. The parent's authority is sustained and may still aid the child in settling upon his or her own occupational identity.

By this account, it can be assumed that there exist children whose perceptions can be characterized as psychological and who are mature beyond their ages and are sensitive to parental needs. But there are also sizeable numbers of naive and economic children. Economic children in particular are ones who, in difficult times for their parents, do not demonstrate significant personal or positional identification. The worth of parents is lowered in their eyes and their parents may be distressed that their children do not want to be like them.

In this way, economic difficulty can mar the quality of parent–child relations. Yet the welfare of both the naive and economic child conflicts directly with the advice of a very influential group of economists from the "Chicago School":

> Few trends could so thoroughly undermine the very foundation of our free society as the acceptance by corporate officials of a social responsibility other than to make as much money for their stockholders as possible. This is a fundamentally subversive doctrine. If businessmen do have a social responsibility other than making maximum profits for stockholders, how are they to know what it is? Can self-selected private individuals decide what the social interest is? Can they decide how great a burden they are justified in placing on themselves or their stockholders to serve that social interest?
>
> (Friedman, 1962, pp.133–134)

Accordingly, the correct prescription for industry is to strive for a balance sheet which is as much in the black as possible. If demand falls off, the very first step should be to lay off workers or cut wages. To this end, it is argued that industry should be allowed to act free of government regulations. But from a psychological viewpoint, little could be more subversive to both the goal of profit and to the quality of parent–child relations, a point which was well recognized originally, in fact, by Schumpeter (Section 2.1). In many cases, to pay workers inadequately, or to make them redundant may increase a firm's short-term profits. Yet this policy could have devastating effects on the status and identity of the employee, in some cases leading to an unanticipated loss of production and sales (see the careful documentation provided by Brown, 1977). Moreover, as shown in the depression years, the unbridled application of this policy can contribute to social unrest in the community, not only among workers, but also among their children who may have little with which to identify (Zawadski and Lazarsfeld, 1935). Therefore it is at least arguable to maintain that corporate officials do have a social responsibility other than to cultivate their stockholders' dividends: namely, to chase every avenue to ensure that their employees are able to meet confidently the basic economic needs of their children. Naturally, there are organizations which do demonstrate a considerable degree of concern over this issue. Nevertheless, Western companies generally tend to assume that the work and family worlds of their employees do not conflict. There is even company resistance to studying how corporate stress affects the family and vice versa—though the pressure of long working hours, extensive travel and transfer relocations certainly endangers family stability (Renshaw, 1976).

Economic deterioration and the worth of children to parents

A lowering of the worth of parents to children under economic stress may also be accompanied by a lowering of the worth of children to parents. By far the most blatant illustration comes from the high incidence of child abuse in poor families. It is true that cases of child abuse and neglect are known in all socioeconomic classes and that two socioeconomically similar neighbourhoods may have different rates of abuse and neglect, depending on the availability of "support systems" (Garbarino and Sherman, 1980). Nevertheless, such cases do predominate in lower-class families. Pelton (1978) has shown that although poor people are more subject to public scrunity there is still much evidence which suggests that the relationship between poverty and child abuse and neglect cannot merely be assigned to a faulty reporting system which monitors the poor and not the rich. Even looking at only impoverished families, the greatest child neglect occurs in the poorest of the poor (Giovannoni and Billingsley, 1970). As Gil (1971, p.640) has written:

> Compared to all families in the United States, the income of families of abused children was very low and that of families of non-white abused children even lower. At the time of the abusive incident over 37 percent of the families were receiving public assistance. Altogether nearly 60 percent of the families had received public assistance at some time preceding the abusive incident.

Perhaps there is no better single example of the importance of studying the socioeconomic conditions underlying parent–child relations than child abuse. Pelton charges that to indulge in a myth of classlessness is to reinforce the interests of middle-class professionals who maintain that abuse is a medical problem rather than a poverty problem. Ultimately, this myth serves to divert efforts away from alleviating poverty to supporting a prestigious and glamorous medical model. It assumes a reductionist explanation that abuse is a result of poorly controlled parental impulses whose psychological symptoms can be traced back to biological dysfunctions controllable by drugs. But in order to implement more forceful and direct measures to eliminate a major antecedent of child abuse, it is necessary to recognize how economic strain can affect the family. Because child abuse occurs more frequently under deteriorating economic conditions, it cannot be simply interpreted in terms of mechanistic biological processes (cf. Section 1.1). As Sternberg, Catalano, and Dooley (1981) have recently shown, increases in the incidence of child abuse are preceded by periods of employment loss.

So with the strain of economic difficulty and the weakening of parent–child ties may come the breakdown of rule-following behaviour. Certainly, one worthwhile pursuit for developmental psychologists is to report and publicize the situation of children whose economic needs have not been met (regardless of their parent's efforts and abilities). On this score, as Marie Jahoda (1979) points out, more research was done in the 1930s than during all of the postwar era; and despite the rapt attention given to effort, ability, and outcome in children's perceptions of justice, the effects of need have been neglected (Hook and Cook, 1979, p.435). But in view of the large numbers of those adults who remain inadequately paid or unemployed, this issue merits further study.

8.2 *Promoting Rule-following Behaviour through Identification: The Case of the Japanese Family*

Childrearing in Japan

To protect the naive and economic child by distributing resources on the basis of need, as well as ability and effort, does not necessarily involve the implementation of a socialist or communist system of economic planning. A clear example comes from the tremendous success of industrialization in Japan. In explaining this success, it is necessary to understand the psychological underpinnings of the collective rules which govern the workings of Japanese social organizations (DeVos, 1973, p.187). To this end, writer after writer has observed that the single most important factor contributing to the Japanese economic miracle resides in the strength of parent–child and particularly mother–child identification.

It has been shown recently that some traditional Western views of contemporary Japanese society are not well supported by findings reported in various research articles (cf. Caudill, 1973). For example, arranged marriages persist in Japan. But contrary to popular Western views, many Japanese women appear to be equalitarian in their attitudes toward marriage roles rather than expressing a preference for the male to play a dominant role. This is especially the case among women students enrolled in prestigious colleges and universities (Arkoff, Meredith and Iwahara, 1964; Kalish, Mahoney and Arkoff, 1966). Moreover, in contradiction to the prevalent Western assumption that a high degree of conformity is prevalent in Japanese society, the results of Asch-type tests of conformity suggest that Japanese college students may be no more conformist than their Western counterparts (Frager, 1970).

Where the evidence does converge is in demonstrating a phenomenon which is often missing from the Western stereotype of Japanese society: the intense relationship between mother and child. Japanese women overwhelmingly assign more importance to the role of a mother over that of a wife and individual. They maintain that the most desirable characteristic of an ideal mother is to put the child's welfare ahead of her own (Smith and Schooler, 1978). Consistent with this belief, Japanese mothers spend much more time in close physical proximity with their infants than do their Western counterparts.

The strength of ties between mother and child manifests itself in several ways (Lebra, 1976). First, the Japanese mother usually spends at least one and possibly even two or three years breastfeeding her baby. Breastfeeding is markedly preferred to bottlefeeding and is an aid toward mother–infant communication.

Second, mother and child sleep together on *futon* (bed mats) until another child is born. Then the child is displaced from his mother's bed and goes to sleep with the father or a grandmother. Co-sleeping with a parent, sibling or other relative is very common at least until the age of puberty. Even in large houses with many bedrooms, parents and children often prefer to co-sleep to the extent that co-sleeping of the mother and father is at times precluded. The child's fond memories of the co-sleeping parent serves to facilitate the process of identification (Caudill and Plath, 1966).

Third, the Japanese mother not only sleeps with her child but the two both sleep together, the close skin contact providing a source of mutual gratification. Co-bathing occurs both in the deep Japanese *furo* (bathtub) at home and in the public bathhouses where baby beds are provided.

Fourth, until very recently, babysitters have not been used in Japan.

Whenever she goes outside, a mother has traditionally transported her child in an *onbu* (papoose). Through this device, parental affection is conveyed and mother and child feel each other's warmth. The *onbu* is so enjoyed that some children can only fall asleep while resting there on the mother's back. And though fathers do not use *onbus*, they too experience the closeness of body contact by frequently holding the child in their arms and on their shoulders.

In view of the closeness of these family ties, it makes sense that there are distinct crosscultural differences between Japanese and Western methods of childrearing. For example, the Japanese mother strongly encourages the child to live in harmony with others. Japanese infants as compared with those in the United States are not only less vocal, but less active and less exploratory of their surroundings. Mothers soothe their infant toward passivity, which appears to be a cultural characteristic of Japanese living in Japan; Japanese who have been living in the United States for generations are more like Caucasian Americans in producing active, vocal babies (Caudill and Frost, 1974).

Japanese mothers also take more time to respond to their babies' unhappy vocalizations than do American mothers and thus the unhappy vocalizations of Japanese babies generally last longer. Caudill (1973) interprets this difference in terms of the strong ties between mother and infant. Because the Japanese mother feels she is "part of the baby", she knows what is good for the baby. She responds not according to the distress which the baby is signalling but how she herself feels. By contrast, the American mother regards the baby as more separate from herself. She responds more quickly according to the baby's own signals.

The closeness of mother–infant ties in Japan is evident in the mother's use of disciplinary techniques which appear to be less severe than those used in the West (Kiefer, 1970). Crosscultural studies of maternal socialization behaviour have indicated that Japanese mothers are more likely to use feeling-oriented appeals to gain children's compliance than are American mothers (Conroy, Hess, Azuma and Kashiwagi, 1980). Rather than physical punishment, Japanese parents appeal to their children's capacity for empathy and use the threat of withdrawal of love to maintain obedience. As Lebra (1976, p.153) remarks, the empathy technique seems to be distinctively Japanese. It conveys to the child: "If you don't stop doing that, it is I, your mother who will suffer most. Try to put yourself in my place." Naughty children are warned by their mothers that if help is needed, it will not be forthcoming. They may be threatened with abandonment or of being locked out of the house. A comparable punishment for a Western child in these circumstances would often involve being sent to one's room, locked in or (in the North American sense) "grounded".

Identification and Japanese socioeconomic arrangements

The emphasis which is placed on the unitary and harmonious nature of the family persists in the child's relationship with classmates when he or she enters school. The family, particularly the mother, encourage children to extend their identifications to other members of the class. There is a strong taste for belongingness among classmates and this exists many years after the group has dissolved. To refresh the memory of belonging even kindergarten alumni may hold an annual reunion which continues past middle age (Lebra, 1976, p.26).

The teacher, classmates, and family all support the child during the famous "examination hell" of the Japanese educational system. The responsibility for the child's success at school rests not only with the student but with others as well, especially the mother. As Kiefer (1970) points out, the Japanese school is the training ground for a single team without the institutionalized competition of Western schools which pit students against each other and their teachers. In Japan, the child can as a rule expect the support of the teacher regardless of his or her academic progress. By passing examinations, a child reaffirms a conviction in belongingness, in maintaining ties to parents, teachers and classmates. In succeeding, Japanese students are the beneficiaries of extravagant praise, usually more than is given to their Western counterparts.

In this way, the peer group in the classroom and later in the office or factory comes to be regarded as family and the relationship between home, school, and later employment is a very close one (Kiefer, 1970). As Abegglen (1958) has pointed out, these characteristics of Japanese economic arrangements are very different to those in the West. Not only do workers in Japan have lifetime employment in the company where their promotions are based on length of service, but there is a paternalistic relationship between superior and subordinate and between employer and employee. The rights and duties of the employer and employee are extended to family members. In return for the employee's loyalty to the company, provision by the company is made for most of the employee's basic needs (including housing and facilities for medical treatment, education, and recreation). That the Japanese factory is family-centred and strives to avoid strife among managers and co-workers appears to be at the core of Japanese economic success (Holden, 1980).

Thus compared to Western social organizations, those in Japan are explicitly dedicated to meeting the needs of the worker's family. Because of the Japanese worker's devotion to his or her employer, individual movement from company to company to seek promotions and higher salaries is uncommon. How then does the family and group identifications of the Japanese worker contribute to a sense of fairness?

Evidence from a study by Shaw and Iwawaki (1972) suggests that Americans are more likely to attribute individual responsibility for acts associated with positive outcomes than for acts associated with negative ones. By contrast, Japanese attribute equal individual responsibility within the group in both the positive and negative cases. In this regard, Japanese appear to be more willing to accept blame than are Americans, who in turn are more likely than are Japanese to maintain that they have been the victim of circumstances. Berrien (1966) gave a questionnaire containing measures of 15 social needs (e.g., achievement, deference, dominance and endurance) to a group of American and Japanese college students. Compared to Americans, the Japanese students were less interested in such individualistic pursuits as being recognized as an authority in a special field, in accepting positions of leadership or in solving problems others have found difficult. More than Americans, the Japanese were willing to accept blame personally when things go wrong, work hard, complete one job before taking on another and avoid interruptions in their work.

In this fashion, the intensive identifications of the Japanese provide the foundation for participation in industrial growth. They give rise to individuals working co-operatively in social organizations which are exquisitely tuned for efficiency and quality in production. Economic success in turn is attributed to the joint efforts of many workers rather than to a few at the top of the company hierarchy. It directly reinforces the identifications of workers with companies. It also indirectly reinforces the identifications of children with their parents who are equal to the task of generativity.

Thus it may be said that while Japan has worked toward rapid technological and institutional change, social change has been controlled or purposely prevented (Morsbach, 1977). Owing to a Confucian-centred ethic of harmony and respect for elders and ancestors, the family unit has retained its stability in the midst of tremendous industrialization.

All of this is in sharp contrast to the West where industrialization has radically changed the nature of the family (Section 2.1). In this respect Japan also differs greatly from the Soviet Union. Despite the high degree of parental and state involvement at controlling the peer group in the service of defined objectives (Section 6.3), Soviet economic development was achieved at the expense of disruptions to the traditional social fabric. The repatriation of land and the implementation of national industrialization plans, as well as undercurrents of individualism and romanticism (love marriages and adulterous relationships) imported from Western Europe, have combined to rock the stability of the family. After the revolution of 1917, families and firms were unable to fill the vacuum left by the overthrow of organizations involved in the control of the traditional serf society. Only through the establishment of national bodies was order restored. Yet this was achieved without such intense identifications with family, firms, and other intermediate organizations, a situation which "may be both a cause and effect of the chronic problem of motivation in the Soviet labor force" (Black *et al.*, 1975, p.329).

In the Soviet Union, all labour is harnessed to distant aims which are national in scope, and workers do not have the highly developed sense of loyalty to the immediate goals of the factory so pervasive in Japan. Consequently, Soviet workers may be less likely than their Japanese counterparts to abide by collective rules of their organization in striving to achieve production quotas and the like. The Japanese system, in comparison, appears to be extremely effective in minimizing worker–management disputes and in encouraging the widespread following of rules.

As Japan in the 1980s is a changing society, the above discussion may be based on observations which are already outdated and too few. Yet if this picture is near an accurate contemporary description, it can be proposed that the Japanese case provides an example of rule-following behaviour enhanced within a socioeconomic context of material success and prosperity.

8.3 *The Authoritative Parent and the Cognition–Affection–Conation Trilogy*

Ideology and childrearing

Rule-following is only part of fairness, for sometimes the rules themselves can and ought to be evaluated as unfair. To make rational, independent judgments on the fairness of rules is to apply formal principles. However, there appears to be no clear example of a society in which such a conception of principles of fairness has actually been adopted—though some crosscultural studies are suggestive in this respect. What can be said is that certain socioeconomic conditions may foster family structures conducive toward attaining a principled morality.

Before turning to these conditions, it is necessary to examine the ideology of childrearing practices. Precisely how parents can justify the means and ends of childrearing is a perennially troubling question. Kohlberg and Mayer (1972) have provided an eloquent answer in describing three ideologies which have competed as justifications for the choice of aims in education and childrearing.

The first two of these ideologies are referred to as the "romanticism" and "cultural transmission" schools respectively. The romantic school contains followers of Freud and assumes that what comes from within the child is what is optimal for development. The child should be allowed to work through problems of emotional development. There is a belief that what children do want is what they should want.

By contrast, the cultural transmission school regards the goals of education as a means of adapting the child to society. Within this school are positivists and behaviourists, in company with others of many other persuasions. While the romantic school is child-centred, the cultural transmission school is society-centred. It purports to convey a justification for teaching children vocational skills deemed necessary for industry and the national needs of a society. Most of Western education has been within this academic tradition.

But as Kohlberg and Mayer (p.477) point out, both these ideologies serve to harbour a sort of elitist cult. Romanticism withholds from children tenets of fairness under the pretext that to educate in this way would be indoctrination. Only the psychologist "culture-designer" has the right to confront and resolve unfair situations; the child who is happily educated in the romantic tradition is unaware of these problems. Similarly the cultural transmission school advocates the education of children to conform to the "needs" of society but not to evaluate these needs. Neither ideology actively advocates education for intellectual inquiry and social justice.

In opposition to this elitism stands the school of progressivism which advocates that children should be stimulated to question societal rules in a critical, rational fashion. The development of logically justifiable, universal ethical principles should be the aim of a moral education and childrearing. The child, then, should not be taught a bag of virtues such as "integrity" and "honesty" as defined by the cultural transmission school (though agreement on the precise nature of these virtues is hard to reach). Rather he or she should be exposed to logical arguments for evaluating rules as fair or unfair. As Piaget has maintained (Section 3.1), exposure to sophisticated, rich, and varied peer-group experience should give rise to a consideration of others' interests and intentions. Development then proceeds in stage-like fashion as described by the Kohlberg approach to moral development. This culminates in a systematic method for evaluating the fairness of rules against stealing, cheating, and even terrorism and torture, not in every single case inevitably deciding that to follow the rules is correct (see the discussion by Hare, 1979).

More recently, Kohlberg (1978) has argued that, after a child has developed beyond the stage of judging moral conflicts in terms of issues of law and order (his Stage 4), moral education must be partly "indoctrinative". Rules against stealing and cheating must be imposed on children with their participation in the rule-making and enforcement process as far as is possible. Such indoctrination is necessary to deal directly with the moral behaviour of children who commonly engage in anti-social activities and have not yet come to understand the basis underlying the enactment of collective rules.

How are children able to go beyond this understanding to evaluate the rules with independent and logical judgment in formulating universal ethical principles? This is to be achieved not in the family but in the school and peer group. As noted in the previous chapter, Kohlberg (1969, p.399) does not regard identification or parental influence as especially important for moral development:

> From our point of view . . . (1) family participation is not unique or critically necessary for moral development, and (2) the dimensions on which it stimulates moral development are primarily general dimensions by which other primary groups stimulate moral development.

In line with this assumption, one approach has been to raise moral development through teacher advocacy and group discussion of moral issues affecting classmates. The goal is to build a just community within the school (Power and Reimer, 1978).

Childrearing patterns and the exercising of independent judgment

Kohlberg's philosophical orientation follows that of Kant, Rawls and Hare. Thus it may be presumed to reflect logically valid aims of childrearing and education as defined by the rationalist tradition of Western philosophy. But his empirical stage theory has not been well supported to date. Kohlberg notwithstanding, the overwhelming thrust of the evidence has been to highlight the significance of parental influence (which itself is able to structure the nature of peer-group contact, as shown in Chapter 6).

In this regard, the family may be the "social unit most responsive to rational influence" (Baumrind, 1975, p.140). Efforts have been made to locate childrearing patterns most conducive toward stimulating the rationality inherent in a principled morality. These studies have suggested that a reciprocal and open communicative relationship between children and parents engenders a state of creative tension from which may come principled moral commitments (Garbarino and Bronfenbrenner, 1976). The most notable of the research in this area has come from the work of Diana Baumrind (1971, 1973, 1977).

Initially, preschoolers and their parents in the Berkeley, California, area were observed interacting in structured laboratory situations and during home visits by a trained observer. On this basis three prototypical patterns of childrearing (authoritarian, permissive and authoritative) and their associations with children's behaviour were described:

1. The *authoritarian* parent (reminiscent of Kohlberg and Mayer's cultural transmission culture-designer) does not encourage verbal give-and-take. Obedience and respect for authority are valued as virtues unto themselves. Children of authoritarian parents were observed to show little independence and moderate responsibility.

2. The *permissive* parent (reminiscent of the romantic culture-designer) acts in an acceptant, benign way toward the child and allows as much freedom as is consistent with the child's physical survival. This parent makes few demands on the child for responsibility and order, and uses little punishment. Children of permissive parents were lowest on social responsibility and showed only moderate leadership.

3. The authoritarian pattern is one dominated by the parent; the permissive pattern is characterized by child-dominance in the relationship. The most equalitarian relationship between child and parent is an *authoritative* one. This type of parent attempts to direct the child making liberal use of reason centred around issues in the home. Care is taken to explain the reasons underlying discipline. The child is expected to respect the rights of others and to be independent and responsible. Together with explanations, physical power is used when necessary to enforce demands. Authoritative parents (reminiscent of progressive educators and parents who used "induction" techniques in the Hoffman and Saltzstein study discussed in Section 4.4) had children who were high on both responsibility and leadership.

Many of these childrearing relationships seem to reappear at later ages (Baumrind, 1977). The same preschoolers with authoritative parents, when examined at ages 8-9 years and compared to those from authoritarian and permissive homes, responded positively to intellectual challenges, set high standards for themselves, and demonstrated leadership in the peer group. Somewhat similar findings emerged in a study by Hoffman (1975a) using middle-class fifth-graders from Detroit schools. In the same vein, Elder (1963) examined the relationship between autonomy and parents' explanations underlying rules, as reported by adolescent subjects. Those who perceived themselves to possess self-confidence and independence in decision-making also reported that their parents made use of explanations.

There are reasons to believe that significant discrepancies exist among Western countries in the extent of authoritative childrearing. Here a study by Kandel and Lesser (1969) is particularly revealing. A survey was made in the United States and Denmark of adolescent's perceptions of the nature of their parental interactions. While the Danish adolescents reported predominately democratic patterns in which they participated with their parents in making joint decisions, the American adolescents perceived their relationships as predominantly authoritarian in which the parent makes all the decisions relevant to the child. Compared to the Americans, the Danish parent was more likely to provide explanations, had more open communication and fewer rules. The Danish adolescents also perceived themselves to be more independent in judgment than the Americans. Kandel and Lesser speculate that Danish parents with young children are less permissive than American ones giving rise to more self-direction in their children as adolescents.

In this regard, a common belief has been that it is difficult to use reason effectively with young children, and certainly in experimental studies it has been shown that younger children need more concrete reasons than do older ones, with reference to the consequences of specific misbehaviour rather than to a generalized rule (LaVoie, 1974; Parke, 1974). However, naturalistic research which assumes a high ecological validity suggests that an abstract form of explanation for the parent's actions contributes to the effectiveness of discipline, even for very young children.

In one innovative study (Zahn-Waxler, Radke-Yarrow and King, 1979), the subjects were one-and-a-half to two-and-a-half years old. The mothers of the children were trained in techniques of recording their own reactions to distresses their child had caused to others (such as hitting innocent playmates) and his or her subsequent reparations. A strong relationship was found between reparations and mothers' affectively delivered explanations given with "cognitive clarity" and intense "emotional investment". In particular, mothers' statements of generalized principles and values about not hurting others (such as "People are not for hitting. You must never poke anyone's eyes. You can talk about biting but you cannot ever do it") were most predictive of reparations. There was also a significant positive relationship between the mother's moralizing and the use of physical punishment, suggesting that both reasoning and power can be combined effectively even at a very early age.

Such a policy of exercising *rational* authority on young children is wholly within the progressive approach. Though early moral development may largely involve having to do what others insist, it does not follow that childrearing must be authoritarian. To insist forcefully on a child's showing concern for others coupled with giving an explanation why this should be so is not a violation of children's rights. As Deardon (1968, p.173) has observed, "It would be sheer sentimentality . . . to suppose that the child is always right', or that consideration for others or a love of fairness are learned without ever reluctantly having to forego what one desires."

Authoritative childrearing, family structure, and socio-economic conditions

The presence of authoritative childrearing seems linked to the structure of power and authority in the family which in turn is influenced by socioeconomic conditions. In most Western countries until quite recently, the mother traditionally has had nearly complete responsibility for day-to-day childrearing (Lopata, 1971, pp.183–184). So it is hardly surprising that the mother has appeared more influential than the father in research on identification.

On this subject, many studies have shown that children view mothers more frequently than fathers as a source of comfort and love (Britton and Britton, 1971; Longstreth and Rice, 1964; Smelser, 1964).

Thus at least with regard to personal identification, the mother comes out ahead. However, it is reasonable to ask whether mother identification predominates in all families regardless of the ability of one parent to influence the other's behaviour. In some families either the mother or father is perceived by the child as dominant; in others, conjugal relationships are seen as equalitarian. To examine whether the perceived distribution of power between the parents is related to children's identifications, Bowerman and Bahr (1973) gave questionnaires to over 18 000 high-school students in Ohio and North Carolina. Their identifications were measured by responses to questions such as "Would you like to be the kind of person your mother (father) is?" and "How much do you depend on your mother's (father's) opinions to influence your ideas of right and wrong?" As a measure of power, the children were asked "When important family problems come up, which parent usually has the most influence in making the decision? The results indicated that, regardless of perceived power, females had higher identification scores with mothers than with fathers—the difference being greatest when the father is weaker and least when he is perceived as dominant. By contrast, males identified more strongly with whichever parent is perceived to be dominant. As with the predominantly equalitarian Danish adolescents in the Kandel and Lesser study, there were no differences between parents in the degree of identification perceived by American children from equalitarian homes. Overall, adolescents who perceived their parents' relationship as equalitarian were highest in identification, while those who perceived the mother as dominant were lowest.

As Bowerman and Bahr observe, equalitarian families can be assumed to have high levels of agreement between the parents. Other research has shown that parental agreement is associated with success in school situations (van der Veen, 1965). In this connection, father identification may be indirectly enhanced by the approval of the mother. With their mothers' approval, adolescent boys are more likely to describe themselves as similar to their fathers (Helper, 1955), though it may be that similar occupational aspirations on the part of the child are associated with father–son conflict—a finding which requires additional investigation (Tesser, 1980). Furthermore, there is evidence to suggest that middle-class wives may influence their husbands' behaviour toward the child more than is the opposite case (Hoffman, 1963).

Presumably, in the low-conflict home where the husband agrees with his wife's childrearing practices, the father would gain the approval of the mother, thus facilitating the child's identification with him. Conversely, in the high-conflict home children would tend to "de-idealize" their parents and not identify, a situation which may be most pronounced in the relationship between divorcing parents (Hetherington, 1979). In this respect, conflict and divorce are like child abuse: they are "intimately related" to poverty (Brandwein, Brown and Fox, 1974). The poorer the family, the greater the incidence of divorce.

Why would a wife approve of her husband? Again one major reason is because he is successful in his career and has a sense of status, identity and generativity. If not, family stress may result, the husband may lose his wife's approval and consequently become less of a model with which his children can identify. In his important study of American families living through the Depression, Elder (1974) comments that unemployment and a sudden loss in income often severely disrupted relations between the husband and wife. In particular, the middle-class father suffered a loss in prestige before other family members. In some cases of extreme deprivation, the wife totally took over in making important financial and household decisions without her husband's consultation or knowledge. When economic hardship struck and the mother became the dominant figure in the household, the father then became vulnerable to criticism and ridicule as a poor provider. It was often seen as shameful that the mother had to fill the traditional male role of breadwinner.

In present-day working-class families, maternal employment may imply that the father has failed. Evidence from a Montreal study indicates difficulties in the father–son relationship (Gold and Andres, 1978). By contrast, middle-class mothers are employed in higher-status and better-paid occupations. They are more content with their work and are more likely to pursue careers out of achievement aspirations rather than economic necessity. Consequently, maternal employment can have positive ramifications provided it is not accompanied by guilt. In the middle-class family free of economic stress, both sons and daughters may have more valued perceptions of the employed mother. The children are encouraged to be independent and to share in household chores. In addition, the father tends to spend more time with his children.

But as Lois Wladis Hoffman (1979) has cautioned, the nature of the family in industrialized society is in rapid flux with increasing rates of divorce, as well as increasing rates of maternal employment even among women who remain married. For this reason, the present and future conditions underlying these changes may not be adequately characterized even by studies which are relatively recent. To this end, many areas of social and personality development remain to be explored, including comparisons of the effects of mother-custody and father-custody on children of divorced parents (for a start in this direction, see Santrock and Warshak, 1979).

8.4 Epilogue: Childrearing and Changing Socioeconomic Conditions

In summary, identification is associated with the development of a fair and principled morality based on rules and principles. The identification process may be enhanced under non-stressful economic conditions where provision is made for the needs of families outside of the breadwinner's efforts and abilities. In comparison, under economic stress, the quality of parent–child relations deteriorates and conflict between the parents may be accentuated. Children tend not to identify with parents and parents tend to neglect and even abuse children. All in all, the research on fairness and moral development permits six conclusions to be drawn:

1. A picture of fairness as a rational attribute in children is incomplete without an examination of the socioeconomic context of the family.

2. This context is associated with the nature of the affective-conative strivings underlying identification.

3. Cognitive development is an important part of moral development. The more intelligent the child, the more likely is he or she to comprehend and evaluate rules. However, a "cool" cognition alone cannot be equated with fairness. To this end, identification must be considered a possible, pervasive process in moral development, and as an integral feature of a "hot" cognition involving the thoughts and decisions that have high affective or conative importance to the person.

4. As the family may be the social unit most capable of generating rational influences, the family conditions under which identification is enhanced may be usefully examined.

5. In the case of rule-following behaviour, a socioeconomic context in which the needs of families are met may be most conducive for identification. Economic deprivation in the service of some particular ideology or interest group may have damaging effects on the stability of the family unit. It would be expected that if economic deterioration were curtailed or reversed, the quality of parent–child relations would improve.

6. In the case of principled behaviour and the fair and logical evaluation of rules, identification may be enhanced in families with an authoritative, democratic structure. These are led by parents who set high standards for their children and who encourage, with warmth and affection, the exercising of independent, rational judgment. Under such conditions, children may be stimulated to strive for fairness to disadvantaged persons. As Baldwin

(1899/1973, p.519) remarked years ago in discussing the conditions of a genuinely democratic society: "This is the socialist ideal; but it can be attained only by the rise of individuals who erect such an ideal *first in its personal form*" (original italics). That is, a just society which is fair to its less fortunate members can only be constituted by leaders in positions of social power who have been willing to make personal sacrifices without self-interest.

Behaviourism traditionally has served as the applied psychology of the *status quo*, of educators striving to maintain obedience in the classroom as well as of technologists aiming to consolidate top positions in a social hierarchy. Ironically, the cognitive revolution which was to replace behaviourism in the mainstream of psychology now appears to have filled a similar function (Sampson, 1981). As Cofer (1981, p.52) has recently lamented "Where, in cognitive theory, are the strong urges and the 'hot' emotions or passions which have been central to thinking in respect to motivation and emotion for so long?" In the case of moral development, the cognitive-developmental approach glosses over the affect and motivation which provide self-definition and meaning to the individual's moral rules and principles. By restricting itself to hypothetical moral dilemmas and the "cool" side of cognition, the approach has circumnavigated the historical and socioeconomic contexts of actual moral behaviour. Thus it misses much of the richness contained in the hot cognition of identification and gives an incomplete picture of children's fairness. Moreover, it does not in the least challenge the existing ideology and socioeconomic arrangements of society.

To give a fuller account of fairness, attention must be diverted to the historical and socioeconomic conditions of childhood. In this connection, it is clear that Western society is undergoing profound changes which will inevitably affect the structure of the family. The energy crisis—real or contrived—may result in less reliance on the automobile. Perhaps a sense of geographical closeness will be brought back, conducive to maintaining stable family communities in large urban areas. With the advent of global communication systems, other cultures, particularly in the Far East, may become a potent influence on the interconnected worlds of work and family.

With increasing maternal employment and economic independence, it might be expected that the male-dominated family is on the decline. Together with the increasing divorce rate and proportion of one-parent families, this phenomenon will almost certainly affect children's perceptions of their mothers and fathers in terms of the influence parents can wield over their children's moral development. In developing rational objectives for childrearing and moral education, there would seem to be no reason why fathers should not take on equally affectionate and warm roles and be every bit as "motherly" as actual mothers.

But the winds of change are blowing, and careful studies are required to document historical developments in family structure. The social and cognitive factors affecting children's fairness are in need of more extensive crosscultural and longitudinal study. There is a lot to be done.

References

Abegglen, J. C. *The Japanese factory: Aspects of its social organization*. Glencoe, Illinois: The Free Press, 1958.

Acock, A. C., and Bengtson, V. L. Socialization and attribution processes: actual versus perceived similarity among parents and youth. *Journal of Marriage and the Family*, 1980, *42*, 501–515.

Allen, V. L., and Newtson, D. Development of conformity and independence. *Journal of Personality and Social Psychology*, 1972, *22*, 18–30.

Appel, Y. H. Developmental differences in children's perception of maternal socialization behavior. *Child Development*, 1977, *48*, 1689–1693.

Arkoff, A., Meredith, G., and Iwahara, S. Male dominant and equalitarian attitudes in Japanese, Japanese-American, and Caucasian-American subjects. *Journal of Social Psychology*, 1964, *64*, 225–229.

Armsby, R. E. A reexamination of the development of moral judgments in children. *Child Development*, 1971, *42*, 1241–1248.

Aronfreed, J. The effects of experimental socialization paradigms upon two moral responses to transgression. *Journal of Abnormal and Social Psychology*, 1963, *66*, 437–448.

Aronfreed, J. The origins of self-criticism. *Psychological Review*, 1964, *71*, 193–218.

Aronfreed, J. The problem of imitation. In L. P. Lipsitt and H. Reese (Eds.), *Advances in child development and behaviour, Vol. 4*. New York and London: Academic Press, 1969.

Aronfreed, J., Cutick, R. A., and Fagan, S. A. Cognitive structure, punishment, and nurturance in the experimental induction of self-criticism. *Child Development*, 1963, *34*, 281–297.

Aronson, E., Bridgeman, D. L., and Geffner, R. The effects of cooperative classroom structure on student behavior and attitudes. In D. Bar-Tal and L. Saze (Eds.), *Social Psychology of Education*. Washington, D.C.: Hemisphere, 1978.

Austin, V. D., Ruble, D. N., and Trabasso, T. Recall and order effects as factors in children's moral judgments. *Child Development*, 1977, *48*, 470–474.

Bakeman, R., and Brown, J. V. Early interaction: Consequences for social and mental development at three years. *Child Development*, 1980, *51*, 437–447.

Baldus, B., and Tribe, V. The development of perceptions and evaluations of social inequality among public school children. *Canadian Review of Sociology and Anthropology*, 1978, *15*, 50–60.

Baldwin, J. M. *Social and ethical interpretations in mental development*, 2nd edition. London: Macmillan, 1899. (Reissued, Arno Press: New York, 1973.)

Baldwin, J. M. *Mental development in the child and the race*. London: Macmillan, 1906.

Bandura, A. Social-learning theory of identificatory processes. In D. A. Goslin (Ed.), *Handbook of socialization theory and research*, Chicago: Rand McNally, 1969.

Bandura, A. Analysis of modeling processes. In A. Bandura (Ed.), *Psychological modeling: Conflicting theories*. Chicago: Aldine, 1971.

Bandura, A. Self-reinforcement processes. In M. J. Mahoney and C. J. Thoresen (Eds.), *Self-control: Power to the person*. Monterey, California: Brooks-Cole, 1974.

Bandura, A. Self-efficacy: Towards a unifying theory of behavioural change. *Psychological Review*, 1977, *84*, 191–215(a).

Bandura, A. *Social learning theory*. Englewood Cliffs, New Jersey: Prentice-Hall, 1977(b).

Bandura, A. The self system in reciprocal determinism. *American Psychologist*, 1978, *33*, 344–358.

Bandura, A. Self-referent thought: The development of self-efficacy. In J. H. Flavell and L. D. Ross (Eds.), *Development of social cognition*. New York: Cambridge University Press, 1981.

Bandura, A., and McDonald, F. J. Influence of social reinforcement and the behaviour of models in shaping children's moral judgments. *Journal of Abnormal and Social Psychology*, 1963, *67*, 274–281.

Bandura, A., Adams, N. E., and Beyer, J. Cognitive processes mediating behavioral change. *Journal of Personality and Social Psychology*, 1977, *35*, 125–139.

Bandura, A., Grusec, J. E., and Menlove, F. L. Observational learning as a function of symbolization and inventive set. *Child Development*, 1966, *37*, 499–506.

Bandura, A., Ross, D., and Ross, S. A. Transmission of aggression through imitation of aggressive models. *Journal of Abnormal and Social Psycbology*, 1961, *63*, 575–582.

Baumrind, D. Current patterns of parental authority. *Developmental Psychology Monograph*, 1971, *4* (No. 1, Pt. 2).

Baumrind, D. The development of instrumental competence through socialization. *Minnesota Symposia on Child Psychology*, 1973, *7*, 3–46.

Baumrind, D. Socialization determinants of personal agency. Paper presented at the Biennial Meeting of the Society for Research in Child Development, New Orleans, 1977.

Bearison, D. J. The construct of regression: A Piagetian approach. *Merrill-Palmer Quarterly*, 1974, *20*, 21–30.

Bearison, D. J., and Isaacs, L. Production deficiency in children's moral judgments. *Developmental Psychology*, 1975, *11*, 732–737.

Beaudichon, J. Nature and instrumental function of private speech in problem-solving situations. *Merrill-Palmer Quarterly*, 1973, *19*, 117–135.

Bem, D., and Allen, A. On predicting some of the people some of the time: The search for cross-situational consistencies in behavior. *Psychological Review*, 1974, *81*, 506–520.

Berkowitz, L. Social norms, feelings, and other factors affecting helping behavior and altruism. In L. Berkowitz (Ed.), *Advances in experimental social psychology*. New York and London: Academic Press, 1972.

Berlyne, D. E. *Structure and direction in thinking*. New York: Wiley, 1965.

Berndt, T. J. The effect of reciprocity norms on moral judgment and causal attribution. *Child Development*, 1977, *48*, 1322–1330.

Berrien, F. K. Japanese values and the democratic process. *Journal of Social Psychology*, 1966, *68*, 129–138.

Bettelheim, B. Individual and mass behaviour in extreme situations. *Journal of Abnormal and Social Psychology*, 1943, *38*, 417–452.

Bixenstine, V. E., DeCorte, M. S. and Bixenstine, B. A. Conformity to peer-sponsored misconduct at four grade levels. *Developmental Psychology*, 1976, *12*, 226–236.

Bizman, A., Yinon, Y., Mivtzari, E., and Shavit, R. Effects of the age structure of the kindergarten on altruistic behaviour. *Journal of School Psychology*, 1978, *16*, 154–160.

Black, C. E., Jansen, M. B., Levine, H. S., Levy, M. J., Rosovsky, H., Rozman, G., Smith, H. D., and Starr, S. F. *The modernization of Japan and Russia*. New York: The Free Press, 1975.

Blaney, N. T., Stephan, C., Rosenfield, E., Aronson, E., and Sikes, J. Interdependence in the classroom: a field study. *Journal of Educational Psychology*, 1977, *69*, 121–128.

Blasi, A. Bridging moral cognition and moral action: A critical review of the literature. *Psychological Bulletin*, 1980, *88*, 1–45.

Blatt, M. M., and Kohlberg, L. The effects of classroom moral discussion upon children's level of moral judgement. *Journal of Moral Education*, 1975, *2*, 129–161.

Block, J. H., Haan, N., and Smith, M. B. Socialization correlates of student activism. *Journal of Social Issues*, 1969, *25*, 143–177.

Bloor, D. The regulatory function of language: An analysis and contribution to the current controversy over Soviet theory. In J. Morton and J. Marshall (Eds.), *Psycholinguistics: Developmental and pathological*. Ithaca, New York: Cornell University Press, 1977.

Boehm, L., and Nass, M. Social class differences in conscience development. *Child Development*, 1962, *33*, 565–574.

Bolstad, O. D., and Johnson, S. M. The relationship between teachers' assessment of students and the students' actual behaviour in the classroom. *Child Development*, 1977, *48*, 570–578.

Bowerman, C. E., and Bahr, S. J. Conjugal power and adolescent identification with parents. *Sociometry*, 1973, *36*, 366–377.

Bowers, K. S. Situationism in psychology: An analysis and a critique. *Psychological Review*, 1973, *80*, 307–336.

Bowlby, J. *Maternal care and mental health*. Geneva: World Health Organization, 1951.

Bowlby, J. *Child care and the growth of love*, 2nd edition. Harmondsworth, Middlesex: Penguin Books, 1965.

Bowlby, J. *Attachment*. London: Hogarth Press, 1969.

Bowlby, J., Ainsworth, M. D., Boston, M., and Rosenbluth, D. The effects of mother-child separation: A follow-up study. *British Journal of Medical Psychology*, 1956, *29*, 212–247.

Brainerd, C. J. Judgments and explanations as criteria for the presence of cognitive structures. *Psychological Bulletin*, 1973, *79*, 172–179.

Brandt, L. W. Behaviorism—The psychological buttress of late capitalism. In A. R. Buss (Ed.), *Psychology in a Social Context*. New York: Irvington, 1979.

Brandwein, R. A., Brown, C. A., and Fox, E. M. Women and children last: The social situation of divorced women and their families. *Journal of Marriage and the Family*, 1974, *36*, 498–514.

Braungart, R. G. Parental identification and student politics. *Sociology of Education*, 1971, *44*, 463–475.

Braungart, R. G. Youth and social movements. In S. E. Dragastin and G. H. Elder, Jr. (Eds.), *Adolescence in the life cycle: Psychological change and social context.*, New York: Wiley, 1975.

Brennan, F. G., Bjelke-Peterson, R. v., and another, *ex parte* Plunkett. *Melbourne University Law Review*, 1979, *12*, 284–291.

Breznitz, S., and Kugelmass, S. Intentionality in moral judgment: Developmental stages. *Child Development*, 1967, *38*, 469–479.

Britton, J. H., and Britton, J. O. Children's perceptions of their parents: A comparison of Finnish and American children. *Journal of Marriage and the Family*, 1971, *33*, 214–218.

Brodbeck, A. J. Language, consciousness and character education: A sketch of social science conflict with some resolutions. In C. H. Faust and J. Feingold (Eds.), *Approaches to education for character: Strategies for change in higher education*. New York: Columbia University Press, 1969.

Brody, G. H., and Henderson, R. W. Effects of multiple model variations and rationale provision on the moral judgments and explanations of young children. *Child Development*, 1977, *48*, 1117–1120.

Bronckart, J. P. The regulating role of speech: A cognitivist approach. *Human Development*, 1973, *16*, 417–439.

Bronfenbrenner, U. Freudian theories of identification and their derivatives. *Child Development*, 1960, *31*, 15–40.

Bronfenbrenner, U. Response to pressure from peers versus adults among Soviet and American school children. *International Journal of Psychology*, 1967, *2*, 199–207.

Bronfenbrenner, U. Reaction to social pressure from adults versus peers among Soviet day-school and boarding-school pupils in the perspective of an American sample. *Journal of Personality and Social Psychology*, 1970, *15*, 179–189(a).

Bronfenbrenner, U. *Two worlds of childhood*. New York: Russell Sage Foundation, 1970(b).

Bronfenbrenner, U. *A report on longitudinal evaluations of pre-school programs. Vol. 2. Is early intervention effective?* Washington, D.C.: D.H.E.W. Publication No. (OHD) 74-25, 1974.

Bronfenbrenner, U. Toward an experimental ecology of human development. *American Psychologist*, 1977, *32*, 514–532.

Broughton, J. M. The cognitive-developmental approach to morality: A reply to Kurtines and Greif. *Journal of Moral Education*, 1978, *8*, 81–96.

Brown, G. *Sabotage*. Nottingham: Spokesman Books, 1977.

Brown, R. *Social Psychology*. New York: Collier-Macmillan, 1965.

Bruner, J. S. The course of cognitive growth. *American Psychologist*, 1964, *19*, 1–15.

Bryan, J. H. You will be advised to watch what we do instead of what we say. In D. J. DePalma and J. H. Foley (Eds.), *Moral development: Current theory and research*. Hillsdale, New Jersey: Lawrence Erlbaum Associates, 1975.

Bryant, P. E. Critical notice. *Journal of Child Psychology and Psychiatry*, 1971, *12*, 305–311.

Bryant, P. E. *Perception and understanding in young children*. London: Methuen, 1974.

Buckley, N., Siegel, L. S., and Ness, S. Egocentrism, empathy, and altruistic behaviour in young children. *Developmental Psychology*, 1979, *15*, 329–330.

Burt, C. Experimental tests of general intelligence. *British Journal of Psychology*, 1909, *3*, 94–177.

Burton, R. V. Generality of honesty reconsidered. *Psychological Review*, 1963, *70*, 481–499.

Burton, R. V. Honesty and dishonesty. In T. Lickona (Ed.), *Moral development and behaviour*. London: Holt, Rinehart and Winston, 1978.

Cairns, R. B. *Social development*. San Francisco: W. H. Freeman, 1979.

Candee, D. Structure and choice in moral reasoning. *Journal of Personality and Social Psychology*, 1976, *34*, 1293–1301.

Caudill, W. The influence of social structure and culture on human behaviour in modern Japan. *Journal of Nervous and Mental Diseases*, 1973, *157*, 240–257.

Caudill, W., and Frost, L. A comparison of maternal care and infant behavior in Japanese-American, American, and Japanese families. In W. P. Lebra (Ed.), *Youth, socialization and mental health*. Honolulu: University Press of Hawaii, 1974.

Caudill, W., and Plath, D. W. Who sleeps by whom? Parent-child involvement in urban Japanese families. *Psychiatry*, 1966, *29*, 344–366.

Chandler, M. J., Siegal, M., and Boyes, M. C. The development of moral behavior: Continuities and discontinuities. *International Journal of Behavioral Development*. 1980, *3*, 323–332.

Chomsky, N. *Syntactic structures*. The Hague: Mouton, 1957.

Chomsky, N., and Herman, E. S. *The Washington connection and third world fascism: The political economy of human rights*. Boston: South End Press, 1980.

Clarke, A. M., and Clarke, A. D. B. (Eds.), *Early experience: Myth and evidence*. London: Open Books, 1976.

Cofer, C. N. The history of the concept of motivation. *Journal of the History of the Behavioral Sciences*, 1981, *17*, 48–53.

Cogswell, F. Some defects in modern Canadian poetry. *Pacific Quarterly*, 1979, *4*, 192–196.

Cohen, D. *J. B. Watson: The founder of behaviourism: a biography*. London: Routledge and Kegan Paul, 1979.

Cohen, G. *The psychology of cognition*. London and New York: Academic Press, 1977.

Cohen, L. J. On the psychology of prediction: Whose is the fallacy? *Cognition*, 1979, *7*, 385–407.

Cohen, L. J. Whose is the fallacy? A rejoinder to Daniel Kahneman and Amos Tversky. *Cognition*, 1980, *8*, 89–92.

Cohen, R. Altruism: Human cultural or what? In L. Wispe (Ed.), *Altruism, sympathy and helping. Psychological and sociological principles*. New York and London: Academic Press, 1978.

Cohen, S. E., and Beckwith, L. Preterm infant interaction with the caregiver in the first year of life and competence at age two. *Child Development*, 1979, *50*, 767–776.

Colby, A. Evolution of a moral-developmental theory. In W. Damon (Ed.) *New directions in child development, Number 2*. San Francisco: Jossey-Bass, 1978.

Colby, A., Kohlberg, L., and Gibbs, J. A longitudinal study of moral development. Paper presented at the Biennial Meeting of the Society for Research in Child Development, San Francisco, 1979.

Conroy, M., Hess, R. D., Azuma, H., and Kashiwagi, K. Maternal strategies for regulating children's behavior: Japanese and American families. *Journal of Cross-Cultural Psychology*, 1980, *11*, 153–172.

Constanzo, P. R., Grumet, J. F., and Brehm, S. S. The effects of choice and source of constraint on children's attribution of preference. *Journal of Experimental Social Psychology*, 1974, *10*, 352–364.

Cook, H., and Stingle, S. Co-operative behaviour in children. *Psychological Bulletin*, 1974, *81*, 918–933.

Coombs, J. R., and Meux, M. Teaching strategies for value analysis. In L. E. Metcalf (Ed.), *Values education*. Washington, D.C.: National Council for the Social Sciences, 1971.

Cowan, P. A., Langer, J., Heavenrich, J., and Nathanson, M. Social learning and Piaget's cognitive theory of moral development. *Journal of Personality and Social Psychology*, 1969, *11*, 261–274.

Cowdry, R. A., Keniston, K., and Cabin, S. The war and military obligations: Private attitudes and public actions. *Journal of Personality*, 1970, *38*, 525–549.

Crockenberg, S. B., and Nicolayev, J. Stage transition in moral reasoning as related to conflict experienced in naturalistic settings. *Merrill-Palmer Quarterly*, 1979, *25*, 185–192.

Cronbach, L. J., and Meehl, P. E. Construct validity in psychological tests. *Psychological Bulletin*, 1955, *52*, 281–302.

Damon, W. *The social world of the child.* San Francisco: Jossey-Bass, 1977.

Damon, W. Why study social-cognitive development? *Human Development*, 1979, *22*, 206–211.

Danziger, K. *Socialization.* Harmondsworth, Middlesex: Penguin Books, 1971.

Danziger, K. The social origins of modern psychology. In A. R. Buss (Ed.), *Psychology in a Social Context*, New York: Irvington, 1979.

Darlington, R. B., Royce, J. M., Snipper, A. S., Murray, H. W., and Lazar, I. Preschool programs and later school competence of children from low-income families. *Science*, 1980, *208*, 202–204.

Davidson, F. H. Ability to respect persons compared to ethnic prejudice in childhood. *Journal of Personality and Social Psychology*, 1976, *34*, 1256–1267.

De Vos, G. A. *Socialization for achievement.* Berkeley: University of California Press, 1973.

DeVries, R. Relationships among Piagetian, IQ, and achievement assessments. *Child Development*, 1974, *45*, 746–756.

Deardon, R. F. *The philosophy of primary education.* London: Routledge and Kegan Paul, 1968.

Deci, E. L., and Ryan, R. M. The empirical exploration of intrinsic motivation processes. In L. Berkowitz (Ed.), *Advances in Experimental Social Psychology, Volume 13.* New York and London: Academic Press, 1980.

Dembroski, T. M., and Pennebaker, J. W. Reactions to severity and nature of threat among children of dissimilar socioeconomic levels. *Journal of Personality and Social Psychology*, 1975, *31*, 338–342.

Dennis, W. Animism and related tendencies in Hopi children. *Journal of Applied Social Psychology*, 1943, *38*, 21–37.

Depalma, D. J., and Foley, D. J. *Moral development: Current theory and research.* Hillsdale, New Jersey: Lawrence Erlbaum Associates, 1975.

Devereux, E. C. The role of peer-group experience in moral development. In J. P. Hill (Ed.), *Minnesota Symposia on Child Psychology, Vol. 4.* Minneapolis: University of Minnesota Press, 1970.

Dienstbier, R. A., Hillman, D., Lehnhoff, J., Hillman, J. and Valkenaar, M. C. An emotion-attribution approach to moral behaviour: Interfacing cognitive and avoidance theories of moral development. *Psychological Review*, 1975, *82*, 299–315.

Dlugokinski, E. L., and Firestone, I. J. Other-centredness and susceptibility to charitable appeals: Effects of perceived discipline. *Developmental Psychology*, 1974, *10*, 21–28.

Dodwell, P. C. Relation between the understanding of the logic of classes and of cardinal number in children. *Canadian Journal of Psychology*, 1962, *16*, 152–160.

Donaldson, M. *Children's minds.* Glasgow: Fontana, 1978.

Dooley, D., and Catalano, R. Economic change as a cause of behavioral disorder. *Psychological Bulletin*, 1980, *87*, 450–468.

Dorr, D., and Fry, S. Relative power of symbolic adult and peer models in the modification of children's moral choice behavior. *Journal of Personality and Social Psychology*, 1974, *29*, 335–341.

Druck, A. B. Recognition of sentences with moral themes: Developmental aspects of organization in memory. Unpublished doctoral dissertation, Adelphi University, 1974.

Ebbeson, E. B., Bowers, R. J., Phillips, S., and Snyder, M. Self-control processes in the forbidden toy paradigm. *Journal of Personality and Social Psychology*, 1975, *31*, 442–452.

Edelman, M. S., and Omark, D. R. Dominance hierarchies in young children. *Social Science Information*, 1973, *12*, 103–110.

Edwards, C. P., and Lewis, M. Young children's concepts of social relations: Social functions and social objects. In M. Lewis and L. A. Rosenblum (Eds.), *The child and its family*. New York: Plenum, 1979.

Eisenberg, P., and Lazarsfeld, P. F. The psychological effects of unemployment. *Psychological Bulletin*, 1938, *35*, 358–390.

Eisenberg-Berg, N. Development of children's prosocial moral judgment. *Developmental Psychology*, 1979, *15*, 128–137.

Eisenberg-Berg, N., and Hand, M. The relationship of preschoolers' reasoning about prosocial moral conflicts to moral behaviour. *Child Development*, 1979, *50*, 356–363.

Elardo, P. T., and Caldwell, B. M. The effects of an experimental social development program on children in the middle childhood period. *Psychology in the Schools*, 1979, *16*, 93–100.

Elder, G. H. Parental power legitimation and its effect on the adolescent. *Sociometry*, 1963, *26*, 50–65.

Elder, G. H. *Children of the Great Depression*. Chicago: University of Chicago Press, 1974.

Elkind, D. *Children in adolescence: Interpretive essays on Jean Piaget*. New York: Oxford University Press, 1970.

Elkind, D., and Dabek, R. F. Personal injury and property damage in the moral judgements of children. *Child Development*, 1977, *48*, 518–522.

Epstein, S. The stability of behaviour: I. On predicting most of the people much of the time. *Journal of Personality and Social Psychology*, 1979, *37*, 1097–1126.

Epstein, S. The stability of behaviour: II. Implications for psychological research. *American Psychologist*, 1980, *35*, 790–806.

Erikson, E. H. *Identity: Youth and crisis*. New York: Norton, 1968.

Farrell, B. A. Psychoanalytic theory. *New Scientist, June*, 1963.

Farrell, B. A. *The standing of psychoanalysis*. Oxford: Oxford University Press, 1981.

Feldman, N. S., Klosson, E. C., Parsons, J. E., Rholes, W. S., and Ruble, D. N. Order of information presentation and children's moral judgements. *Child Development*, 1976, *47*, 556–559.

Feuer, L. S. *The conflict of generations: The character and significance of student movements*. New York: Basic Books, 1969.

Fishbein, M., and Azjen, I. Attribution of responsibility: A theoretical note. *Journal of Experimental Social Psychology*, 1973, *9*, 148–153.

Fishkin, J., Keniston, K., and MacKinnon, C. Moral reasoning and political ideology. *Journal of Personality and Social Psychology*, 1973, *27*, 109–119.
Fishman, J. R., and Solomon, F. Youth and social action: I. Perspectives on the student sit-in movement. *American Journal of Orthopsychiatry*, 1963, *33*, 872–882.
Flacks, R. The liberated generation: An exploration of the roots of student protest. *Journal of Social Issues*, 1967, *23*, 52–75.
Flavell, J. H. Stage-related properties of cognitive development. *Cognitive Psychology*, 1971, *2*, 421–453.
Flavell, J. H. An analysis of cognitive-developmental sequences. *Genetic Psychology Monographs*, 1972, *86*, 279–350.
Flavell, J. H., and Wohlwill, J. F. Formal and functional aspects of cognitive development. In D. Elkind and J. H. Flavell (Eds.), *Studies in cognitive development*. New York: Oxford University Press, 1969.
Ford, M. E. The construct of egocentrism. *Psychological Bulletin*, 1979, *86*, 1169–1188.
Forsyth, D. R. A taxonomy of ethical ideologies. *Journal of Personality and Social Psychology*, 1980, *39*, 175–184.
Frager, R. Conformity and anti-conformity in Japan. *Journal of Personality and Social Psychology*, 1970, *15*, 203–210.
Freedman, J. L., and Fraser, S. C. Compliance without pressure: The foot-in-the-door technique. *Journal of Personality and Social Psychology*, 1966, *4*, 195–202.
Freud, A., and Dann, S. An experiment in group upbringing. In R. Eissler *et al.* (Eds.), *The Psychonanalytic Study of the Child. Vol. 6*. New York: International Universities Press, 1951.
Freud, S. *An autobiographical study*. London: Hogarth Press, 1935.
Freud, S. *The origins of psychoanalysis*. London: Image Press, 1954.
Freud, S. *Civilization and its discontents*. London: Hogarth Press, 1961 (originally published, 1930).
Freud, S. The ego and the id. In J. Strachey (Ed.), *The complete psychological works of Sigmund Freud. Vol. XIX*, London: Hogarth Press, 1961 (originally published, 1923).
Freud, S., and Breuer, J. *Studies on hysteria*. London: Hogarth Press, 1956.
Friedman, M. *Capitalism and freedom*. Chicago: University of Chicago Press, 1962.
Furman, W., and Masters, J. C. Peer influence on resistance to deviation. *Developmental Psychology*, 1980, *16*, 229–236.
Furman, W., Rahe, D. F., and Hartup, W. W. Rehabilitation of socially withdrawn preschool children through mixed-age and same-age socialization. *Child Development*, 1979, *50*, 915–922.
Furth, H. G. Young children's understanding of society. In H. McGurk (Ed.), *Issues in childhood social development*. London: Methuen, 1978.
Furth, H. G., Baur, M., and Smith, J. E. Children's conceptions of social institutions: A Piagetian framework. *Human Development*, 1976, *19*, 341–347.
Garbarino, J., and Brofenbrenner, U. *The socialization of moral judgement and behaviour in cross-cultural perspective*. New York: Holt, Rinehart and Winston, 1976.
Garbarino, J., and Sherman, D. High risk neighborhoods and high risk families: The human ecology of child maltreatment. *Child Development*, 1980, *51*, 188–198.
Gibbs, J. C. Kohlberg's stages of moral judgment: A constructive critique. *Harvard Educational Review*, 1977, *47*, 43–61.
Gil, D. G. Violence against children. *Journal of Marriage and the Family*, 1971, *33*, 637–647.

Giovannoni, J., and Billingsley, A. Child neglect among the poor: A study of parental inadequacy in families of three ethnic groups. *Child Welfare*, 1970, *49*, 196–204.

Gold, D., and Andres, D. Developmental comparisons between ten-year-old children with employed and nonemployed mothers. *Child Development*, 1978, *49*, 75–84.

Goldfarb, W. Effects of psychological deprivation in infancy and subsequent stimulation. *American Journal of Psychiatry*, 1945, *102*, 18–33.

Goldschmidt, M. L. T., and Bentler, P. M. *Concept Assessment Kit*. San Diego: Educational Testing Service, 1968.

Gottman, J., Gonso, J., and Rasmussen, B. Social interaction, social competence, and friendship in children. *Child Development*, 1975, *46*, 709–718.

Grim, P. F., Kohlberg, L., and White, S. H. Some relationships between conscience and attentional processes. *Journal of Personality and Social Psychology*, 1968, *8*, 239–252.

Grusec, J., and Ezrin, S. A. Techniques of punishment and the development of self-criticism. *Child Development*, 1972, *43*, 1273–1288.

Grusec, J. E. Some antecedents of self-criticism. *Journal of Personality and Social Psychology*, 1966, *4*, 244–252.

Grusec, J. E., Kuczynski, J., Rushton, P., and Simutis, Z. M. Modelling direct instruction and attributions: Effects on altruism. *Developmental Psychology*, 1978, *14*, 51–57.

Gutkin, D. C. The effect of systematic story changes on intentionality in children's moral judgments. *Child Development*, 1972, *43*, 187–195.

Haan, N. Hypothetical and actual moral reasoning in a situation of civil disobedience. *Journal of Personality and Social Psychology*, 1975, *32*, 255–270.

Haan, N. Two moralities in action contexts: Relationships to thought, ego regulation, and development. *Journal of Personality and Social Psychology*, 1978, *36*, 286–305.

Haan, N., Langer, J., and Kohlberg, L. Family patterns of moral reasoning. *Child Development*, 1976, *47*, 1204–1206.

Haan, N., Smith, M. B., and Block, J. Moral reasoning of young adults: Political-social behaviour, family background, and personality correlates. *Journal of Personality and Social Psychology*, 1968, *10*, 183–201.

Habermas, J. *Legitimation Crisis*. Boston: Beacon Press, 1975.

Halford, G. S. *The development of thought*. Hillsdale, New Jersey: Lawrence Erlbaum Associates, 1982.

Hamlyn, D. W. The logical and psychological aspects of learning. In R. S. Peters (Ed.), *The concept of education*. London: Routledge and Kegan Paul, 1967.

Harari, H., and McDavid, J. W. Situational influence on moral justice: a study of "finking". *Journal of Personality and Social Psychology*, 1969, *11*, 240–244.

Hare, R. M. *The language of morals*. Oxford: Oxford University Press, 1952.

Hare, R. M. *Freedom and reason*. Oxford: Oxford University Press, 1963.

Hare, R. M. On terrorism. *Journal of Value Inquiry*, 1979, *13*, 241–249.

Harris, M. B. The effects of performing one altruistic act on the likelihood of performing another. *Journal of Social Psychology*, 1972, *88*, 65–73.

Harrower, M. R. Social status and the moral development of the child. *British Journal of Educational Psychology*, 1934, *4*, 75–95.

Hartig, N., and Kanfer, F. H. The role of verbal self-instructions in children's resistance to temptation. *Journal of Personality and Social Psychology*, 1968, *25*, 259–267.

Hartshorne, H., and May, M. A. *Studies in the nature of character. Vol. I: Studies in deceit*. New York: Macmillan, 1928.

Hartshorne, H., May, M. A., and Maller, J. B. *Studies in the nature of character. Vol. II: Studies in self-control*. New York: Macmillan, 1929.

Hartshorne, H., May, M. A., and Shuttleworth, F. K. *Studies in the nature of character. Vol. III: Studies in the organization of character*. New York: Macmillan, 1930.

Havighurst, R. J., and Neugarten, B. L. *American Indian and white children*. Chicago: University of Chicago, 1955.

Hebb, D. O. What psychology is about. *American Psychologist*, 1974, *29*, 71–87.

Hebble, P. W. The development of elementary schoolchildren's judgment of intent. *Child Development*, 1971, *42*, 1203–1215.

Heirich, M. *The spiral of conflict*. New York: Columbia University Press, 1971.

Helper, M. M. Learning theory and the self concept. *Journal of Abnormal and Social Psychology*, 1955, *51*, 184–194.

Henle, M. Why study the history of psychology? *Annals of the New York Academy of Science*, 1976, *270*, 14–20.

Herbert, E. A., Gelfand, D. M., and Hartman, D. P. Imitation and self-esteem as determinants of self-critical behaviour. *Child Development*, 1969, *40*, 421–430.

Hess, J. L. Piaget sees science dooming psychoanalysis. *New York Times, 19 October*, 1972.

Hetherington, E. M. Divorce: A child's perspective. *American Psychologist*, 1979, *34*, 851–858.

Hetherington, E. M., and Frankie, G. Effects of parental dominance, warmth and conflict on imitation in children. *Journal of Personality and Social Psychology*, 1967, *6*, 119–125.

Higgins, E. T. Social class differences in verbal communicative accuracy: A question of "which question?". *Psychological Bulletin*, 1976, *83*, 695–714.

Hilgard, E. R. The trilogy of mind: Cognition, affection, and conation. *Journal of the History of the Behavioral Sciences*, 1980, *16*, 107–117.

Hinde, R. A. *Biological bases of human behaviour*. New York: McGraw-Hill, 1974.

Hoffman, L. W. Maternal employment: 1979. *American Psychologist*, 1979, *34*, 859–865.

Hoffman, M. L. Personality, family structure, and social class as antecedents of parental power assertion. *Child Development*, 1963, *34*, 869–884.

Hoffman, M. L. Moral development. In P. Mussen (Ed.), *Carmichael's manual of child psychology*, 3rd edition. New York: Wiley, 1970.

Hoffman, M. L. Identification and conscience development. *Child Development*, 1971, *42*, 1071–1082.

Hoffman, M. L. Altruistic behavior and the parent–child relationship. *Journal of Personality and Social Psychology*, 1975. *31*, 937–943(a).

Hoffman, M. L. Moral internalization, parental power, and the nature of parent–child interaction. *Developmental Psychology*, 1975, *11*, 228–239(b).

Hoffman, M. L. Empathy, role-taking, guilt, and development of altruistic motives. In T. Lickona (Ed.), *Moral development and behavior*. New York: Holt, Rinehart and Winston, 1976.

Hoffman, M. L. Personality and social development. *Annual Review of Psychology*, 1977, *28*, 295–321(a).

Hoffman, M. L. Sex differences in empathy and related behaviours. *Psychological Bulletin*, 1977, *84*, 712–722(b).

Hoffman, M. L. Development of moral thought, feeling and behavior. *American Psychologist*, 1979, *34*, 958–966.
Hoffman, M. L. Moral development in adolescence. In J. Adelson (Ed.), *Handbook of adolescent psychology*. New York: Wiley, 1980.
Hoffman, M. L., and Saltzstein, H. D. Parent discipline and the child's moral development. *Journal of Personality and Social Psychology*, 1967, *5*, 45–57.
Hogan, R. Theoretical egocentrism and the problem of compliance. *American Psychologist*, 1975, *30*, 533–540.
Holden, C. Innovation: Japan races ahead as U.S. falters. *Science*, 1980, *210*, 751–754.
Hollos, M. and Cowan, P. A. Social isolation and cognitive development: logical operations and role-taking abilities in three Norwegian school settings. *Child Development*, 1973, *44*, 630–641.
Holstein, C. B. Irreversible, stepwise sequence in the development of moral judgment: A longitudinal study of males and females. *Child Development*, 1976, *47*, 51–61.
Hook, J. G., and Cook, T. D. Equity theory and the cognitive ability of children. *Psychological Bulletin*, 1979, *86*, 429–445.
Horn, J. L., and Knott, P. D. Activist youth of the 1960's: Summary and prognosis. *Science*, 1971, *171*, 979–985.
Houssiadas, L., and Brown, L. B. Egocentrism in language and space perception: an examination of the concept. *Genetic Psychology Monographs*, 1980, *101*, 183–214.
Hull, C. L. *Principles of behavior*. New York: Appleton-Century-Crofts, 1943.
Hunt, J. McV. Psychological development: Early experience. In L. W. Porter and M. R. Rosenweig (Eds.), *Annual Review of Psychology, Vol. 30*. Palo Alto, California: Annual Reviews, 1979.
Ianotti, R. J. Effect of role-taking experiences on role-taking, empathy, altruism and aggression. *Developmental Psychology*, 1978, *14*, 119–124.
Imamoglu, E. O. Children's awareness and usage of intention cues. *Child Development*, 1975, *46*, 39–45.
Inhelder, B., and Piaget, J. *The growth of logical thinking from childhood to adolescence*. New York: Basic Books, 1958.
Inhelder, B., Bovet, M., and Sinclair, H. Developpement et apprentissage. *Psychologie*, 1967, *26*, 1–23.
Jahoda, G. Immanent justice among West African children. *Journal of Social Psychology*, 1958, *47*, 241–248.
Jahoda, G. The construction of economic reality by some Glaswegian children. *Journal of Social Psychology*, 1979, *9*, 115–127.
Jahoda, M. The impact of unemployment in the 1930's and the 1970's. *Bulletin of the British Psychological Society*, 1979, *32*, 309–314.
James, W. *The principles of psychology, Vol. II*. London: Macmillan, 1890.
Jarvis, P. E. Verbal control of sensori-motor performance: A test of Luria's hypothesis. *Human Development*, 1968, *11*, 172–183.
Jensen, L. C., and Hughston, K. The relationship between type of sanction, story content, and children's judgments which are independent of sanction. *Journal of Genetic Psychology*, 1973, *122*, 49–54.
Jensen, L. C., and Murray, M. Facilitating development of four moral concepts among kindergarten and first grade children. *Journal of Educational Psychology*, 1978, *70*, 936–944.

Johnson, R. C. A study of children's moral judgement. *Child Development*, 1962, *33*, 327–354.

Kadushin, A. *Adopting older children.* New York: Columbia University Press, 1970.

Kadushin, C. The managed texts: Prose and qualms. *Change, March*, 1979.

Kagan, J. The concept of identification. *Psychological Review*, 1958, *65*, 296–305.

Kagan, J., and Klein, R. E. Cross-cultural perspectives on early development. *American Psychologist*, 1974, *28*, 947–961.

Kagan, J., Lapidus, D. R., and Moore, M. Infant antecendents of cognitive functioning: A longitudinal study. *Child Development*, 1978, *49*, 1005–1023.

Kagan, S., and Madsen, M. C. Experimental analyses of cooperation and competition of Anglo-American and Mexican children. *Developmental Psychology*, 1972, *6*, 49–59.

Kahneman, D., and Tversky, A. On the psychology of prediction. *Psychological Review*, 1973, *80*, 237–251.

Kahneman, D., and Tversky, A. On the interpretation of intuitive probability: a reply to Jonathan Cohen. *Cognition*, 1979, *7*, 409–411.

Kalish, R. A., Mahoney, M., and Arkoff, A. Cross-cultural comparisons of college student marital role preferences. *Journal of Social Psychology*, 1966, *68*, 41–47.

Kandel, D., and Lesser, G. S. Parent–adolescent relationships and adolescent independence in the United States and Denmark. *Journal of Marriage and the Family*, 1969, *31*, 348–358.

Kanfer, F. H., and Duerfeldt, P. H. Age, class standing, and commitment as determinants of cheating in children. *Child Development*, 1968, *39*, 545–557.

Karniol, R., and Ross, M. The development of causal attributions in social perception. *Journal of Personality and Social Psychology*, 1976, *34*, 455–464.

Keasey, C. B. Implications of cognitive development for moral reasoning. In D. J. DePalma and J. M. Foley (Eds.), *Moral development: current theory and research*, Hillsdale, New Jersey: Lawrence Erlbaum Associates, 1975.

Keniston, K. The sources of student dissent. *Journal of Social Issues*, 1967, *23*, 108–137.

Keniston, K. *Radicals and militants.* Lexington, Massachusetts: D. C. Heath, 1973.

Kessen, W. *The child.* New York: John Wiley, 1965.

Kiefer, C. W. The psychological interdependence of family, school, and bureaucracy in Japan. *American Anthropologist*, 1970, *72*, 66–75.

Knight, G. P., and Kagan, S. Acculturation of prosocial and competitive behaviors among second and third-generation Mexican-American children. *Journal of Cross-Cultural Psychology*, 1977, *8*, 273–284(a).

Knight, G. P., and Kagan, S. Development of prosocial and competitive behaviours in Anglo-American and Mexican-American children. *Child Development*, 1977, *48*, 1385–1394(b).

Koestler, A. *The ghost in the machine.* London: Hutchinson, 1967.

Kohlberg, L. The development of modes of moral thinking and choice in the years ten to sixteen. Unpublished doctoral dissertation, University of Chicago, 1958.

Kohlberg, L. Moral development and identification. In H. Stevenson (Ed.), *Child psychology: 62nd yearbook of the National Society for the Study of Education*, Chicago: University of Chicago Press, 1963(a).

Kohlberg, L. The development of children's orientations toward a moral order. I. Sequence in the development of moral thought. *Human Development*, 1963, *6*, 11–33(b).

Kohlberg, L. Stage and sequence: the cognitive-developmental approach to socialization. In D. A. Goslin (Ed.), *Handbook of socialization theory and research*, Chicago: Rand McNally, 1969.

Kohlberg, L. Stages of moral development as a basis for moral education. In C. M. Beck, B. S. Crittenden, and E. V. Sullivan (Eds.), *Moral education: Interdisciplinary approaches*. Toronto: University of Toronto Press, 1971.

Kohlberg, L. Continuities in childhood and adult moral development revisited. In P. B. Baltes and K. W. Schale (Eds.), *Life span developmental psychology: Personality and Socialization*. New York and London: Academic Press, 1973.

Kohlberg, L. Moral stages and moralization: the cognitive-developmental approach. In T. Lickona (Ed.), *Moral development and behavior*. New York: Holt, Rinehart and Winston, 1976.

Kohlberg, L. The measurement and meaning of moral development. Paper presented at the 86th Annual Convention of the American Psychological Association, Toronto, 1978(a).

Kohlberg, L. Revisions in theory and practice of moral development. In W. Damon (Ed.), *New directions in child development*, Volume 2. San Francisco: Jossey-Bass, 1978(b).

Kohlberg, L., and Elfenbein, D. The development of moral judgements concerning capital punishment. *American Journal of Orthopsychiatry*, 1975, *45*, 614–640.

Kohlberg, L., and Gilligan, C. The adolescent as philosopher: the discovery of self in a postconventional world. *Daedalus*, 1971, *100*, 1051–1086.

Kohlberg, L., and Kramer, R. B. Continuities and discontinuities in childhood and adult moral development. *Human Development*, 1969, *12*, 93–120.

Kohlberg, L., and Mayer, R. Development as the aim of education. *Harvard Educational Review*, 1972, *42*, 449–496.

Kohlberg, L., and Turiel, E. Moral development and moral education. In G. S. Lesser (Ed.), *Psychology and educational practice*. Glenview, Illinois: Scott Foresman, 1971.

Kohlberg, L., Colby, A., Gibbs, J., Speicher-Dubin, B., and Power, C. Assessing moral stages: a manual. Unpublished manuscript, Harvard University, 1977.

Kohn, M., and Rosman, B. L. A social competence scale and symptom checklist for the preschool child: Factor dimensions, theory cross-instrument generality, and longitudinal persistence. *Developmental Psychology*, 1972, *6*, 445–452.

Kohn, M. L. Social class and parent–child relationships: an interpretation. *American Journal of Sociology*, 1968, *74*, 47–480.

Kraut, R. E., and Lewis, S. H. Alternate models of family influence on student political ideology. *Journal of Personality and Social Psychology*, 1975, *31*, 791–800.

Krebs, D., and Rosenwald, A. Moral reasoning and moral behavior in young adults. *Merrill-Palmer Quarterly*, 1977, *23*, 77–87.

Krebs, D. L. Altruism—An examination of the concept and a review of the literature. *Psychological Bulletin*, 1970, *73*, 258–302.

Kuhn, D. Imitation theory and research from a cognitive perspective. *Human Development*, 1973, *16*, 157–180.

Kuhn, D. Short-term longitudinal evidence for the sequentiality of Kohlberg's early stages of moral judgement. *Developmental Psychology*, 1976, *12*, 162–166.

Kuhn, T. S. *The structure of scientific revolutions*, 2nd edition. Chicago: University of Chicago Press, 1970.

Kurdek, L. E. Perspective taking as the cognitive basis of children's moral development: a review of the literature. *Merrill-Palmer Quarterly*, 1978, *24*, 3–28.

Kurtines, W., and Greif, E. B. The development of moral thought: Review and evaluation of Kohlberg's approach. *Psychological Bulletin*, 1974, *81*, 453–470.

LaVoie, J. C. Cognitive determinants of resistance to deviation in seven-, nine-, and eleven-year-old children of low and high maturiry of moral judgement. *Developmental Psychology*, 1974, *10*, 393–403.

Lamb, M. E. (Ed.), *The role of the father in child development*. New York: Wiley, 1976.

Lane, J., and Anderson, N. H. Integration of intention and outcome in moral judgement. *Memory and Cognition*, 1976, *4*, 1–5.

Langston, K. P. *Political socialization*. New York: Oxford, 1969.

Lebra, T. S. *Japanese patterns of behaviour*. Honolulu: University Press of Hawaii, 1976.

Lee, L. C. The concomitant development of cognitive and moral modes of thought: A test of selected deductions from Piaget's theory. *Genetic Psychology Monographs*, 1971, *83*, 93–146.

Lee, L. C. *Personality development in childhood*. Monterey, California: Brooks/Cole, 1976.

Leeds, R. Altruism and the norm of giving. *Merrill-Palmer Quarterly*, 1963, *9*, 226–236.

Lemerise, T., and Pinard, A. Synchronie ou asynchronism génétique dans la solution d'un ensemble de tâches numériques élémentaires. *Enfance*, 1971, *jan.-mars*, 17–30.

Leming, J. S. Intrapersonal variations in stage of moral reasoning among adolescents as a function of situational context. *Journal of Youth and Adolescence*, 1978, *4*, 405–416.

Lenneberg, E. H. *Biological foundations of language*. New York: Wiley, 1976.

Lepper, M. R. Dissonance, self-perception and honesty in children. *Journal of Personality and Social Psychology*, 1973, *25*, 65–74.

Lepper, M. R., Green, D., and Nisbett, R. E. Undermining children's intrinsic interest with extrinsic reward: A test of the over-justification hypothesis. *Journal of Personality and Social Psychology*, 1973, *28*, 129–137.

Lerner, E. *Constraint and the moral judgement of children*. Menasha, Wisconsin: Banta, 1937(a).

Lerner, E. The problem of perspective in moral reasoning. *American Journal of Sociology*, 1937, *43*, 249–269(b).

Lerner, M. J., and Miller, D. T. Just world research and the attribution process: Looking back and ahead. *Psychological Bulletin*, 1978, *85*, 1030–1051.

Lickona, T. An experimental test of Piaget's theory of moral development. Paper presented at the Society for Research in Child Development, Philadelphia, 1973.

Lickona, T. Research on Piaget's theory of moral development. In Lickona, T. (Ed.), *Moral Development and Behavior*. New York: Holt, Rinehart and Winston, 1976.

Lieberman, M. Estimation of moral judgement level using items whose alternatives form a graded scale. Unpublished doctoral dissertation, University of Chicago, 1971.

Liebert, R. M., and Allen, M. K. Effects of rule structure and reward magnitude on the acquisition and adoption of self-reward criteria. *Psychological Reports*, 1967, *21*, 445–452.

Lipset, S. M., and Wolin, S. S. (Eds.), *The Berkeley student revolt*. New York: Doubleday, 1965.

Locke, J. *An essay concerning human understanding*. Oxford: Clarendon Press, 1690/1975.

London, P. The rescuers: Motivational hypotheses about Christians who saved Jews from the Nazis. In J. Macaulay and L. Berkowitz (Eds.), *Altriuism and helping behavior*. New York and London: Academic Press, 1970.
Longstreth, L E. Revisiting Skeets' final study: A critique: *Developmental Psychology*, 1981, *17*, 620–625.
Longstreth, L. E., and Rice, R. E. Perceptions of parental behavior and identification with parents by three groups of boys differing in school adjustment. *Journal of Educational Psychology*, 1964, *55*, 144–151.
Looft, W. R. The psychology of more. *American Psychologist*, 1971, *26*, 561–565.
Lopata, H. *Occupation: Housewife*. New York: Oxford University Press, 1971.
Lovaas, O. I. Interaction between verbal and nonverbal behavior. *Child Development*, 1961, *32*, 329–336.
Lucker, W. G., Rosenfield, D., Sikes, J., and Aronson, E. Performance in the interdependent classroom: A field study. *American Educational Research Journal*, 1976, *13*, 115–123.
Lukes, S. Chomsky's betrayal of truths. *The Times Higher Education Supplement*, 1980, 7 *November* (No. 418).
Luria, A. *The role of speech in the regulation of normal and abnormal behaviours*. Oxford: Pergamon, 1961.
MacRae, D. A test of Piaget's theories of moral development. *Journal of Abnormal and Social Psychology*, 1954, *49*, 14–18.
Maccoby, E. E. The development of moral values and behaviour in childhood. In J. A. Clausen (Ed.), *Socialization and Society*, Boston: Little, Brown, 1968.
Maccoby, E. E. *Social Development*. New York: Harcourt Brace Jovanovich, 1980.
Mackenzie, B. D. *Behaviourism and the limits of scientific method*. London: Routledge & Kegan Paul, 1977.
Macrae, D. A test of Piaget's theories of moral development. *Journal of Applied Social Psychology*, 1954, *49*, 14–18.
Markarenko, A. S. *The collective family*. New York: Doubleday, 1967.
Masserman, J. H., Weckkin, S., and Terris, W. "Altruistic" behaviour in rhesus monkeys. *American Journal of Psychiatry*, 1964, *121*, 584–585.
Masters, J. C., and Pisarowicz, P. A. Self-reinforcement and generosity following two types of altruistic behaviour. *Child Development*, 1975, *46*, 313–318.
McDougall, W. *An introduction to social psychology*, 22nd edition. London: Methuen, 1931.
McKechnie, R. J. Between Piaget's stages: A study in moral development. *British Journal of Educational Psychology*, 1971, *41*, 213–217.
McLaughlin, G. H. Psychologic: A possible alternative to Piaget's formulation. *British Journal of Educational Psychology*, 1963, *33*, 61–67.
McNamee, S. Moral behaviour, moral development and motivation. *Journal of Moral Education*, 1978, *7*, 27–31.
Meacham, J. A. Verbal guidance through remembering the goals of actions. *Child Development*, 1978, *49*, 188–193.
Mead, G. H. *Mind, self and society*. Chicago: University of Chicago Press, 1934.
Medinnus, G. R. Immanent justice in children: A review of the literature and additional data. *Journal of Genetic Psychology*, 1959, *94*, 253–262.
Meichenbaum, D., and Asarnow, J. Cognitive-behaviour modification and meta-cognitive development: Implications for the classroom. In P. C. Kendall and S. D. Hollon (Ed.), *Cognitive-behavioural interventions: Theory, research and procedures*. New York and London: Academic Press, 1979.

Meichenbaum, D., and Goodman, J. Training impulsive children to talk to themselves: A means for developing self-control. *Journal of Abnormal Psychology*, 1971, 77, 115–126.

Melville, H. *Moby Dick*. New York: Dutton, 1895.

Miller, N. E., and Dollard, J. *Social learning and imitation*. New Haven: Yale University Press, 1941.

Miller, S. A., Shelton, J., and Flavell, J. H. A test of Luria's hypothesis concerning the development of verbal self-regulation. *Child Development*, 1970, *41*, 651–655.

Millham, J. Two components of need for approval score and their relationship to cheating following success and failure. *Journal of Research in Personality*, 1974, *8*, 378–392.

Mischel, W. *Personality and assessment*. New York: Wiley, 1968.

Mischel, W., and Gilligan, C. Delay of gratification, motiviation for the prohibited gratification, and response to temptation. *Journal of Applied Social Psychology*, 1964, *69*, 411–417.

Mischel, W., and Mischel, H. N. A cognitive social-learning approach to morality and self-regulation. In T. Lickona (Ed.), *Moral development and behaviour*. New York: Holt, Rinehart and Winston, 1976.

Mitford, J. *Hons and rebels*. London: Victor Gollancz, 1960.

Monahan, J., and O'Leary, K. D. Effects of self-instruction on rule-breaking behaviour. *Psychological Reports*, 1971, *29*, 1059–1066.

Moran, J. J., and Joniak, A. J. Effect of language on preference for responses to a moral dilemma. *Developmental Psychology*, 1979, *3*, 337–338.

Morsbach, H. An intensive "triangular" study (Japan–USA–Europe) of socio-psychological variables. *Annals of the New York Academy of Science*, 1977, *285*, 221–226.

Muson, H. Moral thinking: Can it be taught? *Psychology Today*, 1979, *12*, 48–68.

Mussen, P., Harris, S., Rutherford, E., and Keasey, C. B. Honesty and altruism among preadolescents. *Developmental Psychology*, 1970, *3*, 169–194.

Mussen, P. H., and Eisenberg-Berg, N. *Roots of caring, sharing and helping*. San Francisco: W. H. Freeman, 1977.

Najarian-Svajian, P. H. The ideal of immanent justice among Lebanese children and adults. *Journal of Genetic Psychology*, 1966, *109*, 57–66.

Nicolayev, J. and Philips, D. C. On assessing Kohlberg's stage theory of moral development. In D. B. Cochrane, C. M. Hamm, and A. C. Kazepides (Eds.), *The domain of moral education*. New York: The Paulist Press, 1979.

Nisbett, R. E., and Wilson, T. D. Telling more than we can know: Verbal reports on mental processes. *Psychological Review*, 1977, *84*, 231–259.

Nissen, H. W., and Crawford, M. P. A preliminary study of pool sharing behaviour in young chimpanzees. *Journal of Comparative Psychology*, 1936, *22*, 383–419.

Novak, M. A., and Harlow, H. Social recovery of monkeys. *Developmental Psychology*, 1975, *11*, 453–455.

O'Connor, N., and Hermelin, B. Cognitive deficits in children. *British Medical Bulletin*, 1971, *27*, 227–232.

O'Leary, K. D. The effects of self instruction on immoral behavior. *Journal of Experimental Child Psychology*, 1968, *6*, 297–301.

Oden, S., and Asher, S. Coaching children in social skills for friendship making. *Child Development*, 1977, *48*, 495–506.

Omark, D. R., and Edelman, M. S. A comparison of status hierarchies in young children: an ethological approach. *Social Science Information*, 1975, *14*, 87–107.

Omark, D. R., Omark, M., and Edelman, M. Formation of dominance hierarchies in young children. In T. R. Williams (Ed.), *Psychological Anthropology*. The Hague: Mouton, 1975.
Ozols, E., and Gilmore, J. B. Respecting children: Moral reasoning when right conduct joins punishing outcomes. *Canadian Journal of Behavioral Science*, 1978, *10*, 296–307.
Palmer, F. H., and Semlear, T. Early intervention as compensatory education. In R. M. Liebert, R. W. Poulos, and G. S. Strauss (Eds.), *Developmental Psychology*, 2nd edition. Englewood Cliffs, New Jersey: Prentice-Hall, 1977.
Parke, R. D. Rules, roles, and resistance to deviation: Recent advances in punishment, discipline, and self-control. *Minnesota Symposia on Child Psychology*, 1974, *8*, 111–143.
Parke, R. D. Perspectives on father–infant interaction. In J. D. Osofsky (Ed.), *Handbook of Infant development*. New York: Wiley, 1979.
Parsons, J. E., Ruble, D. N., Klosson, E. C., Feldman, N. S., and Rholes, W. S. Order effects on children's moral and achievement judgements. *Developmental Psychology*, 1976, *12*, 357–358.
Pavlov, I. P. *Conditioned reflexes*. London: Oxford University Press, 1927.
Peck, R. F., and Hauighurst, R. J. *The psychology of character development*. New York: Wiley, 1960.
Peele, S. Reductionism in the psychology of the eighties: Can biochemistry eliminate addiction, mental illness, and pain? *American Psychologist*, 1981, *36*, 807–818.
Pelton, L. H. Child abuse and neglect: The myth of classlessness. *American Journal of Orthopsychiatry*, 1978, *48*, 609–617.
Perry, D. G., and Perry, L. C. Effects of anger arousal and competition on aggressive behaviour. *Journal of Child Psychology and Psychiatry*, 1976, *17*, 145–149.
Peters, R. S. What is an educational process? In Peters, R. S. (Ed.), *The concept of education*. London: Routledge and Kegan Paul, 1967.
Peters, R. S. The place of Kohlberg's theory in moral education. *Journal of Moral Education*, 1978, *8*, 147–157.
Piaget, J. *Judgement and reasoning in the child*. New York: Harcourt, 1928.
Piaget, J. *The moral judgement of the child*. London: Routledge and Kegan Paul, 1932 (1977 edition, Penguin Books, Harmondsworth).
Piaget, J. Jean Piaget. In E. G. Boring, H. Werner, H. S. Langfeld and R. M. Yerkes (Eds.), *A history of psychology in autobiography, Volume IV*. Worcester, Massachusetts: Clark University Press, 1952.
Piaget, J. The general problems of psychobiological development of the child. In J. M. Tanner and B. Inhelder (Eds.), *Discussion on child development: Proceedings of the World Health Organization study group on the psychobiological Development of the Child, Vol. IV*. New York: International Universities Press, 1960.
Piaget, J. *Play, dreams and imitation*. London: Routledge and Kegan Paul, 1962.
Piaget, J. *Six psychological studies*. New York: Random House, 1967.
Piaget, J. Piaget's theory. In P. H. Mussen (Ed.), *Carmichael's manual of child psychology, Vol. I*, 3rd edition. New York: Wiley, 1970.
Piaget, J. *Science of education and the psychology of the child*. New York: Viking, 1971.
Piaget, J. Intellectual evolution from adolescence to adulthood. *Human Development*, 1972, *15*, 1–12.
Pliner, P., Hart, H., Kohl, J., and Saari, D. Compliance without pressure: Some further data on the foot-in-the-door technique. *Journal of Experimental and Social Psychology*, 1974, *10*, 17–22.

Plunkett, M., and Summy, R. Civil liberties in Queensland: A nonviolent political campaign. *Social Alternatives*, 1980, *1*, 73–90.

Polyani, K. Our obsolete market mentality. *Commentary*, 1947, *3* (*February*), 109–117. (Reprinted in G. Galton (Ed.), *Primitive, archaic, and modern economies: Essays of Karl Polanyi*. Boston: Beacon Press, 1968.)

Popper, K. R. *Conjectures and refutations*, 5th edition. London: Routledge and Kegan Paul, 1974.

Power, C., and Reimer, J. Moral atmosphere: an educational bridge between moral judgement and action. In W. Damon (Ed.), *Moral development: new directions for child development, Number 2*. San Francisco: Jossey-Bass, 1978.

Putnam, H. Reductionism and the nature of psychology. *Cognition*, 1973, *2*, 479–502.

Ramey, C. T., Farran, D. C., and Campbell, F. A. Predicting IQ from mother–infant interactions. *Child Development*, 1979, *50*, 804–814.

Rawls, J. Justice as fairness. *Philosophical Review*, 1958, *57*, 164–194.

Rawls, J. *A theory of justice*. Cambridge, Massachusetts: Harvard University Press, 1971.

Renshaw, J. R. An exploration of the dynamics of the overlapping worlds of work and family. *Family Process*, 1976, *15*, 143–165.

Rest, J. R. Development in moral judgment research. *Developmental Psychology*, 1980, *16*, 251–256.

Rest, J. R., Davison, M. L., and Robbins, S. Age trends in judging moral issues. A review of cross-sectional, longitudinal, and sequential studies of the Defining Issues Test. *Child Development*, 1978, *49*, 263–279.

Rieff, P. *Freud: The mind of a moralist*. London: Methuen, 1965.

Riegel, K. F. Influence of economic and political ideologies on the development of developmental psychology. *Psychological Bulletin*, 1972, *78*, 129–141.

Rockwell, R. C., and Elder, G. H. Jr., Economic deprivation, and problem behavior: Childhood and adolescence in the Great Depression. Paper presented at the Biennial Meeting of the Society for Research in Child Development, San Francisco, 1979.

Rose, S. E. R., and Rose, H. Do not adjust your mind, there is a fault in reality—ideology in neurobiology, *Cognition*, 1973, *2*, 479–502.

Rosen, B. C. Social class and the child's perception of the parent. *Child Development*, 1964, *35*, 1147–1153.

Rosenhan, D., and White, G. Observation and rehearsal as determinants of prosocial behaviour. *Journal of Personality and Social Psychology*, 1967, *5*, 424–431.

Rosenhan, D. L. The natural socialization of altruistic autonomy. In J. Macaulay and L. Berkowitz, (Eds.), *Altruism and helping behavior*. New York and London: Academic Press, 1970.

Rosenthal, T. L., and Zimmerman, B. J. *Social learning and cognition*. London and New York: Academic Press, 1978.

Rubin, K. H. Role taking in childhood: some methodological considerations. *Child Development*, 1978, *49*, 428–433.

Rubin, K. H., and Trotter, K. T. Kohlberg's moral judgment scale: some methodological considerations. *Developmental Psychology*, 1977, *13*, 535–536.

Ruble, D. N., Feldman, N. S., and Boggiano, A. K. Social comparison between young children. *Developmental Psychology*, 1976, *12*, 192–197.

Rule, B. G., and Duker, P. Effects of intentions and consequences on children's evaluations of aggressors. *Journal of Personality and Social Psychology*, 1973, *27*, 184–189.

Rushton, J. P. Socialization and the altruistic behavior of children. *Psychological Bulletin*, 1976, *83*, 898–913.
Russell, J. *The acquisition of knowledge*. London: Macmillan, 1978.
Rutter, M. Maternal deprivation. *Child Development*, 1979, *50*, 283–305.
Rybash, J. M., Sewall, M. B., Roodin, P. A., and Sullivan, L. Effects of age of transgressor, damage, and type of presentation on kindergarten children's moral judgments. *Developmental Psychology*, 1975, *11*, 874.
Sagi, A., and Hoffman, M. L. Empathic distress in the newborn. *Developmental Psychology*, 1976, *12*, 175–176.
Sampson, E. E. Studies of status congruence. In L. Berkowitz (Ed.), *Advances in experimental social psychology, Vol. 4*. New York and London: Academic Press, 1969.
Sampson, E. E. Psychology and the American ideal. *Journal of Personality and Social Psychology*, 1977, *35*, 767–782.
Sampson, E. E. Scientific paradigms and social values: Wanted—A scientific revolution. *Journal of Personality and Social Psychology*, 1978, *36*, 1332–1343.
Sampson, E. E. Cognitive psychology as ideology. *American Psychologist*, 1981, *36*, 730–743.
Santrock, J. W. Moral structure: the interrelations of moral behavior, moral judgment, and moral affect. *Journal of Genetic Psychology*, 1975, *127*, 201–213.
Santrock, J. W., and Warshak, R. A. Father custody and social development in boys and girls. *Journal of Social Issues*, 1979, *35*, 112–125.
Santrock, J. W., Smith, P. C., and Bourbeau, P. E. Effects of social comparison on aggression and regression in groups of young children. *Child Development*, 1976, *47*, 831–837.
Schaffer, H. R. Social learning and identification. In E. A. Lunzer and J. F. Morris (Eds.), *Development in human learning*. London: Staples Press, 1968.
Scheck, D. C., and Emerick, R. The young male adolescent's perception of early child-rearing behavior: the differential effects of socioeconomic status and family size. *Sociometry*, 1976, *39*, 39–52.
Schumpeter, J. *Capitalism, socialism, and democracy*. New York: Harper and Row, 1950.
Scriven, M. Psychology without a paradigm. In L. Breger (Ed.), *Clinical-cognitive psychology*. Englewood Cliffs, New Jersey: Prentice-Hall, 1969.
Shaffer, D. R. *Social and personality development*. Monterey, California: Brooks/Cole, 1979.
Shantz, C. U. The development of social cognition. In M. Hetherington (Ed.), *Review of child development research, Vol. 5*. Chicago: University of Chicago Press, 1975.
Shaw, M. E., and Iwawaki, S. Attribution of responsibility by Japanese and Americans as a function of age. *Journal of Cross-Cultural Psychology*, 1972, *3*, 71–81.
Shepherd, G. A critique and extension of Bronfenbrenner's Moral Dilemma test. *International Journal of Psychology*, 1977, *12*, 207–217.
Shevrin, H., and Dickman, S. The psychological unconscious: A necessary assumption for all psychological theory? *American Psychologist*, 1980, *35*, 421–434.
Shultz, T. R., and Butkowsky, I. Young children's use of the scheme for multiple sufficient causes in the attribution of real and hypothetical behavior. *Child Development*, 1977, *48*, 464–469.
Shure, M. B., and Spivack, G. Interpersonal problem-solving as a mediator of

behavioral adjustment in preschool and kindergarten children. *Journal of Applied Developmental Psychology*, 1980, *1*, 29–44.

Siegal, M. Socialization and the development of adult respect. *British Journal of Psychology*, 1979, *70*, 83–86.

Siegal, M. Children's perceptions of adult economic needs. *Child Development*, 1981, *52*, 379–382.

Siegal, M. Identification as a process in moral development. Unpublished paper, University of Queensland, 1982.

Siegal, M., and Francis, R. Parent–child relations and cognitive approaches to moral judgment and behavior. *British Journal of Psychology*, in press.

Siegel, L. S. Infant perceptual, cognitive, and motor behaviours as predictors of subsequent cognitive and language development. *Canadian Journal of Psychology*, 1979, *33*, 382–395.

Silvern, L. E., Waterman, J. M., Sobesky, W., and Ryan, V. L. Effects of a developmental model of perspective-taking training. *Child Development*, 1979, *50*, 243–246.

Skeels, H. M. Adult status of children from contrasting early life experiences: A follow-up study. *Monographs of the Society for Research in Child Development*, 1966, *31*.

Slaby, R. G. Verbal regulation of aggression and altruism. In J. DeWit and W. W. Hartup (Eds.), *Determinants and origins of aggressive behavior*. The Hague: Mouton, 1974.

Slater, P. E. Toward a dualistic theory of identification. *Merrill-Palmer Quarterly*, 1961, *7*, 113–126.

Sluckin, A. M., and Smith, P. K. Two approaches to the concept of dominance in preschool children. *Child Development*, 1977, *48*, 917–923.

Smelser, W. T. Adolescent and adult occupational choice as a function of family socioeconomic history. *Sociometry*, 1963, *26*, 393–409.

Smith, K. C., and Schooler, C. Women as mothers in Japan: The effects of social structure and culture on values and behavior. *Journal of Marriage and the Family*, 1978, *40*, 613–620.

Smith, M. B., Haan, N., and Block, J. Social-psychological aspects of student activism. *Youth and Society*, 1970, *1*, 261–288.

Snow, C. E., and Hoefnagle-Hohle, M. The critical period for language acquisition: Evidence from second language learning. *Child Development*, 1978, *49*, 1114–1128.

Snyder, M., and Cunningham, M. R. To comply or not comply: Testing the self-perception explanation of the "Foot-in-the-door" phenomenon. *Journal of Personality and Social Psychology*, 1975, *31*, 64–67.

Somerville, S. C. The pendulum problem: Patterns of performance defining developmental stages. *British Journal of Educational Psychology*, 1974, *44*, 266–281.

Spivack, G., and Shure, M. B. *Social adjustment of young children*. San Francisco: Jossey-Bass, 1974.

Staub, E. The use of role playing and induction in children's learning of helping and showing behavior. *Child Development*, 1971, *42*, 805–817.

Staub, E. *Positive social behavior and morality, Vol. 2: Socialization and development*. New York and London: Academic Press, 1979.

Staub, E. C. To rear a prosocial child: Reasoning, learning by doing, and learning by teaching others. In D. J. DePalma and J. M. Foley (Eds.), *Moral development:*

Current theory and research. Hillsdale, New Jersey: Lawrence Erlbaum Associates 1975.

Steinberg, L. D., Catalano, R., and Dooley, D. Economic antecedents of child abuse and neglect. *Child Development*, 1981, *52*, 975–985.

Steinlieb, J. L., and Youniss, J. Moral judgments one year after intentional or consequence modeling. *Journal of Personality and Social Psychology*, 1975, *31*, 895–897.

Stephenson, G. M., and Barker, J. Personality and the pursuit of distributive justice: An experimental study of children's moral behavior. *British Journal of Social and Clinical Psychology*, 1972, *11*, 207–219.

Stephenson, G. M., and White, J. H. An experimental study of some effects of injustice on children's moral behavior. *Journal of Experimental Social Psychology*, 1968, *4*, 460–469.

Stephenson, G. M., and White, J. H. Privilege, deprivation, and children's moral behavior: An experimental clarification of the role of investments. *Journal of Experimental Social Psychology*, 1970, *6*, 167–176.

Sternlieb, J. L., and Youniss, J. Moral judgments one year after intentional or consequence modeling. *Journal of Personality and Social Psychology*, 1975, *31*, 895–897.

Strayer, F. F., Wareing, S., and Rushton, J. P. Social constraints on naturally occurring preschool altruism. *Ethology and Sociobiology*, 1979, *1*, 3–11.

Strayer, J. A naturalistic study of emphatic behaviours and their relation to affective states and perspective-taking skills in preschool children. *Child Development*, 1980, *51*, 815–822.

Suls, J., and Kalle, R. J. Intention, damage, and age of transgressor as determinants of children's moral judgments. *Child Development*, 1978, *49*, 1270–1273.

Taylor, C. *The explanation of behaviour*. London: Routledge and Kegan Paul, 1964.

Tesser, A. Self-esteem maintenance in family dynamics. *Journal of Personality and Social Psychology*, 1980, *39*, 77–91.

Thurer, G. *Free and Swiss*. London: Oswald Wolff, 1970.

Tizard, B., and Hodges, J. The effect of early institutional rearing on the development of eight-year-old children. *Journal of Child Psychology and Psychiatry*, 1978, *19*, 99–118.

Tower, R. B. Parents' self-concepts and preschool children's behaviors. *Journal of Personality and Social Psychology*, 1980, *39*, 710–718.

Tsujimoto, R. N., and Nardi, P. M. A comparison of Kohlberg's and Hogan's theories of moral development. *Social Psychology*, 1978, *41*, 235–245.

Tuddenham, R. N. Theoretical regularities and individual idiosyncracies. In M. B. Green, M. P. Ford, and G. B. Flamer (Eds.), *Measurement and Piaget*. New York: McGraw-Hill, 1971.

Uranowitz, S. W. Helping and self-attributions: A field experiment. *Journal of Personality and Social Psychology*, 1975, *31*, 852–854.

Urbain, E. S., and Kendall, P. C. Review of social-cognitive problem-solving interventions with children. *Psychological Bulletin*, 1980, *88*, 109–143.

Urmson, J. O. Saints and heroes. In A. I. Melden (Ed.), *Essays in moral philosophy*. Seattle: University of Washington Press, 1958.

Utech, D. A., and Hoving, K. L. Parents and peers as competing influence on the decisions of children of differing ages. *Journal of Social Psychology*, 1969, *78*, 267–274.

Van der Veen, F. The parent's concept of the family unit and child adjustment. *Journal of Counseling Psychology*, 1965, *12*, 196–200.
Von Wright, J. M., and Niemela, P. On the ontogenetic development of moral criteria. *Scandinavian Journal of Psychology*, 1966, *7*, 65–75.
Vygotsky, L. S. *Thought and language*. Cambridge, Massachusetts: MIT Press, 1962.
Walster, E. Assignment of responsibility for an accident. *Journal of Personality and Social Psychology*, 1966, *14*, 101–113.
Walster, E., and Walster, G. W. Equity and social justice. *Journal of Social Issues*, 1975, *31*, 21–43.
Warnock, G. J. *The object of morality*. London: Methuen, 1971.
Watson, J. B. *Psychological care of infant and child*. New York: W. W. Norton, 1928.
Watson, J. B. John Broadus Watson. In Carl Murchison (Ed.), *A history of psychology in autobiography, Vol. III*. New York: Russell and Russell, 1930.
Watson, J. B. *Behaviourism*, 2nd edition. London: Routledge and Kegan Paul, 1931.
Wegner, D. M., and Vallacher, R. R. *Implicit Psychology*. New York: Oxford University Press, 1977.
Weiner, B., and Peter, N. A cognitive-developmental analysis of achievement and moral judgments. *Developmental Psychology*, 1973, *9*, 290–309.
Werner, E. E. *Cross-cultural child development*. Monterey, California: Brooks/Cole, 1979.
Westby, D. L., and Braungart, E. G. Class and politics in the family backgrounds of student political activists. *American Sociological Review*, 1966, *31*, 690–692.
White, C. B., Bushnell, N., and Regnemer, J. L. Moral development in Bahamanian school children: A 3-year examination of Kohlberg's stages of moral development. *Developmental Psychology*, 1978, *14*, 58–65.
White, G. M. Immediate and deferred effects of model observation and guided and unguided rehearsal on donating and stealing. *Journal of Personality and Social Psychology*, 1972, *21*, 139–148.
White, P. Limitations on verbal reports of internal events: A refutation of Nisbett and Wilson and of Bem. *Psychological Review*, 1980, *87*, 105–112.
White, R. Ego and reality in psychoanalytic theory. *Psychological Issues*, 1963, *3*.
White, S. H. Evidence for a hierarchical arrangement of learning processes. In L. P. Lipsitt and C. C. Spiker (Eds.), *Advances in child development and behaviour*. New York and London: Academic Press, 1965.
White, S. H. The learning theory tradition and child psychology. In P. H. Mussen (Ed.), *Carmichael's manual of child psychology*, 3rd edition. New York: Wiley, 1970.
White, S. H. Children in perspective. *American Psychologist*, 1979, *34*, 812–814.
Whiteman, P. H., and Kosier, K. P. Development of children's moralistic judgments: age, sex, IQ, and certain personal-experiential variables. *Child Development*, 1964, *35*, 843–850.
Whittaker, D., and Watts, W. A. Personality characteristics of a nonconformist youth subculture: A study of the Berkeley non-student. *Journal of Social Issues*, 1969, *25*, 65–89.
Winder, C. L., and Rau, L. Parental attitudes associated with social deviance in pre-adolescent boys. *Journal of Applied Social Psychology*, 1962, *64*, 418–424.
Wright, D. *The psychology of moral behaviour*. Harmondsworth, Middlesex: Penguin Books, 1971.
Wright, H. F. *Recording and analyzing child behavior*. New York: Harper and Row, 1967.

Yussen, S. Characteristics of moral dilemmas written by adolescents. *Developmental Psychology*, 1977, *13*, 162–163.

Zahn-Waxler, C., Radke-Yarrow, M., and King, R. A. Child-rearing and children's prosocial initiations toward victims of distress. *Child Development*, 1979, *50*, 319–330.

Zalkind, S. S., Gaugler, E. A., and Schwartz, R. M. Civil liberties, attitudes and personality measures: Some exploratory research. *Journal of Social Issues*, 1975, *31*, 77–91.

Zawadzki, B., and Lazarsfeld, P. The psychological consequences of unemployment. *Journal of Social Psychology*, 1935, *6*, 224–251.

Zigler, E., and Trickett, P. K. IQ, social competence, and evaluation of early education programs. *American Psychologist*, 1978, *33*, 789–798.

Zimmerman, B. J., and Bell, J. A. Observer verbalization and abstraction in vicarious rule learning, generalization and retention. *Developmental Psychology*, 1972, *7*, 227–231.

Subject Index